PRAISE FOR ORGA

PLANNING AND

MW00860603

Building a forward-looking OP&A unit is crucial at these times of increasing economic disruption. Any business's most critical asset is its people. For organizations to survive, these people need efficient and effective management, deployment and development. It comes as no surprise that Rupert Morrison has produced an outstanding analysis of how this can be done. He illustrates how OP&A can leverage data to gain a detailed examination of every member of the organization and determine their optimal development path. At the same time, he demonstrates OP&A's role in the daily management of the organization and when facilitating major change. This book is so much more than an optional read.

Ian Kantor, Founder, Investec

Practice and research show that organization capabilities have far more impact on stakeholder outcomes than individual competencies. Rupert Morrison masterfully offers ideas and specific analytical tools and cases on planning, transformation, workforce, and technology to improve organizations. Anyone interested in creating more effective organizations will find this an exceptional guide.

Dave Ulrich, Rensis Likert Professor, Ross School of Business, University of Michigan, and Partner, The RBL Group

In this book Rupert offers a compelling guide for executive and practitioner alike. If you truly believe that people are your organization's greatest asset and you have been frustrated with previous efforts to make a workforce transformation real, then look no further. Blending strategy, finance, workforce planning and analytics, this book offers a logical, evidence-based process for introducing OP&A as a new capability in your organization. Doing so will ensure that you can achieve sustained and measurable workforce success. Highly recommended.

David Stroud, Director, Workforce Insight Pty

If you enjoyed *Data-Driven Organization Design*, the prequel to this book, then you'll love *Organizational Planning and Analysis*. Rupert is one of the genuine thought leaders in our field. He first outlined the key concepts outlined in this book to me as a guest on the *Digital HR Leaders* podcast. I was captivated. If you want to understand how to use data and analysis to build organizational capabilities through workforce planning and drive business success, then this is the book for you.

David Green, co-author of *Excellence in People Analytics*, Managing Partner at Insight222 and host of the *Digital HR Leaders* podcast

Rupert Morrison's timely new book is a practical read for any business leader needing to steer their organization through volatility, uncertainty and change. Just as the Finance function has embraced the need for both backward-looking operational and forward-focused planning capabilities, the same is now true for the HR People function in any enterprise. Read this book and learn from one of the best. Developing your organization planning and analysis capabilities can transform your enterprise performance and culture.

Nick Araco Jr, Chief Executive Officer AchieveNEXT

Any company serious about strategy execution needs to establish an OP&A function. This excellent book not only describes the *why* and the *what*, it also delves into the *how*. It should be read not just by HR professionals and consultants but by every executive in the C-Suite who understands that world class talent management is the starting point of any successful transformation.

Bernhard Raschke, Chief Transformation Officer, RS Group

In his new book, Rupert astutely illustrates applying systems theory to organizational planning for driving outcomes in a complex environment. He gives us courage to rethink planning as a dynamic and insightful process to build long term organizational capabilities.

Shradha Prakash, VP, Future of Work, Org Design and Talent Enablement at Prudential Financial

Rupert's approach to the forward-looking HR function is both pragmatic and overdue. We are now at a time when HR and Finance are at the same table and business performance is linked closely to workforce capability. Introducing a familiar framework to HR is needed as we continue to move and transform our organizations with insight and agility.

Daniel Zrno, Ability Map

We all know, in theory, that planning and analysis founded on good data is an organizational must. Getting the theory into day-to-day practice is more problematic. Rupert Morrison clearly and carefully lays out why and how to do this. What's not to follow in his guidance? The benefits are huge.

Naomi Stanford, organization design author and consultant

Executives spend significant amounts of time and energy analysing market trends, building strategic plans and financial modelling. *Organizational Planning and Analysis* is an important reminder to focus equally on building a right-sized and efficient organization that fosters execution excellence to navigate the further of work. Why? As the fundamental working contract between employers and employees shifts, the C-suite must show urgency and sophistication in driving retention. Rupert offers practical advice and sophisticated solutions to build an organization that is not only relevant to customers, but also personally relevant to an ever-evolving workforce. The savvy reader will take away new insights around how to ensure the right people are doing the right work in the right way and with sustainable alignment.

Beau River, Partner at Vantage Leadership Consulting and Adjunct Lecturer at Northwestern University's Masters of Science in Learning and Organizational Change

A practical guide to using data to continuously optimize organizational performance, aligning for innovation, agility and productivity. A must-build muscle for all organizations today.

Kent McMillan, Managing Director, Global Organization Strategy and Design Lead, Accenture

Leadership is about taking an organization from one place to another knowing that the movement can only come from the people. This book shows how data can power alignment, speed and purpose on the journey.

Pär Åström, President Gardena Division, Husqvarna Group

In a world where business leaders are told to reflect properly and plan effectively, this book equips them with the right questions to ask and a framework for generating continuous performance. Ultimately, it ushers in a leadership approach that is confident and clear in the face of an increasingly volatile and opaque business landscape. Essential reading.

John Brown, Founder and CEO, Don't Cry Wolf

Simplicity is something hard to achieve. OP&A is a simple yet very effective concept to solve one of the most complex challenges that organizations face today. This is an essential read to anyone in charge of teams.

Thiago R Kiwi, Head of Marketing and Communications at Headspring Executive Development

Organizational Planning and Analysis

Building the capability to secure business performance

Rupert Morrison

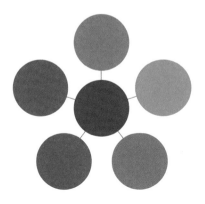

KoganPage

First published in Great Britain and the United States in 2022 by Kogan Page Limited

2nd Floor, 45 Gee Street	1518 Walnut Street, Suite 1100	4737/23 Ansari Road
London EC1V 3RS	Philadelphia PA 19102	Daryaganj
United Kingdom	USA	New Delhi 110002
www.koganpage.com		India

© Rupert Morrison 2022

ISBNs

Hardback	978 1 3986 0587 9
Paperback	978 1 3986 0581 7
Ebook	978 1 3986 0586 2

British Library Cataloguing-in-Publication Data

A CIP record for this book is available from the British Library.

Library of Congress Control Number
2022942425

Typeset by Integra Software Services, Pondicherry
Printed and bound in Great Britain by Henry Ling Limited, at the Dorset Press, Dorchester DT1 1HD
Kogan Page books are printed on paper from sustainable forests.

CONTENTS

ABOUT THE AUTHOR

Rupert Morrison is an entrepreneur, economist and visionary in Data-Driven Organizational Management. He is the author of *Data-Driven Organization Design*, the prequel to this book.

Rupert started life on a sheep station in Wairarapa, New Zealand. After studying Economics, he began his career in Management Consulting with a focus on supply chain, organization design and transformation work. This role saw him work with many of the world's largest companies in multiple sectors (automotive, FMCG, mining, government agencies, pharmaceutical and private equity). This work led him to believe businesses were missing out on the opportunity to take greater control of these programmes in a more sustainable and data-driven way through the use of technology.

It was this belief that inspired him to found software solutions company Concentra Analytics Limited in 2008, and launch orgvue – the organizational design and planning platform – in 2011. Under his steer, the firm has become one of the fastest growing technology companies in the UK (Sunday Times Tech Track 100, 2011) and orgvue has become a revolutionary platform for human resources (Gartner's Cool Vendor in Human Capital Management, 2014). In 2018 Rupert secured $61 million in funding to further the expansion of the business. orgvue has been adopted by the world's largest companies to solve complex organizational design and planning challenges by using data to better understand and manage the workforce and make fearless decisions about the future.

This book is a labour of love and a homage to the hundreds of client projects Rupert has delivered over the past 25 years as well as the many lessons he has learned along the way. Rupert spends much of his time evangelizing about the data-driven approach to organizational design and planning at conferences and in the media.

Away from professional life, Rupert lives with his wife and three sons in London. He's a rugby fanatic – both as a follower of the All Blacks and as a coach of his local junior team – and an Ironman competitor.

FOREWORD

Meeting Rupert for the first time wasn't quite the experience I was expecting. During the first few minutes of my interview, each case example on my proudly delivered CV was forensically deconstructed. His conclusion was the same, delivered in an increasingly withering tone: every assignment had taken too long, involved too many consultants, and had been too expensive (based on his annoyingly accurate estimates). It wasn't personal: Rupert had trodden the same time-based, Excel- and PowerPoint-dependent consulting path I had, but he had had the vision and tenacity to develop better ways to deliver lasting impact. I was just another consultant who thought being data-driven meant driving a few spreadsheets. The 'interview' provided a Damascene moment as Rupert drew the most compelling, simple and practical organization design framework I had ever seen on the glass wall of his office. To this day, it is the only compelling, simple and practical organization design framework I have seen. His final point: this wasn't just a framework. This was the orgvue data model. I was converted.

In *Data-Driven Organization Design* – the prequel to this book – Rupert demonstrates how his framework is applied. No esoteric theories or academic concepts; just one page with six components of the organization system and nothing more statistically complex than gaps between targets and actuals. The organization as a system? We've known this for decades. But through his framework and with orgvue Rupert provided the means to connect the components with data to bring clarity over complexity. Good luck managing without this.

Rupert continues to combine his practical approach, deep expertise and tenacious zeal to shape the industry by providing a playbook for leaders to build their Organization Planning and Analysis (OP&A) capability. In a context where change is the only constant, the need to be adept at adapting and plan with confidence has never been greater. From organization design as transformational episodes to Organization Planning and Analysis as a continuous, professional discipline, this book provides the blueprint to make this real. Rupert provides valuable insight on the mindsets, capabilities, methods and processes needed within the OP&A function to work hand in hand with the established counterpart of Financial Planning and

Analysis. Any leader needing to steer their organization through volatility, uncertainty, complexity and ambiguity will benefit from his approach.

HR needs to get data-driven. It owns a critical mandate to ensure the right people with the right skills are doing the right work in the right numbers, but without data-driven approaches this role is at best an aspiration and more likely a cliché. How do you know if you have the right people, or whether they have the right skills needed to perform in their roles, or whether their time and effort are being spent doing the right work, and whether the workforce has the right number of people for today, and for tomorrow? If you don't have the data to inform decisions and the capability for analysing and planning the performance of the organization, you're in trouble. You may as well proclaim 'people are our greatest asset' while parts of the workforce risk becoming an increasingly expensive liability.

Steve Kelly

ACKNOWLEDGEMENTS

•

I owe so much to so many.

To Steve Kelly for contributing significantly to the thinking in every chapter of this book, in the same way that you did with the second edition of *Data-Driven Organization Design*. Thanks too for providing the foreword and for all your work in getting the images over the line. Thank you for your good humour and enthusiasm throughout. Your input has been invaluable.

To Kai Berendes and Magne Myrtveit for your tireless work on the workforce planning chapters. Your contribution strengthened those chapters immeasurably.

To Mike Bobek for your significant contribution to the thinking around agile methodology. I am delighted to have been able to include the agile case study in the book.

To my colleagues who reviewed the chapters meticulously at various stages of the writing process and provided specific suggestions and insights. Special mentions need to go to Alberto Acuña, Tim Archer and Sebastien Berlioz. Thank you for engaging in debate and sharpening the thinking. Thanks too to James Don-Carolis, Darshan Baskaran, Deb Semple, Christian Folkestad, Matthew Stewart , Chris Houghton, Mike Doherty and Jennifer Cheung, not to mention John Brown from Don't Cry Wolf.

To the graphic design team: Andreea Teodorescu, Anna Triantafillou and Arron Wilson at Ocular, New Zealand.

Thanks to Katherine Hartle for your tremendous support in the writing of this book, ensuring readability and coherence throughout.

To everyone on the orgvue – thank you for your unswerving enthusiasm, support and effort, which are taking our company from strength to strength. This book is born out of your work.

To Lucy Carter at Kogan Page for your expertise, support and for being so flexible in the publishing process.

To all my clients who I am unable to mention by name. Thank you for placing your faith in me and for your continued trust and support.

To my family: my father who passed over 30 years ago and my mother. To Henk and Alexandra, my four brothers and dear sister, my special Uncle

Erik, Aunt Marg and dear Gran. To my three gorgeous boys, Hugh, Alec and Peter, who give me a reason to keep going every day.

To my dear wife Vanessa. Everyone who knows me well knows that none of this would have been possible without you. To you, Vanessa, the biggest thanks of all.

PART ONE

Introduction

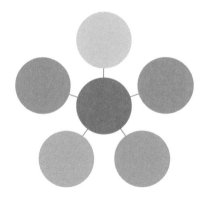

1.1

Organizational Planning and Analysis

Introduction

Imagine jumping into a time machine and transporting yourself five, 10 or 15 years into the future. Imagine being able to view and understand your business at these future points: how it has adapted to societal changes, megatrends and technological innovations; what your customers' needs are, how this has impacted the design of your organization and the people and capabilities needed to deliver on future business goals. Now imagine hopping back in your time machine to the present day, armed with these powerful insights. Such a concrete understanding of how your organization will need to adapt in the future in response to disruptive change would allow you to stay two steps ahead, making changes (large or small) to your organization design *before* the market and evolving environment demanded them. You wouldn't have to predict the future, you would know it, and your competitors wouldn't stand a chance.

Of course, what I'm asking you to imagine is impossible; we can't ever know for certain what the future holds. But that doesn't mean we shouldn't try to understand what lies ahead. Adopting a future-focused, **'What-If' mindset** is essential for organizations to adapt at speed and survive in a world of disruptive change. We may not have a time machine, but we do have tools and techniques which we can use to model and plan. We can continually ask 'What-If' questions to understand the impact that various options available to us might have and be ready to adapt and capitalize on opportunities when they present themselves. This is **scenario modelling**, a valuable tool which enables businesses to evaluate the impact of unexpected changes and future events. Done well, it gives organizations a window into best- and worst-case scenarios, aiding decision-making around immediate actions as well as longer-term plans.

In most organizations, scenario modelling is the preserve of the Finance function, and specifically the area of finance devoted to **Financial Planning and Analysis (FP&A)**. Chief financial officers (CFOs) use scenario modelling to estimate the impact of events on cash flow and the value of a business. I believe that limiting this type of modelling and planning to finance is short-sighted. This book argues for a new core capability called Organizational Planning and Analysis (or OP&A for short). This capability could sit within the People function, although it may also sit within Transformation or even FP&A. Wherever it sits, it ought to form a core part of an organization's central nervous system, working in unison with FP&A to enhance the precision of activities such as scenario modelling. In just the same way as the Finance function has a need for both backward-looking operational and forward-focused planning capabilities, the same is true for the People function. Leveraging many of the modelling techniques used by FP&A, OP&A allows businesses to ensure that both the organization system and the required workforce are in place to execute strategy on a perpetual basis.

This book is a sequel to my first book, *Data-Driven Organization Design*, in which I explain how and why organizations can use data and analytics to design their organization system. There is an important distinction to make between *designing* an organization at a specific point in time and *planning* one over time. Planning an organization over time – the subject of the book that you now hold in your hands – involves optimizing the performance of the organization's system on an ongoing basis against a set of shifting targets. Elements of what you will find in these pages were incorporated in a short chapter at the end of the second edition of *Data-Driven Organization Design*, but there wasn't sufficient room to delve into the level of detail necessary to implement the advice in practice. That is what this book seeks to do. My aim is to help you to find the right critical questions to ask and answer them so that you can respond to strategic goals:

- Where are we underperforming and why is this happening?
- Where is investment required and at what point?
- Where are efficiencies needed and at what point to hit our financial targets?
- Where do we need to maximize productivity?

Change and uncertainty are constants, and they are not easy conditions in which to lead. This chapter begins by looking at today's disrupted world (while making the point that disruption is not new) and some of the factors to consider when operating within this context. I then go on to look at the importance of planning, and why planning still matters in a volatile and uncertain world. I introduce a tool which was presented to me at a conference: Duke Corporate Education's Agile Dashboard, at the centre of which is a four-point model which helps leaders to adopt agile ways of thinking and make confident decisions. As part of this discussion, I look at scenario modelling and Real Option Pricing and explain the concept of volatility. There is a need to think of the range of possible outcomes rather than just the expected, as the expected will always be wrong. The remainder of the chapter is dedicated to the role of OP&A in helping organizations to navigate these uncertain times, and the lessons that can be learned from FP&A colleagues. The chapter ends with an introduction to the work of OP&A.

Navigating disruption and change

The first thing to say about disruption is that it shouldn't be feared. The second thing to say – and contrary to how it is so often written about and discussed – is that disruption is not new. To claim that it is shows an ignorance of history and a lack of empathy for past generations. Austrian-American economist Joseph Schumpeter popularized the term 'creative disruption' back in 1942 when he argued that the constant evolution of industries revolutionizes the economic structure they are part of, thereby creating a new one. The brilliant Richard Rumelt has argued that there has been less change between 1970 and 2020 than there was between 1870 and 1920.[1] Businesses have always needed to adapt to change. It is a fact of business life and our economic system. Yes, the past 50 years have seen the rise of information technology, globalization, the rise of China and the fall of the Soviet Empire, but between 1870 and 1920 there was the advent of electricity, transportation and urbanization. Pick any period since the beginning of the Industrial Revolution and you will see evidence of massive intergenerational change. In 1840, my great-grandfather took his family on a four-month voyage to New Zealand, which was the start of radical change for his family. His world changed as much as, if not more than, mine has. We should not talk about change as something new and surprising. We just need to learn to deal with it. If rapid, transformational change did at some point cease, *then* we'd be talking about unprecedented times.

The most successful organizations are those able to adapt to this ongoing change. They are not static, but dynamic, ever-changing systems. Back in the year 2000, General Electric (GE) released their annual report in which Jack Welch, the Chief Executive Officer (CEO) at the time, said: 'We've long believed that when the rate of change inside an institution becomes slower than the rate of change outside, the end is in sight. The only question is when.'[2] The story of GE can be used to illustrate this point. Four years after it was formed in 1892, the company became part of the Dow Jones Industrial Average, and was one of the original 12 companies to be included. It was there, on and off, until 2018, when it became the last of those companies to leave.[3] After Welch stepped down from being CEO in 2001, the company hit troubled times. The fact that GE has fallen so far in the past few years makes his statement even more resounding.

Today the powerful forces we see, such as industry transformation; emerging economies; major economic or political movements; digital innovations like automation; and megatrends like environmentalism can bring enormous opportunity. Harnessing this opportunity requires business leaders to be both informed about the future possibilities for their organization and brave enough to embrace necessary change at speed. Those that manage it can reap enormous rewards (think of Apple, Amazon or Tesla). Those that fail to innovate in response to change often do so at their peril. Nowhere is this shown more clearly than in the number of times firms have remained in the Standard and Poor 500 (S&P 500) Index over the last few decades. The index, brought to life in a biennial Corporate Longevity Report from Innosight, shows a steady decline in corporate lifespans and an increasing churn rate of companies, due to either a decline in market value or an acquisition. In the late 1970s, S&P 500 companies had an average tenure of 30 to 35 years. According to Innosight's 2021 report, this is likely to drop to 15 to 20 years by 2030. Added to this, in 2015 there were 12 US-based, venture-backed private companies valued at $5 billion or higher, but in 2020 there were 28.[4]

The report also highlights that the Covid-19 pandemic led to accelerated innovation in certain industries, especially in sectors which saw the most disruption. This disruption was already happening before Covid struck, but Covid accelerated innovation and led to the growth of three 'hybrid industries':

1 digital healthcare (seeing a convergence in healthcare, biotech and pharma – think of all the Zoom consultations with doctors)

2 retail-tainment (in which retail, consumer and entertainment came together)

3 e-mobility (incorporating energy, utilities and transportation sectors)

Unsurprisingly, these three broad sectors saw the most innovation and the highest levels of churn on the S&P 500 Index between 2018 and 2020. Consider these figures highlighted in the 2021 report:

- In healthcare, biotech and pharma, eight companies exited the Index and seven joined.

- In the energy, transportation and utilities sector, 14 companies exited the Index and six joined.

- During the same time period in the retail, consumer and entertainment sector, 12 exited the Index and six joined.

The key takeaway for me is that business leaders need to work harder to adapt. Like many before us, we're operating in a world of Volatility, Uncertainty, Complexity and Ambiguity (VUCA), which are uncomfortable contexts for human beings to cope with. We're not particularly cut out for making decisions under these circumstances, especially decisions which could lead to failure and ultimately reflect badly on ourselves. For many people, the natural inclination is to either stick their head in the sand or overthink a situation to minimize the chance of making a mistake. This might take the form of amassing too much information and becoming over-whelmed by data. This can lead to analysis paralysis, inaction and missed opportunities. The good news is that by adopting the right mindset, having the right tools at your disposal and the right capability within your organi-zation, it is possible to feel comfortable and even confident within these seemingly uncomfortable circumstances. Later in the chapter I'll discuss the importance of having the right capability and tools to do this effectively, but first I'll look at the mindset needed to succeed. A large part of this is under-standing **systems thinking** and the impact interconnected relationships can have on the evolution of organizations over time. This is also important to understand when performing scenario modelling so that you can adapt and innovate in line with emerging trends.

The importance of systems thinking

One of my favourite examples of systems thinking is a phenomenon named Dutch Disease. In 1959, natural gas was discovered in the Netherlands.

You'd be forgiven for assuming this would have been great for the Dutch economy – after all, gas means money, better business opportunities and more jobs. But this wasn't the case. After the gas was discovered, unemployment increased. Why? Because the discovery led to an appreciation of the Dutch currency, and the price of exports went up. The markets couldn't afford the increases, so Dutch businesses lost out. This, in turn, meant cuts and job losses. One part of the system (in this case, the economics system – the oil and gas industry) had a hidden connection with another part of the system (the manufacturing industry).

An organization is not dissimilar to an economy. Both are volatile, and difficult to manage and understand as a whole; and both have tangible and intangible drivers. Like an economy, how an organization evolves over time is best understood from a systems perspective and an appreciation of how a change in one part of the system affects something elsewhere. The world is continually changing, and without adopting a future-focused mindset which also seeks to understand cause and effect, businesses will fail to keep up with the ever-increasing pace of disruption.

In mid-2021, I had the honour of chairing a conference for the Corporate Research Forum (CRF), during which I heard Dave Snowden, a management consultant and researcher in the field of complexity science and knowledge management, discuss considerations for businesses operating in the modern-day environment. He talked about his well-known Cynefin framework, which helps decision makers make sense of their business contexts and understand cause and effect so they can tailor their actions accordingly. I was struck by the emphasis Snowden puts on the need for businesses to differentiate between *complicated* contexts and systems, and *complex* contexts and systems.

Snowden's Cynefin framework is comprised of five domains which describe the different contexts in which an organization operates:

1   Clear – If a context is clear, the cause and effect relationship is predictable and easy to understand. You can know with certainty that if you do x, you will get y. The result is always the same and you can be very sure of the outcome.

2   Complicated – If a context is complicated, there is still a relationship between cause and effect, but that relationship is much less obvious, and expertise is needed to understand it. Those experts perform analysis and gather insight to work out the relationships. In this domain there may be several solutions to the challenge. Insight can be used to inform future outcomes.

3   Complex – Complex contexts and complicated contexts are often understood to be the same thing, but they are different. In complex contexts, cause and effect relationships become intertwined and non-linear. It is only possible to understand outcomes in hindsight and impossible to predict using foresight. If you replayed a scenario time after time, it is likely you would get a different outcome each time.

4   Chaotic – In chaotic contexts there is no perceivable relationship between cause and effect and it is impossible to make sense of outcomes, even in hindsight.

5   Disorder – In disordered situations, it's difficult to see which of the other four domains applies.[5]

For each domain, Snowden recommends that a different problem-solving approach is applied. For example, in simple contexts it should be obvious what action to take, whereas in complicated contexts decisions can't be made without performing some degree of analysis first. Many organizations operate as if their business contexts are either simple or complicated. Experts perform backward-looking analysis to understand why things are the way they are, and this insight informs future actions. But in a world of VUCA, this isn't enough. VUCA plunges businesses into the third, complex domain, where situations or problems must be probed to uncover the unknowns, to gain an understanding of how x has led to y.

The difference between complicated and complex contexts can be understood in terms of chess and poker. Chess is complicated, but it is all-knowable, and you can work to understand it. It can be solved by creating algorithms, and a certain amount of it comes down to rote learning and memorizing patterns. Poker, on the other hand, is complex and unpredictable. It's a game of uncertainty, of calculating probabilities and adapting to constant change each time a new card is played. In poker you place your bets without having all the information to hand. Too often, people see business as a chess board rather than a poker game. They produce linear plans based on previous experience and get taken by surprise if something unforeseen comes along and derails that plan. They fail to factor in uncertainty, apply systems thinking or consider a range of potential future conditions which could impact the organization. In turn, they are ill prepared to act quickly when disruption comes knocking. Planning matters, and it should be done for a range of different scenarios.

Why planning matters: Be adept at adapting

Against the backdrop of our VUCA world, you may wonder if there's any point planning for the future. If things are so uncertain and volatile, is it necessary to devise a plan that's likely to get knocked off course? **Agile methodology** is becoming increasingly orthodox, so can't organizations simply leverage these methods to react to changing circumstances, using the information available to them at the time? The truth is that disruption increases the importance of planning. It's not only about having the capability to pivot, but foreseeing the need, and pivoting faster than everyone else. In our global world, speed matters in an increasing number of markets. If you can prepare your business for a range of possible contingencies, and understand the implications of each one, you can take quick and decisive action with a high level of confidence. Planning is what helps you to see change through as quickly as possible and gives you the best chance of beating your competitors to succeed in your markets.

I'm a huge sports enthusiast. I love to play it, watch it, and for many years I've coached a junior rugby team. I am endlessly struck by the parallels which can be drawn between the worlds of business and sport. In rugby, not only is there a need for a sound game plan (known as a playbook) but also to react and adapt as circumstances evolve during a game. Predicting these circumstances is difficult as so much depends on the other team: what they bring to the game on that day, how they react to you and how you react to them. Some sports are continuous, such as soccer, and some have structured set plays (meaning that the game is stopped for a period before the ball is returned to open play). In American football the game is stopped in between plays so the team can regroup and decide how to approach the next one based on what is going well, and what isn't. It's very similar to a game of chess. The coach decides which players should be on the field and the moves they should be making. These decisions can be made while the ball is out of play. Conversely, soccer is a continuous game with no set plays. Players on the pitch have a game plan but they need to constantly react to evolving circumstances.

Rugby is a game of both. There are structured set plays but, in between, the game is continuous, and the players make decisions in real time. This is one of the hardest things to coach in rugby. Players need to scan the space ahead of them and see threats and opportunities so that they can make a great decision in milliseconds. It is known as 'heads-up rugby'. The idea is to exploit the opposing team's weaknesses. Many people struggle to put their heads up and see the space, and it is the same in business.

Another difficult thing to coach in rugby is how to communicate what you see to others. We call this information sharing, and the speed of play makes it a tricky thing to do. Barking out words isn't the same thing as communication. Kids will often shout 'pass' or call out the name of the person with the ball. If you're that person, all you hear is white noise and it can be completely debilitating. But if you hear someone shout 'on your left' or 'space left', that's useful *information*. They are not just words that make your head buzz. You can then make a decision and act. The same is true in business. A meaningful language is needed so that swift and decisive action can be taken.

A good rugby player who scans the space seems to have more time to make decisions. A great rugby player seems to have all the time in the world. They see space early and work hard off the ball to get to where the ball is going to be before everyone else. The question is, how do you give yourself more time in business? As play breaks down and things become unstructured, how do you maintain a **heads-up mindset** to see what is in front of you and make confident decisions so that you can win? How do you act like a great quarterback and decide not to do a set play because you've seen something ahead of you? The analysis provided by a great OP&A Team should give senior management more time and space to see what's ahead and react faster. The methods, techniques and tools I explain throughout this book are intended to give you the confidence to be able to react quickly, making better decisions earlier, and with a level of belief that means you can sleep at night. One such tool was introduced to me by Joseph Perfetti while I was chairing the CRF conference: Duke University Corporate Education's Agile Dashboard.[6]

The Agile Dashboard

The Agile Dashboard is a tool used to encourage leaders to adopt agile ways of thinking and leading to enable fast decision-making in uncertain times. At its heart is the SUDD model, which consists of four parts:

1. CAN I **SCAN** THE ENVIRONMENT TO SEE THE ROAD AHEAD?

Scanning the horizon to understand the road ahead relates to much of what I've discussed so far in this chapter. Organizations need the capability to collect data related to the external market system and track **leading indicators**. They also need the capability to effectively plan, spot trends, understand likely technological innovations and predict how their customer needs and behaviours will change over the next five years. Might your customers look elsewhere for more sustainable or convenient solutions, or could you be overlooking a new set of customers who would not have found you before?

It's also important to consider who your competitors are likely to be in five years' time. A great point made in the Innosight report is that 'Your new competitive landscape depends not on your history but on your strategy'. Think about your strategy and how you intend to innovate and adapt in response to emerging trends in your market. Where will that take you, and what will your new competitive landscape look like when you get there?

2. CAN I **UNDERSTAND** WHAT I AM LOOKING AT AND MAKE SENSE OF THE INFORMATION?

There's no point in data for data's sake. It needs to be understood to gain **actionable insight**. This involves getting into the 'why': the root causes of why the data you are looking at is showing what it is showing. In Chapter 4.2 I explain the importance of using hypotheses to investigate and get to the 'so what' of any data uncovered.

3. CAN I **DISCERN** THE CHOICES BY CREATING OPTIONS AND FLEXIBILITY?

The third point on the Agile Dashboard is the one that excites me the most: that of optionality. To fully understand the choices available to you, scenario modelling can be performed to create **options**. Probability can be attached to those options to understand the most likely outcomes of your actions and decisions that you make.

Scenario modelling is all about asking 'What-If' questions across a range of possible future scenarios to ensure that your organization is better prepared to react quickly in the face of disruption. It involves thinking through all the possible eventualities which could have an impact on your plan, and what your best course of action would be if those eventualities occurred. In the film *Avengers: Infinity War*, Dr Strange uses the Time Stone to model millions of alternative future scenarios (14,000,605 in fact). His head whips from left to right at supersonic speed, and in doing so he views 'all the possible outcomes' of the battle with the enemy Thanos.[7] In all those millions of outcomes, he sees only one in which the Avengers win, so he knows for certain how he needs to proceed. Sadly, none of us has a Time Stone or Dr Strange's superpower any more than we have a time machine to help us zip to the future, but we can work out the probability that if we do x, y will happen, and we can work this out over a range of possible scenarios. Working out probability in a complex world is difficult, but you can give it your best shot.

I'll illustrate this with an example of an economic technique I learned over 20 years ago: that of **Real Option Pricing (ROP)**. In finance terms, an option is essentially a contract which gives the buyer the right to buy an asset at a specified time in the future, at a price determined at the time the option is sold. It's a game of risk and taking bets, and I've always loved it. I'm a fan of its counterintuitive nature, and after learning about it I experienced a paradigm shift in how I thought about investment. At the heart of the technique is the idea that there is never one single outcome of investing in an option, but a range of potential outcomes. These outcomes can be used to calculate the level of risk in different scenarios. When investing, you communicate an expected return, but also provide a range of outcomes which demonstrates the level of risk. In a fast-moving, uncertain market environment, defining the range of uncertainty is critical to understanding the risk of a decision.

The greater the level of uncertainty and volatility of an outcome, the greater the level of risk; and the greater the level of risk, the greater the option value. In other words, uncertainty and volatility drive up the value of an option. Understanding the options and the level of risk attached to each helps you to see where to place your bets. This is where you need to think like a poker player, assessing probabilities, reacting quickly by making small bets and investments. Some bets you'll win and some you'll lose, but that's how you learn so that you can be better prepared next time around. The most important thing, in my view, is to guard against being too risk averse. Many businesses are held back and miss out on opportunities because they fall into this trap. Experience has shown me that the larger the organization, the harder it is to persuade people to go for it. This is why start-ups often have such a strong chance in uncertain markets. Having comparatively few decision makers means they can assess the level of uncertainty and risk at speed and reach decisions far more quickly.

4. CAN I **DECIDE** AND ACT WITH IMPERFECT INFORMATION?

How much information do you need to make a decision? Colin Powell, the late US secretary of state, famously had a 40/70 rule. This involved putting off decision-making until you have at least 40 per cent of the available information, while not waiting until you have over 70 per cent. Less than 40 per cent and you'll be relying too heavily on guess work, but over 70 per cent is likely to delay you beyond the point where the decision needs to be made. I see this in a friend of mine who is a venture capitalist. His experience is such that he can make an investment decision within an hour. He competes with speed, writing term sheets on the spot, and submitting them to the companies he wants to invest in while others are probably stuck doing the analysis. He's an extreme example – his experience is such that he automatically knows which data is relevant and which isn't. Less experienced venture capitalists can't make such lightning-fast decisions, but success depends on being able to deal with a level of ambiguity and acting with imperfect information. This is true for any type of business. I love data. It runs through my blood, and I get a kick out of using it to analyse, understand, predict and plan. But there is no point in analysis for analysis's sake, or in getting so embroiled in it that it slows you down to the point of missing out to a faster competitor.

The importance of organizational capabilities

A crucial point to make about the Agile Dashboard is that organizations need the right capabilities to employ its principles well. Capability is needed to collect data, track leading indicators, perform analysis and create action-able insight. The right skills and technology are also needed to perform scenario modelling. The importance of organizational capabilities is also at the heart of Dave Snowden's thinking, specifically the relative significance of organizational *capabilities* over individual *competencies*. For him, **interface design** and how people connect and interact within the organization system are far more important than who people are as individuals, and the competencies that they hold. I couldn't agree more. In fact, everything put forward in this book as well as its prequel is about seeing the whole and understanding connections to maximize performance. One of my favourite quotes of all time is from Dave Ulrich, a professor, author and management consultant who I greatly admire: 'People can be champions, but organizations win championships… it's not talent or people which provide competitive edge, but organization systems. The key question is how to build an organization as a system to win in the marketplace.'[8]

I want to be clear about the difference between **competencies** and **capabilities**. While individual people have competencies, organizations have teams and capabilities in which processes, systems, culture and people (with the right competencies) come together to execute organizational strategy. As Figure 1.1.1 shows, in a core capability, you need the right people, with the right competencies to do the work. Competencies include people's skills, behaviours, knowledge and cognition (for more on competencies see Chapter 1.2). You also need the right systems and processes to enable that work to be done. A future-focused mindset and culture is also important for setting expectations about how work should be carried out within the capability.

FIGURE 1.1.1   The components of a core capability

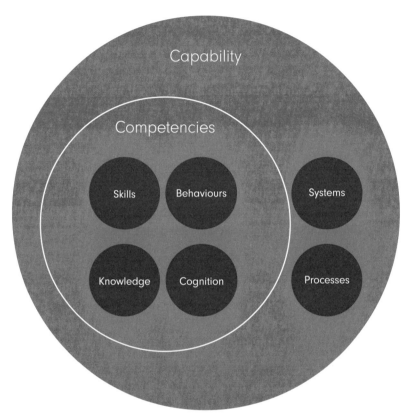

A new core capability is needed: OP&A

This book puts forward the case for a new core, strategically focused capability to manage and track the performance of the organization system on an ongoing basis, to perform organization design work, to plan the size and cost of the workforce and maintain strategic alignment. I am therefore not only arguing for the need to see past individual competencies to organizational capabilities, but also for a new capability to be introduced, the job of which is to maximize the spectrum of capabilities within the organization.

Despite commentators maligning the People function for years for not being sufficiently strategic and future-oriented, the problem has not yet been satisfactorily solved. In most organizations, the People function's focus is still firmly fixed on historical data, looking backwards rather than forwards. In fact, based on hundreds of organizations I have worked with, and asked the question of, and dozens where I have performed activity analysis, at least 98 per cent of time is spent on transactional tasks. Consider these facts:

- 82 per cent of HR executives don't have the right people to execute their strategy[9]
- 65 per cent of children entering school now will work in jobs that don't yet exist[10]

Research carried out in 2019 by the Centre for Economics and Business Research into the economic benefits of workforce planning and analytics revealed that productivity growth rate is twice as high for organizations that invest in people planning capabilities.[11] For the UK economy that equates to £10.4 billion, and for the US economy it equates to $92.2 billion. These figures are not only significant at an individual business level, but at a macroeconomic one too. To me, the introduction of an OP&A capability into organizations is a no-brainer, and yet the amount of time a typical People function spends on activities such as organization design, workforce planning and people analytics is between zero and 2 per cent. The simple truth is that most People functions currently don't have the tools and capabilities necessary to help organizations proactively prepare for disruption and change. Two things are clear:

1 Operational Human Resources (HR), which is concerned with the immediate needs of the workforce (as opposed to planning for the future), is no longer sufficient to meet the needs of the modern organization.

2 There is an ever-increasing requirement for the People function to become more data-driven, and for those within it to adopt a more future-oriented mindset, allowing for activities such as people analytics, ongoing organization design and workforce planning, workforce visualization and analysis, scenario modelling, transition management and succession planning. These activities are not nice-to-haves but are vital for future proofing business in the face of disruptive change. Without them, organizations can find themselves in a cycle of event-based and large-scale reactive transformation.

After a period of interviewing candidates for a CFO role, I had become accustomed to hearing about the same topic – that of the need to separate the Finance Team into those with responsibility for FP&A, conducting activities such as scenario modelling, and those with responsibility for day-to-day financial operations. This key message made me think: how can future-focused FP&A be truly effective without a real understanding of *organizational* needs both now and in the weeks, months and years ahead? Surely, for FP&A to provide a truly accurate picture, it should work in tandem with analysis and planning from the People function to understand how Roles, Positions and People in organizations are likely to change over the short, medium and long term and impact on the bottom line? And then it dawned on me: the answer is staring us in the face. To better serve the organization, the People function needs look no further than Finance for a well-established blueprint to follow to form its own strategically focused capability.

FP&A: A blueprint for OP&A to follow

As a function, Finance is broadly broken into two pieces: there are those who deal with transactional, operational tasks such as payroll; financial control; accounting and financial reporting; and operational management reporting. These activities make up around 78 per cent of the work of the Finance function and are integral to the day-to-day running of a business.[12] Without them, businesses couldn't survive. The remaining 22 per cent is comprised of forward-looking planning, monitoring and analysis which falls under the umbrella of FP&A. The mindset of those performing FP&A activities is vital for the success of the function. The CFO is the FP&A Leader, and they think like futurists. They budget and forecast financial performance. They perform analysis; they model and plan and pull the levers that add value to the business, generating actionable insight to allow quick and accurate decision-making. In their analyses they don't only look at **lagging indicators** such as revenue but also leading indicators such as how many leads there are in the sales funnel or sales funnel conversion rates. The FP&A Leader speaks a language that senior management understands (everyone gets the concept of a bottom line) and is therefore a much-valued advisor to the Executive Team, particularly when reformulating strategy from a financial perspective. In many organizations, they are seen to have the greatest insight into organizational needs and the capability of the business to perform now, and in the future. In truth, they rarely have access to the level of detail necessary to truly understand the work and the workforce. This is where OP&A comes in.

Taking lessons from the Finance function, the People function can be divided similarly. The core, day-to-day tasks associated with the People function are essential to the very existence of organizations and should take up around 75 per cent of the work that the function does. These include tasks such as talent acquisition and employee onboarding, Learning and Development, employee lifecycle management, dispute resolution and compensation and benefits. But, as Figure 1.1.2 shows, the work of the People function should not stop there. The remaining 25 per cent should be focused on OP&A:

- organization design
- workforce planning
- **position lifecycle management** (managing current and future total size and cost of the workforce based on positions opening and closing)
- advanced and predictive analysis
- scenario modelling
- transition management
- succession planning
- tracking and monitoring organizational performance

FIGURE 1.1.2   Finance provides a model for the People function to adopt

Day-to-day, backward-looking	Forward-looking
Continuous processes necessary to sustain the business but do not drive strategic advantage.	Analysis and planning to anticipate changes and prepare the organization for the future.

Finance

Finance operations	Financial planning and analysis
→ Credit control and payables → Accounting and financial reporting → Operational management reporting → Controls and treasury	→ Budgeting and forecasting financial performance → Evaluates new projects and investment opportunities → Optimizes financing structure → Analyses financial and operational

HR

HR operations	Organizational planning and analysis
→ Employee Lifecycle Management → Talent acquisition and employee onboarding → Compensation and benefits → Learning and development → Governance and controls	→ Organization design → Workforce planning → Position Lifecycle Management → Advanced and predictive analysis → Future talent planning

Successful People Teams consider leading indicators such as the number of employees churning within three months, the number of CVs being submitted to the company and the quality of new hires. In short, the support provided by OP&A helps with vital tasks which prepare the business for the future. OP&A Leaders need a place in the boardroom alongside FP&A, influencing and advising the Executive Team about strategic options based on insight gained from analysis of data.

How this book will help you

This book sets out the case for implementing OP&A in your organization. It takes you through the work of the capability when it is both 'business as usual' and at times of large-scale transformation. It also explains how to get the capability up and running in your own organization.

It is my strong belief that OP&A will change the way that the People function serves organizations, both now and in the future. You might consult in this field, or work within an organization's People function. You might be an HR Business Partner, a Chief People Officer (CPO), or work as part of an Organizational Effectiveness Team. You may be one of a growing number of organizational planning analysts. You might be a CFO working in FP&A and wanting to understand how you can work better with the People function to form a more complete view of the future organization. If you are involved in any way with people data, ongoing organization design, or workforce planning, this book will help you to navigate the path ahead.

My aim is to help you to identify crucial business questions to ask such as:

1 Are we executing our strategy? How can we improve on our ability to deliver our strategy from an organization design perspective? Are we fit for purpose?

2 What is our people cost today and how is it likely to look in the future? Does this track against plan? Is the plan right?

3 How do we know who's doing what work and who should be doing it? What skills are we lacking?

4 Where can we make efficiency savings in headcount, processes or by location to support our long-term goals?

5 How can we make decision-making less bureaucratic and streamline the work we need to do to sustain the business?

Answering these sorts of questions is easy if you have the right capability. The difficult part is knowing which ones to ask. This book will help you to develop the right mindset so that you can isolate the right questions.

Structure of the book

This book takes you through the work performed by the OP&A function: organization design, transformation and continual optimization, workforce planning and analysis, and culminates with advice on how to put the systems, processes and technology in place to enable OP&A capability.

The remainder of Part One consists a resumé of my first book, *Data-Driven Organization Design*, as the concepts discussed therein are essential to understand to fully grasp the work of OP&A. Next, I look at the work of FP&A, as well as the mindset needed to do it. My intention is to arm you with the tools and language necessary to work collaboratively with your FP&A colleagues.

In Part Two I look at the work performed by the OP&A function in terms of making organization redesigns real and optimizing those designs over time. I take you through a four-step process: 1. Prepare to execute; 2. Assess impacts and plan communications; 3. Manage talent transitions and consultation; 4. Ongoing optimization.

Part Three looks at the six steps for workforce planning: building an as-is baseline; top-down supply projections; top-down demand planning; bottom-up position planning; finalizing budgets and targets; and analysing and monitoring.

Part Four looks at the different types of analysis that can be done as well as the challenges faced in both the analysis and the reporting of that analysis. I consider common statistical traps which are easy to fall into, as well as dashboard design and the necessity to get the amount of data 'just right' to be able to tell the story you want to tell.

Finally, in Part Five, I look at how to make OP&A real in your own organization. The chapters in this part serve as a case study for how to implement the advice given throughout *Data-Driven Organization Design* and this book.

To help bring the discussion to life, I have included a case study through-out based on a fictional organization named Hokupaa. This is a continuation of the case study in *Data-Driven Organization Design*. While inspired by my own experiences, I have changed many details to protect people and simplify the story.

Final thoughts

OP&A is all about integrated thinking. It's about understanding how one thing impacts another in an organization, and about bringing together siloed planning for greater alignment and understanding. There are seven points of integration which I will explain throughout this book.

The first is time horizons. When designing an organization, you do it for a single photographic snapshot in time, but when planning an organization, you do it to maintain organizational health *over time*. This requires you to think with different time horizons: short, medium and long term. When taking a short-term view, you look to the next month or quarter. A medium-term view involves looking 12 to 18 months ahead (a good example of this is an annual budget). Planning over the long term requires a multi-year outlook. These different time horizons are applied both when scenario planning and when workforce planning.

The second point of integration is demand and supply. Workforce planning is about the demand and supply of the workforce over time. By integrating the demand (the planned workforce) with the supply (the actual workforce) you can understand the likely cost of your workforce over time as well as the competencies that your organization is likely to need into the future. You can also identify headcount and competency gaps between demand and supply. Once you know the gaps, you can work to find the root cause for why they exist to get the supply of workers back on track. The chapters of Part Three cover workforce planning in detail.

The third point of integration is **top-down** and **bottom-up** thinking. These terms are spoken about a lot generally in business. When it comes to OP&A, they are applied to workforce planning. Top-down helps you to get started – it sets the direction and provides high-level guestimates to anchor your thought. Bottom-up planning brings a reality check. Do those high-level guestimates make sense? It involves validating, iterating and learning as you iterate. OP&A brings together top-down budgeting and business planning assumptions done by workforce planners and bottom-up position planning done by individual teams. The top-down assumptions are based on business drivers and targets and provide a model plan. The teams then outline what they think they need to be able to execute this plan. Part Three looks at the difference between these two activities.

The fourth point is the integration of high-level aggregation and individual-level detail. Activities such as talent mapping and succession planning require data at an individual level to understand who the potential candidates are for a role and where people might move to in the organization at a future date. As the role of OP&A is also to understand trends and make predictions and assumptions, data also needs to be aggregated: gathered and presented in a summarized form. There are a great many ways in which data can be aggregated to understand how the organization system is functioning and predict how it can expect to function in the future.

OP&A also integrates planning and the employee and position lifecycles. The employee lifecycle model helps employers to understand how the people they hire engage with their organization. Much like the customer lifecycle, employees go through a journey consisting of six steps – attraction; recruitment; onboarding; development; retention; separation – and they experience the organization differently at each one of them. OP&A can help businesses understand how the employee lifecycle impacts on the supply of workers by giving an integrated view of factors which contribute to flight risk and attrition, such as the employee experience, flexibility and reward. I explain the position lifecycle in Chapter 3.3. In its lifecycle, a position also transitions through six steps from being planned to being closed. OP&A tracks positions through their lifecycles to understand the number of open positions at any one time, closing them or keeping them open as necessary, depending on the need identified in top-down and bottom-up workforce planning.

The last two points relate to the integration of people. As already explained, OP&A brings together Finance and HR to build a cohesive workforce plan. With the right technology, OP&A can work in tandem with FP&A to create true alignment and collaboration on the overall business goals. OP&A can provide a comprehensive understanding of the cost of the workforce over time, as well as the required headcount and competencies over time to execute strategy. It can also provide insight into the divergence of actuals from targets. I describe the interface between FP&A and OP&A in more detail in Chapter 5.3.

Finally, OP&A is all about integrating business operations and people. As I explain in Chapter 1.2, the organization system is comprised of six inter-related components, each of which forms a dataset: **objectives**; **activities**;

competencies; **roles**; **positions**; and **people**. OP&A ensures that the workforce is fully integrated with the needs and goals of the business. Data brings transparency to the hidden truths of the organization to give a clear picture of how work in the organization is carried out and the performance of the workforce.

These seven points are brought to life throughout the chapters of this book. They build on the principles discussed in *Data-Driven Organization Design*. To help you recap, the next chapter provides a whistle-stop tour of the main concepts. These are vital to understand before getting to grips with the work of OP&A.

REMEMBER THIS

1 Disruption is not new. It's been around since at least 1840.

2 Organizations with the capability to plan for disruptive change and make rapid, confident decisions related to the organization and the workforce will outperform their competitors.

3 Model scenarios and continually ask 'What-If' questions to understand the impact of various available options. This enables organizations to be 'adept at adapting' and capitalize on opportunities when they present.

4 Maintain a heads-up mindset to scan the horizon and see the space in front of you.

5 The concept of volatility can be understood through Real Option Pricing.

6 A new core capability is needed: Organization Planning and Analysis (OP&A), to anticipate changes and prepare the organization for the future.

Notes

1 Rumelt, R (2012) *Good Strategy/Bad Strategy: The difference and why it matters*, Profile Books Ltd.

2 General Electric (2000) *Annual Report 2000*. www.annualreports.com/HostedData/AnnualReportArchive/g/NYSE_GE_2000.pdf (archived at https://perma.cc/3F39-SA4Z)

3 Reuter, D (2018) A look back at General Electric's 129-year journey from American manufacturing icon to fallen giant, *Business Insider*. www.businessinsider.com/ the-rise-and-fall-of-general-electric-2019-8?amp (archived at https://perma.cc/ TUG4-7PAB)

4 Viguerie, P, Calder, N and Hindo, B (2021) 2021 corporate longevity forecast, *Innosight*. www.innosight.com/insight/creative-destruction/ (archived at https://perma.cc/A5PN-R2C4)

5 For more on the Cynefin Framework, visit https://thecynefin.co/about-us/ about-cynefin-framework/ (archived at https://perma.cc/M5FT-F5CC)

6 For more on Duke Corporate Education's Agile Dashboard, visit www.dukece. com/insights/closer-look-at-agile-dashboard/ (archived at https://perma.cc/ D847-45XB)

7 *Avengers: Infinity War* (2018) Directed by Anthony Russo and Joe Russo [feature film], Walt Disney Studios Motion Pictures.

8 Ulrich, D (2019) The role of the HR Business Partner in a digital age, MyHRFuture, 27 August. www.myhrfuture.com/digital-hr-leaders-podcast/ 2019/8/27/role-of-the-hr-business-partner-in-a-digital-age (archived at https://perma.cc/8HCY-MWBT)

9 SHL (2018) Global assessment trends report. www.shl.com/en/assessments/ trends/ (archived at https://perma.cc/4LMG-VNZN)

10 World Economic Forum (2016) *The Future of Jobs: Employment, skills and workforce strategy for the Fourth Industrial Revolution*. www3.weforum.org/ docs/WEF_Future_of_Jobs.pdf (archived at https://perma.cc/2EMC-TA5U)

11 Centre for Economics and Business Research (2019) Large firms underinvesting in raising productivity say leading economists. www.orgvue.com/news/ large-firms-underinvesting-in-raising-productivity-say-leading-economists (archived at https://perma.cc/SC7P-VGFW)

12 Driscoll, M (2015) Metric of the month: How finance people spend their time. www.cfo.com/budgeting/2015/12/metric-month-finance-people-spend-time (archived at https://perma.cc/Q4EL-Y5CJ)

1.2

Data-Driven Organization Design

Introduction

Data-Driven Organization Design (or D-DOD, as I shall refer to it throughout this book) is the process of designing organizations with datasets which reflect the main components of the organization system. These datasets give clarity on where the organization is heading, the results that need to be achieved and how well the organization is set up to deliver necessary outcomes today and in the future. They allow you to collect and sort data on your employees and the work that they do in a way that is practical and relevant to the organization.

This chapter serves as a summary of my book *Data-Driven Organization Design*. It is important to understand the principles within it before attempting activities such as workforce planning or career path mapping. OP&A provides the capability to evolve the design on an ongoing basis but getting the design right is a crucial first step. I don't mean for this chapter to provide a comprehensive guide to D-DOD, but rather to give you a high-level understanding of the overarching principles.

Too often, organization design is seen as a structural matter: of organization charts and who reports to whom. D-DOD is about more than this. It maps out all the elements of an organization's design to ensure that the *right people*, with the *right skills*, are doing the *right work*, in the *right numbers* with *real alignment* to achieve strategic objectives.

D-DOD is comprised of three stages:

1 macro operating design

2 micro detailed design

3 Making it Real

The **macro operating design** relates to what most people think of when they hear the words 'organization design'. It's the kind of all-encompassing design that brings about a change to the operating model and results in large-scale transformation. The **micro detailed design** is what it sounds like – it's the detail. It involves defining all the elements of the design across the organization system so that the macro operating model is implementable. *Data-Driven Organization Design* delves into these first two stages, and only touches on Stage 3. *Organizational Planning and Analysis* is less about the design and more about the 'doing'. A large component of the book in your hands is about Stage 3 – **Making it Real**. This chapter gives a whistle-stop tour of the first two stages. But first, I will explain some core foundations which underlie D-DOD.

The organization is a system

Understanding the organization as a system is at the heart of D-DOD. It is made up of components – datasets containing target and actual data which allow you to monitor organizational performance. These datasets bring transparency to hidden connections so that seemingly unpredictable scenarios can be foreseen.

The D-DOD datasets fall into two groups: **Roles, Positions and People (RPP)** and **Objectives, Activities and Competencies (OAC)**. Understanding the difference between Roles, Positions and People is fundamental to D-DOD:

- Roles are designed to deliver the strategy. They are designed with pieces of OAC which create targets for the role.
- Positions are the specification and number of roles planned over time: for example, the scope or location.
- People are individuals (be they employees or external contractors) holding a position, performing a role.

Figure 1.2.1 provides the key to understanding the **organization system** and the connections between the different components. These connections provide a framework to analyse, design, plan and monitor the organization system. **Target** and **actual data** are shown as well as the **gap** between the two. An example of a gap is the difference between the required number of positions and the current number of people.

FIGURE 1.2.1 The organization system

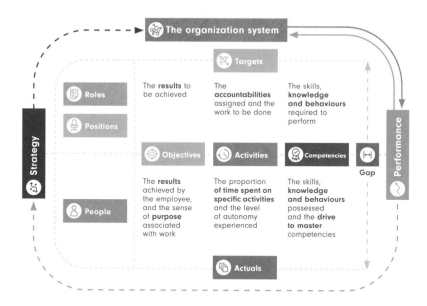

Organization design is not about moving people and positions in organization charts. You need to see the system, how the information flows and hierarchies across the organization to understand how they fit together (for more on hierarchies, see below). In understanding, mapping and modelling these links you can connect the elements together:

- It gives clarity on who is required to do what and for how long.
- It helps ensure everything that needs to be done is covered.
- It avoids duplication of effort or things falling between the cracks.

If there's one key mantra to remember when doing organization design it's this: it is what is *in the box* that counts, not where the box sits on a chart. In Chapter 4.2 I talk about nodes in data. In D-DOD, a box is a node. Say this node is a role, the box will hold information such as title, description, function, sub-function, level or grade. The box will also contain *connections*. A role might be connected to a person, and to different taxonomies, for example the objectives taxonomy or the activity taxonomy.

Organizational data is hierarchical

While it's not fashionable to think of organizations in terms of hierarchical structures, they are inescapable when it comes to D-DOD. Hierarchies (or taxonomies) are needed to manage the organization system and bring control over complexity. They categorize and subcategorize each of the datasets into logical chunks of information. The key taxonomies to develop are those for Objectives, Activities and Competencies. I outline best-practice rules for creating taxonomies in *Data-Driven Organization Design*. Examples are given later in the chapter when I discuss the elements of micro detailed design.

Organizational data is messy (fragmented and incomplete, constantly changing and connected in complex ways)

Most organizations have problems with their organization data. At the highest level, organizations change, there are acquisitions, mergers, and divestments over time. Business units merge and morph, and companies enter new markets and geographies. At the RPP level, people are constantly joining, moving within and leaving the organization. Positions are constantly planned, opened, filled, vacated and closed, and the roles required to deliver the strategy change periodically. All this makes for messy data. It's hard to keep track of unless you find a way to visualize the connections.

Many-to-many relationships exist in the connections between the six interrelated components of the organization system. Figure 1.2.2 demonstrates this using the examples of succession planning and understanding the work being done by the workforce. As the figure shows, many employees can be candidates for the same position, and a single employee can be a succession candidate for many positions.

Visualization is one of the foremost principles of understanding the **links** in the organization system. Rows and tables of data contain lots of information but tell you very little. If used in the right way, visualization can drive performance and aid decision-making. Visualizing information helps to connect the seemingly unconnected, and give deeper and better insights across the organization. It helps you to see things from different angles and perspectives, zooming out to understand the whole or zooming in to understand the detail.

FIGURE 1.2.2 The many-to-many relationships in organization data

People connected to positions

Many employees as succession
candidates for the **same position**

Single employee as succession
candidate for **many positions**

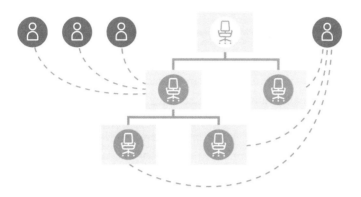

Replicated across **many employees** and **many positions** in the organization

People connected to work activities and processes

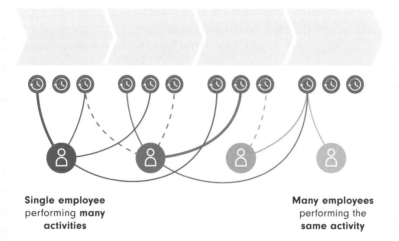

Single employee
performing **many
activities**

Many employees
performing the
same activity

Replicated for **many employees** across **many activities** and processes

By creating, linking and visualizing organization hierarchies, you can achieve a remarkable depth of analysis. You can see the links between individual performance and target objectives, and then delve into whether an individual who is underperforming has missing competencies that are trainable, is overloaded with too many new objectives or is working for a new manager who has historically high levels of attrition on their team.

Macro operating design versus micro detailed design

When most people talk about organization design, they usually mean the big picture stuff – the kind of design that determines the best operating model to execute an organization's strategy. D-DOD separates organization design into two different types: macro operating design and micro detailed design. The former is the big picture; the latter is involved with defining the detail of the components of the organization system. It can be useful to think of these two different types in terms of telescopic and microscopic views of the organization. We need telescopes to understand the universe (macro operating design) and microscopes to understand the detail (micro detailed design). Changing the macro operating design usually causes significant upheaval, and in my view should only be done when absolutely necessary. Far too many organizations get caught in a boom-and-bust cycle of hiring in the good times and firing in the bad. With D-DOD, organization performance is monitored to give insight into when small-scale micro detailed design tweaks might be necessary for the organization to continue executing strategy. In this way, large-scale transformations can largely be avoided. The rest of this chapter outlines the main aspects of macro operating and micro detailed design.

Macro operating design

When considering macro operating design, the most important question is whether the potential upside of doing it is worth the downside cost and risk. Redesigns don't only have implications for organizations. They have a profound effect on all those who go through them. Large-scale intervention is not always (in fact is rarely) necessary and you need an overwhelming **case for change** to embark on it. Micro detailed design interventions are often sufficient in the continuous pursuit of organization performance, even after a change of strategic direction.

If you decide that a long-term step change is needed there is a four-stage, gated process to follow:

1 articulating your strategy and case for change

2 setting your **design principles** and **design criteria**

3 listing potential models and mapping those to the value chain

4 selecting a model and creating a business case

There is not the space to go into each of these stages in detail, but I will outline the main points below.

Stage 1: Articulating your strategy and case for change

Macro operating design starts with your **vision**, **strategy** and **goals**:

- The vision statement is a single statement that explains clearly and specifically where you want to get to over the long term.
- The strategy defines how you are going to achieve your vision. It sets out the direction and scope of the organization over the long term.
- The goals are the intended results you want your organization to achieve based on your strategy and vision.

The goals translate into high-level objectives for the organization. All stakeholders need to agree about these fundamental aspects. They provide purpose for the new design, and enable trade-offs to be made throughout the macro operating design process. They also form the basis of your case for change.

THE CASE FOR CHANGE

The case for change answers why a redesign is necessary and outlines how it will help to deliver business success. There are two main points about the case for change:

1 It must be inextricably linked to the strategy and tied to identifiable problems preventing it from being executed.

2 It is crucial that all stakeholders fully support each point with their heads and their hearts.

Building the case for change starts with identifying the current challenges preventing your organization from achieving its goals and objectives. These challenges should be taken from across functions, organizational levels and geographies. There are two aims:

1 Establish where the risk is.

2 Identify why the problem exists by using root cause analysis.

When building your case for change it's useful to perform two exercises which I describe in full in my book *Data-Driven Organization Design*: 'Imagine your nightmare competitor' and 'Imagine you are moving house'. The first asks people to think about a competitor who could come in and beat you. This competitor may not currently exist, or it may be a company that has the potential to diversify and break into your markets. The second encourages you to imagine you are moving house and apply it to the organization. You ask yourself the following questions:

1 What should you leave behind?

2 What should you take with you?

3 What should you buy new?

It's all about trade-offs and where you place your bets. For a practical application of this technique, see Chapter 5.2.

Once agreed, the case for change is converted into sets of design principles and design criteria that can be used to evaluate alternative operating model **design options**.

Stage 2: Setting your design principles and design criteria

If, at the end of Stage 1, you decide that a full organization redesign is the way forward, the first step is to set out your design principles and design criteria. These are your reference point for any decisions regarding how to change your organization. They bring together your vision, goals, strategy and case for change in a framework that sets the priorities for the design work. Figure 1.2.3 shows how the design principles and criteria link your vision, goals, strategy and case for change. Design principles and criteria are frequently muddled. This is how they differ:

- Design principles are key measurable objectives that are translated into design rules which must hold true irrespective of the design option under consideration.

- Design criteria are critical business goals used in the design process to evaluate which options should be chosen. They are best articulated as an outcome, and it must be possible to identify how success against the criteria would be measured. Design criteria must be listed in order of priority to aid in the decision between different design options.

FIGURE 1.2.3 The design principles and criteria should clearly link back to the vision and goals of the organization

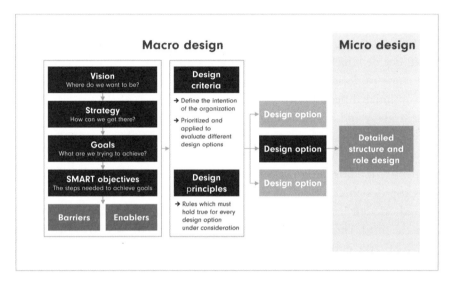

The following would all be considered common design principles:

- There should be no one-to-one reporting relationships.
- Team members should only ever report to someone one or two grades higher than themselves.
- There should only be one person ultimately responsible for any activity or decision.
- There should be no more than three people with veto approval or power.

Principles can be measured and managed. You can quantify how well you are doing against these principles in the micro detailed design phase.

The design criteria guide you on how you want to change your organization and are integral to choosing the right design. Below are examples of some common design criteria:

- Exceed customers' expectations.
- Provide a standardized customer experience.

- Reduce delivery time to customers.
- Innovate faster.
- Enable excellence in execution.
- Minimize cost.

Once you've set out your design criteria, be sure to cross-reference them with all the major elements of your case for change, to check for alignment.

PRIORITIZE YOUR DESIGN CRITERIA

Next, decide which criteria are the most important. This is vital for when you come to decide between different design options, as different models will optimize different criteria. This is a difficult part of the process, but if your strategy and case for change are clear and agreed, it should be possible to reach a consensus. Prioritization requires you to isolate the single design criterion that matters the most. You're not aiming for a top three; you need to identify the *one* design criterion that is the most important on your list. This top design criterion should be significantly more important than the second on your list, and the second should be significantly more important than the third. There are various methods which can be used to prioritize the design criteria, explained in *Data-Driven Organization Design*.

Stage 3: Listing potential models and mapping those to the value chain

Once you have your criteria, it's time to choose a design option which describes what the high-level organization should look like. A design option is a schematic or conceptual model which should enable you to answer the following sorts of questions:

- How will we work across products, channels, customer segments, business units and geography (and which is our primary organizing dimension)?
- How will we interact with customers?
- How will shared business services be provided?
- Where does accountability for key elements of the value chain sit?
- How will the key dimensions of the design option interact?

The option you choose should give you the best possible chance of delivering on your design criteria, especially that single most important one. The rationale behind the decision will be documented in your business case (see Stage 4) and is the logic that will drive the detailing when doing the micro detailed design.

When choosing an option, you will need to make a whole range of trade-offs between desirable but often mutually exclusive factors. Your aim is to meet the largest number of your design criteria and optimize the top one on your list. There are three steps involved in the process.

STEP 1: DEFINE THE HIGH-LEVEL VALUE CHAIN AND SUMMARY PROCESSES

Your **value chain** describes how the 'raw materials' you need for your business (whether that's ideas or parts) can be broken down and transformed into your final product or service. At this point, your aim is to map the high-level value chain and summary processes to the high-level to-be organizational structure. The idea is to build a simple taxonomy as shown in Figure 1.2.4. These summary processes help to define the true scope of each of the structural options.

FIGURE 1.2.4 List of summary processes

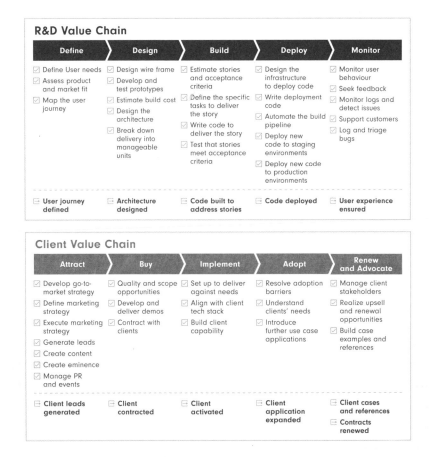

STEP 2: DEVELOP DESIGN OPTIONS

The next step is to develop different design options which will support your design criteria. Start by thinking about the different possible dimensions of design most suited to your organization. These are your **Key Organizational Dimensions (KODs)**. These might be geography, function or customer. Decide how you would rank these KODs, as this will feed into your thinking.

Design dimensions are comprised of frames and features, with a **frame** being the highest-level architectural concept of an organization. For example, in a geographic frame, the organization would be structured by geography, giving autonomy to each region or area, while in a functional frame, the organization would be structured around core functional capabilities which would usually align to professions, e.g. Sales, Marketing, Finance or Operations.

A **feature** is an item which can be incorporated into part of a frame to describe how that area functions. Coming up with a list of design options involves combining frames and features to create **hybrid** or **matrix designs**. You normally need to go through numerous iterations before feeling confident that you have one that will work in practice. The first step is to choose a primary frame which best supports the design criterion at the top of your list. The second is to embed other frames or features into your primary frame to create a hybrid or matrix design option tailored to your own organization. The aim is to end up with a list of three or four options.

STEP 3: ASK HOWWIP QUESTIONS

Step 3 is to understand how each option will work in practice using various methods to map out responsibilities and ask **HOWWIP (How it Will Work In Practice)** questions. This helps to decide which option would be the best to proceed with. The methods are described in *Data-Driven Organization Design*.

Stage 4: Selecting a model and creating a business case

Finally, it's crunch time – it's time to decide which option to choose. If there is a clear option which is best placed to deliver the goals and strategy of the organization, proceed to creating a business case. Most of the time, the option to proceed with is not obvious and trade-offs need to be made to reach a decision. A simple Strengths, Weaknesses, Opportunities and Threats

(SWOT) analysis often suffices. If not, you can progress to doing a weightings analysis. There isn't room here to look at this method in detail, but I do so in *Data-Driven Organization Design*.

Once you've chosen your option, it's time to write the business case, which could follow the following generic headings:

1 recommendation and summary rationale

2 the vision and strategy

3 current must-keep strengths

4 current issues and case for change

5 list of design criteria and principles, including how each principle will be measured

6 options

7 summary of value stream and processes

8 summary of how each option would work

9 recommended option with rationale

10 benefits

11 implementation plans and costs

Macro operating design is about thinking. Thinking about different options and how those options will work in practice. It's about answering a range of fundamental questions and documenting the answers to those questions. For your chosen option to work, micro detailed design is needed to realize your vision. This is the next stage.

Micro detailed design

Micro detailed design defines how all the components in Figure 1.2.1 come together. It is where you ensure that the *right people* with the *right skills* are doing the *right work* in the *right numbers* and in the *right place*. As mentioned above, micro-level adjustments are often needed not only in response to a change to the macro operating model, but to continually optimize performance.

Micro detailed design can be understood in five distinct stages:

1 Build the data foundation.

2 Define and cascade objectives.

3 Optimize work and define accountabilities.

4 Define and manage competencies.

5 Pull it all together.

Stage 1: Build the data foundation

Building the **data foundation** involves two phases:

1 sourcing, consolidating, cleaning and validating data

2 developing a **role grid** and role design

I describe how to go about Phase 1 in Chapter 4.2 of this book, as preparing your data for ongoing OP&A analysis follows the same steps as when doing it for D-DOD. The other side of building your data foundation is role design. Role design is the fundamental building block from which the micro detailed design follows. Its objective is to maintain clarity and consistency so organizations can adapt at speed to changing contexts and plan and manage their evolution to consistently deliver business strategy. As my colleague Otto Pretorius states: 'Role and role grid design means to human capital what the general ledger design means to Finance. Although few see it, it's omnipresent. It anchors design, integrates process and provides context for meaningful analytics.' Without role design, terminology is muddled, roles and positions are thought of interchangeably and leaders do not have a good handle on their workforce and the work that they do.

ROLE DESIGN AND THE ROLE GRID

Against each person in the organization, there is actual data:

- the actual results which have been achieved by each person

- the proportion of time spent on specific activities and the responsibility held for specific activities

- the skills, knowledge and behaviours possessed and demonstrated

Roles are designed in the context of pieces of data. They should be designed to be highly motivating for people. The data creates targets for the role:

- objectives (the results to be achieved)

- activities (the work that needs to be done and the accountabilities that need to be held)
- competencies (the skills, knowledge and behaviours needed to perform the work effectively so that the objectives are met or exceeded)

The data also defines:

- accountabilities to be held
- purpose and mandate
- level and grade
- role family and cluster
- pay benchmarking codes (grade; target base; bonus; long-term incentive plan)

The above list indicates the minimum data required for role design. In Chapter 3.2 I outline the data needed for workforce planning (see Figure 3.2.1).

By defining roles and specifying positions within those roles, it's easy enough to scale up and add further positions when required, which has benefits for workforce planning and budgeting. In this way, roles can be seen as anchor points: essential building blocks in the design, planning and monitoring of the organization system. If they are not clearly defined, organization designs can get bent out of shape, and organizations become ineffective and unlikely to maintain agility and performance over time.

Once roles are designed, they are inserted into a role grid comprising role families and levels of work. Figure 1.2.5 shows an example of a role grid. Role grids provide a data framework for roles and positions, ensuring that data values relating to RPP and OAC, as well as pay and reward, are held in one place and kept in alignment across the organization.

Using Elliot Jacques' method for devising **requisite levels of work**, role grids help to verify whether people are doing work appropriate for their level. There is not the space to delve into Elliot Jacques' requisite levels of work in this chapter. For that, see *Data-Driven Organization Design*.

The role grid also becomes the basis for an organization's design, planning of positions and measurement of gaps, providing the master data for Enterprise Resource Planning and other transactional systems. This naturally leads to the grid providing data to all HR processes: workforce planning; recruitment; compensation; Learning and Development; performance management; and succession and talent planning. It is the anchor from which these HR processes follow. The more accurate and well designed the data, the better the experience when applying these people processes in daily interactions, and the more accurate the monitoring of gaps.

FIGURE 1.2.5 Roles are structured in a role grid determined by levels and role families

Role families

Level of work	Product management	Sales	Development
6	O Chief Executive Officer		
5	O Chief Product Officer	O Chief Revenue Officer	O Chief Technology Officer
4	O Vice President Method & Content O Vice President Product Management	O Vice President Client Success O Vice President PreSales O Vice President Revenue Enablement O Vice President Sales O Vice President Sales Channels	O Vice President Engineering
4S	O Lead Method & Content Consultant	O Lead PreSales Consultant O Lead Sales Executive	O Lead Architect O Technology Operations Lead
3	O Head of Client Capability Development O Head of UX	O Senior Sales Operations Manager	O Head of Quality Assurance O Senior Engineering Manager
3S	O Senior Client Capability Specialist O Product Manager O Senior Method & Content Consultant O Senior UX Designer	O Associate Sales Executive O Senior Channel Development Manager O Senior Channel Development Consultant O Head of Revenue Enablement O Lead Client Success Consultant O Sales Executive O Senior Client Success Consultant O Senior PreSales Consultant O Senior Client Operations Specialist O Technology Partnership Manager	O Architect O Lead Data Engineer O Lead Software Engineer O Senior Data Engineer O Senior Architect O Senior Quality Engineer O Senior Front-End Engineer O Senior Back-End Engineer O Senior Support Engineer
2S	O Digital Learning Technologist O Instructional Designer O UX Designer	O Client Success Consultant O PreSales Consultant O Client Success Operations Specialist	O Quality Engineer O Front-End Engineer O Back-End Engineer O Support Engineer
1S	O Junior Digital Learning Technologist O Junior UX Designer	O Client Operations Agent	O Client Support Agent O Graduate Software Engineer O Graduate Quality Engineer
1		O Enablement Coordinator	

Role families: Roles requiring the same type of functional competencies grouped together

Level of work: Roles with comparable levels of impact, complexity and time span grouped together

ROLE FAMILIES AND ROLE CLUSTERS

Role families are groupings of roles with similar skills, competencies and professional qualifications. Roles within the same family have similar **specialist functional skills** but different efficiency levels within those. Role families provide the anchor point for technical skills which, in turn, can feed into reward strategies. In addition, once roles with similar competencies are grouped together, Operational HR activities such as talent management, Learning and Development and the tracking and planning of vertical career paths become easier to manage.

For workforce planning purposes, role families are broken into clusters of similar levels – I refer to these as **role clusters** throughout this book and explain them in detail in Chapter 3.2.

Stage 2: Define and cascade objectives

Objectives Management (OM) is the process of breaking down your strategic goals (defined in your macro design) into a hierarchy of high-level objectives and sub-objectives. This strategic side of OM is performed by the Executive Team. It is a one-off activity which is revisited annually. OM is also an operational process, as objectives are cascaded throughout the organization by linking them to people and roles. They also need to be maintained over time.

Successful OM helps you to answer the following questions:

- How are strategic goals broken down across your business?
- What progress is being made towards each of these objectives?
- How has organizational performance changed over time?
- Who is responsible for delivering key outcomes?

Objectives should be continually managed and measured, so you have a clear picture of the answers to these questions at any given time. An important note about OM: while objectives can be tracked and managed on an organization-wide level, doing the same to an individual's objectives should not be taken as a measure of their performance. Individual performance is as much about competencies as ability to achieve certain outcomes.

In *Data-Driven Organization Design*, I delve into detail about how to set both high-level goals and objectives as well as how to cascade them with bottom-up input. Cascading top-level objectives throughout the organization involves breaking them down into a hierarchical 'tree' structure. See Chapter 5.3 for an example objectives tree (Figure 5.3.2).

Stage 3: Optimize work and define accountabilities

Stage 3 involves activity analysis and design. It brings transparency on whether the *right people* are doing the *right work*. Good activity design means that everyone knows both what they are doing and what everyone else is doing while making the most of individual competencies. Specifically, it looks at how the amount of time people spend on specific activities can be measured and compared against a target model of roles.

Activity design starts with your value chain. This gets broken down into processes and sub-processes which outline the flow of the work. These, in turn, are broken down into activities. Activities are broken down into **Decisions, Outputs and Tasks** (which I refer to as DOT):

- decisions that need to be made
- outputs that need to be produced
- tasks that need to happen

Collectively, this is known as 'the work'. There are different types of process map, which, in D-DOD, are categorized into levels. A Level 0 map is the summary value chain produced in the macro operating design. It shows the top-level processes for all the core elements of the business. A Level 1 process map breaks down the Level 0 value chain into greater degrees of granularity. It highlights the activities linked to each process.

CLOSING THE GAP BETWEEN THE AS-IS AND TO-BE PROCESSES

Activity design is a process of analysing the actual work being done by the workforce against a target model of processes to understand and close the gap between the two. The gap is closed by optimizing processes using the **Reduce, Reallocate, Improve and Invest (RRII)** process levers (see below).

There is often a question about where you should start: by analysing the as-is work and using those insights to inform your target to-be model; or by creating your to-be processes first to define a target to perform analysis against. In truth, it doesn't matter which way round you do it, as the result is the same. The first step is to build an activity taxonomy. Visit *Data-Driven Organization Design* for detail on how to do this.

CREATE THE TARGET MODEL

Start by running workshops with key stakeholders to define specific improvements you want to achieve. Be led by your design principles and criteria as
well as your objectives, if you've got them. For example:

- Improve efficiency:
  - Consolidate effort by aggregating work – achieve the same output
    with less input.
  - Move work from high-cost resources to lower-cost resources: for
    example, upskill nurses to perform aspects of the work of clinicians.
  - Automate processes.
  - Do the same but faster through improved execution: for example,
    increasing training or upskilling people.
- Save cost:
  - Which activities should you stop doing?
  - Which activities could you outsource? Are there activities which are
    high risk or outside the core skills available to you?
- Facilitate new business priorities:
  - What are you not doing that you should be doing to meet business
    goals?
  - What key things within the case for change need to be prioritized?

LINK THE TO-BE WORK TO TO-BE ROLES

The next stage is to define the to-be roles in terms of processes, activities and
decisions. This is important so that when it comes to performing **Individual
Activity Analysis (IAA),** you can see the gaps between the actual and target
activities. The aim is to map accountabilities to provide a view on what each
role will be doing, and what it will be responsible for. Once you have the
to-be activities and roles defined, you are ready to perform an IAA.

The purpose of an IAA is to understand the work being done in the as-is,
specifically:

- how much time each activity is taking
- which roles or people are doing what

You will then be able to compare this to the to-be model to identify gaps,
spot inefficiencies and create paths to more simple ways of working.

IAA data is gathered through various methods, which can be used in isolation, or, for best results, in combination. How you collect data will depend on your organization. Different methods will be better suited to some participants than others, and whether or not participants use computers will largely determine the methods used:

- Interviews and workshops
  With this method you sit with people doing the work. They say how much time they spend doing it using the Level 1 process map. This can be extrapolated for those doing the same roles.

- Surveys
  Surveys should be sent to a representative sample of people performing roles you want to understand. They should allow participants to select the activities they do from the activity taxonomy and enter the proportion of time they spend on them. Surveys should also aim to collect qualitative data. Ask questions such as:

  o Do you find the work motivating?

  o Can you work with sufficient autonomy?

  o Do you think you should be doing this activity?

- Top-down estimate
  This method is used if you don't have the time or remit to engage with those doing the work. It's therefore less accurate. Start by listing activities in an 'n' grid. One axis is the frequency and the other is the duration of the activity. Multiplying the duration by the frequency gives you the amount of effort required for each activity. The total effort doesn't equal the total supply of hours so you can pro rata the time to supply.

ANALYSING THE AS-IS AGAINST THE TARGET MODEL

Having mapped your as-is activities and collected your data, you can now slice and dice it further to get insight into how the organization really works, as well as doing gap analysis to understand the fit of the actual work to the model. This process helps to bring transparency on fundamental business questions such as:

- Are the right roles working on the right activities?

- Are activities being undertaken as intended, with the right roles **Responsible for, Approving and Doing** the work **(RAD)**?

- Are resources working efficiently?

- How many people and Full-Time Equivalents (FTEs) are involved in each process?

- What is the average cost and range of grades working on each activity?
- How many and which functions or sub-functions are working on each process?
- Are people spending their time on the right work for their role?
- Where does process inefficiency need to be addressed?
- How do regions or business units compare?
- Which activities have either no one or more than one person responsible for them?

IAA data can also be compared against defined targets to understand gaps and overlays between the two. Armed with this analysis, you can start to ask questions. If someone isn't doing a particular activity, why is that? Is it because they don't know they should be doing it? Do they not have time to do it? Should they be doing it, or could the model be wrong?

From this analysis, roles can be clarified by isolating the activities per role which should be stopped, started and continued:

- Activities to stop are those that fall outside the model and are therefore unnecessary.
- Activities to start are those that are not currently begin performed but are defined in the model.
- Activities to continue are those that match the model.

This is the basis for optimizing process efficiency.

OPTIMIZING ACTIVITIES

'Stop, start, continue' is a simplified version of an array of levers that can be pulled to optimize processes. In D-DOD, this is done by using the Reduce, Reallocate, Improve and Invest (RRII) framework. The framework gives a potential eight enhancement levers to pull to project the impact of planned improvements on things such as headcount and cost:

- When *reducing* activities there are two things you can do – stop them completely (i.e. 100 per cent reduction) or reduce them by a certain percentage.
- When *reallocating* activities, you can either consolidate them or reassign them. When consolidating, you rationalize the number of people involved in an activity. This often overlaps with reducing effort. When reassigning, you change who/where and/or the level of those doing the work.

- When *improving* activities, your focus is on either process optimization or outsourcing. Optimizing processes might involve re-engineering or automating work.

- When *investing* in activities, you do the mirror opposite of reduce. There are two forms of investment: increase investment in an existing activity or start a completely new one (the need to do this might have been identified when comparing IAA to the target model).

Once you have identified an appropriate enhancement lever to pull, it's important to scope the opportunity by making assumptions about the impact it might have. It's also good to qualify it by asking subject matter experts and stakeholders what they feel the impact of pulling the levers might be.

Stage 4: Define and manage competencies

Competencies are important for individuals to track their development and should be seen first and foremost as a development rather than performance tool. In D-DOD, as with all components of the organization system, competencies are linked through data to understand actuals versus targets and the gaps in between. Roles are linked to target competency proficiency levels and people are linked to actual proficiency levels.

'Competencies' is an umbrella term encompassing behaviour, cognitions, generic business skills and specialized functional skills. To understand the requirements for someone to be effective in their role, all these different facets of competence need to be considered. **Behavioural competencies** are attributes which shape behaviour. They show how an individual performs their work, conducts themselves and interacts with others. **Cognitive competencies** are related to behaviour but focus more on cognitive functioning: for example, how someone thinks and solves problems. **Generic business skills** and **specialized functional skills** are more technical in nature and refer to generic and specialized functional knowledge and technical abilities.

PUTTING A COMPETENCY FRAMEWORK INTO PRACTICE

The competency framework should enable you to answer:

- Which competencies do people possess at which proficiency level?
- What is the average proficiency level for each competency?
- What and where are the gaps, by person and by competency?
- Where would our training budget get its biggest return?

- Who is above where they need to be?
- Who is improving and by how much over time?
- Who is ready for another role?

STEP 1: CREATE THE COMPETENCY FRAMEWORK

As with all the 'micro system datasets', competency definitions are defined and organized in a taxonomy. An example of a competency taxonomy is given in Chapter 5.3.

STEP 2: CREATE TARGETS FOR ROLES (AND/OR ACTIVITIES)

A large part of creating targets for roles and/or activities is defining proficiency levels for each competency. Proficiencies are helpful as they explain what competencies look like at different levels of the organization. They need to be clearly observable and measurable and described in language that is distinguishing and clear. There are different ways to define proficiency levels. In *Data-Driven Organization Design* I dedicate a few pages to explaining what these are and why, when doing D-DOD, I think it is best to link proficiency levels to Elliot Jacques' requisite organization.

When setting targets for roles, keep it realistic. The appropriate number of competencies will vary from one organization to another. My rule of thumb is to ensure that 90 per cent of roles have 10 to 15 (and a maximum of 18) competencies. No more than seven of these competencies should be behavioural.

Creating archetypes is enormously helpful when mapping competencies to roles. Trying to link every single role to every single competency would take too long and lead to inconsistencies. Instead, map certain types of competencies to areas of the role grid. Some competencies will cut across role families. For example, leaders in all role families will need behavioural competencies such as decision-making or generic business competencies such as business acumen. Other competencies are needed for an entire role family. For example, all salespeople, no matter what their level, will need tenacity and drive.

Competencies are best prioritized so that they do not become long, overwhelming lists. I recommend doing this by using a **swing rating method**. I explain how to do this in *Data-Driven Organization Design*. The method allows you to bucket competencies into 'must haves', 'should haves' and 'could haves'.

STEP 3: POPULATE ACTUALS

Populating actuals can include any combination of:

- self-assessment
- manager assessment
- 360 assessments
- third-party assessments: for example, assessment centres or technical tests

Each of these ways of assessing competence provides data points to enable an understanding of how employees view their own competence as well as how they are viewed by others. There is a lot to think about when applying these methods, including the need to recognize bias, and the fact that there is often a mismatch between how people view themselves and how others view them. Different types of bias can be measured by tracking patterns in data and making choices about any exclusions or adjustments that might be required.

STEP 4: CALCULATE COMPETENCY GAPS

Once you have the targets and have measured the actuals, you can calculate gaps. This can be done at both an individual and aggregate level. Once you know how well someone's competencies fit the role they are currently doing, you can calculate their 'current role fit' to give a **role fit score**. This data can be aggregated in the context of the organization to highlight which positions have the biggest gaps. You can also see which people are most suited to other roles in the organization, based on the competencies they possess but aren't currently using. I explain more about how to do this in Chapter 2.3, as this is a useful way to slate candidates for positions when going through a transformation process.

STEP 5: MANAGE DEVELOPMENT OVER TIME

It's important to measure competencies over time to assess how people are developing. This can be done at an individual or team level.

Stage 5: Pull it all together

RIGHTSIZE THE NUMBER OF POSITIONS

Fundamentally, **rightsizing** refers to the number of FTEs each role requires. It is often taken to mean downsizing, but this is entirely inaccurate. It is also something which is often left to chance, but I believe that the number of FTEs required for each role is too important for this to happen. The number of FTEs required is one of the hardest questions to answer because there is no silver bullet. The answer is often 'it depends'. It depends on the level of productivity; the scale of the organization; the economics of the business and whether there are systems dynamics such as the impact of queues and service level trade-offs. I advocate using six data-driven methods to make these decisions. I call them **FIDRAM**:

- **Fixed roles**
- Incremental percent
- Driver
- Ratio
- Activity
- Modelling

The key to successful rightsizing is picking the right method for the right set of roles. I won't run through these methods here as I draw on them in Chapter 3.2 when explaining how to perform top-down demand planning. The methods are the same. The difference is that when using them to design a to-be organization, you do it for a fixed point in time. When using the methods to determine the optimal size for role clusters over time (as is the case in workforce planning), you use an array of time points.

DEVELOP THE POSITION HIERARCHY

Once you have your rightsizing calculations, you are equipped with the information needed to start building your organization structure. This is the final step in the micro detailed design process and involves structuring the organization into roles and positions. This stage of D-DOD is like building Lego. You have your instruction booklet (the macro operating design) and the Lego blocks (the data contained within the role grid, the activity map and the rightsizing calculations). These blocks are what you will use to build and organization structure according to the instruction booklet.

There is not the space to go into detail about how to build a position hierarchy here, but to give you a flavour, the process consists of four steps:

1 pulling it all together
2 building out the macro structure

3 iterating the detail to develop a complete first draft position hierarchy

4 refining, testing and finalizing

Step 4 is important. The hierarchy should meet as many design principles as possible. But this is also where you meet reality and realize that possibly not everything hoped for in the design will be possible. You may need to make exceptions, but that's ok. So long as these exceptions can be justified to yourself and others, you should go ahead and make them. Gut feel is important in this process.

Final thoughts

It is difficult to distil the essence of D-DOD into a few thousand words, but I hope this chapter has given you a flavour of the high-level principles. I would advise reading it in conjunction with the chapters in Part Five where I explain how to design an OP&A function. Chapters 5.2 and 5.3 serve as a mini case study for progressing through macro operating and micro detailed design.

Once you reach the end of the micro detailed design process, the output is a detailed design for implementation. This is what is taken forward to the processes described in the next part of this book: Making it Real.

REMEMBER THIS

1 The objective of D-DOD is to ensure that the *right people* with the *right skills* are doing the *right work* in the *right way* in the *right numbers* and with *real alignment*.

2 The organization is a system comprised of connected RPP and OAC datasets.

3 In D-DOD, Roles, Positions and People are not the same thing.

4 Organization data contains many-to-many relationships and is messy. Visualizing it helps to understand the connections.

5 D-DOD includes both macro operating design and micro detailed design. Macro operating design should only be pursued if the case for change is overwhelming.

1.3

Financial Planning and Analysis

Introduction

I love interdisciplinary learning. There's nothing better than bringing two seemingly unrelated topics together and exploring what they can develop. Take astrophysics and chemistry. Unifying these two disciplines has given us an understanding of how all the elements of the periodic table are created at the heart of dying stars. Astrophysics is largely concerned with the energy of stars and how, through a natural process of fusion, two atoms join and release heat and power. Chemistry is largely concerned with the elements in the periodic table. Each element has an atomic number defined by the number of protons, electrons and neutrons. A hydrogen atom contains one electron, one proton and no neutrons. Its atomic number is therefore 1. Living stars burn hydrogen, fusing hydrogen atoms together to create helium atoms with two protons and two electrons. Helium, the second number in the periodic table, has an atomic number of 2. When the hydrogen starts to run out, the fuel of the star starts to deplete and the end of its life draws near. The pressure and the heat increase, and other elements start to form in a sequence. First, helium nuclei begin to fuse together, resulting in beryllium – the element with an atomic number of 4. What do you get when you fuse beryllium (4) with helium (2)? An atom with six protons and six electrons, or an atomic number of 6. This element is carbon, the building block of life, which can be reshaped into any number of things, from dirty, dark coal to brilliantly transparent diamonds. As it gets hotter, and the end of the star's life draws closer, the heavier elements are created – magnesium, aluminium and finally iron. Some stars become so heavy that the gravity makes them collapse into a black hole, but with bigger stars, the heat within them becomes so intense that they explode, releasing all 92 chemical elements found on Earth into the atmosphere. Carbon exists in every living thing on the planet. Look at your hand and realize that it was created by dying stars billions of years ago. In other words, you are star dust. With this realization we have fused not only astrophysics and chemistry but also biology.

Two more connected disciplines, but very much back on earth, are HR and Finance. Finance inspired me to coin the term OP&A. I studied economics and finance, and much of my early work was focused on developing financial models, a technique I constantly return to when running or building a business. Only later in life did I generate a deep interest in HR through the fields of organization design and workforce planning, but it felt natural to me to use the modelling techniques I learned in those early days and apply them to HR. To properly understand OP&A, I believe it is fundamental to understand and learn from FP&A. It is it crucial that OP&A should be joined at the hip with FP&A not only in service to the business but also so that OP&A professionals can take some of what their FP&A colleagues do well – in particular some of the tools and techniques that they use – and apply them to their own discipline. As the chapters in Part Three will demonstrate, many of the techniques involved in workforce planning – such as assessing the impact of change and modelling and simulating scenarios – are also leveraged by the FP&A function.

There are many books explaining the ins and outs of the FP&A role. That is not the aim of this chapter. Instead, it aims to build awareness of the work the FP&A function performs, and the perspective and future-focused mindset FP&A professionals inhabit day to day. It also aims to draw out the lessons that OP&A can learn from FP&A and help you to speak the same language as your FP&A colleagues to improve your working relationship. My intention is to keep things simple as I realize that a lot of those reading it will not have had significant financial training. I hope it gives a foundation of understanding and respect, as well as building out your general management acumen. I begin by explaining the need for FP&A in all organizations before continuing to explain the key concepts and terms you need to understand as an OP&A professional to be able to work in unison with your FP&A colleagues. I then explain how FP&A uses planning, budgeting and monitoring to ensure the future financial health of the business, before looking at modelling and sensitivity analysis. Throughout, I draw on a fictional case study showing a financial model of a toll bridge to illustrate the concepts discussed.

Why businesses need FP&A

According to Gartner, FP&A is a 'set of four activities that support an organization's financial health: planning and budgeting, integrated financial planning, management and performance reporting and forecasting and modelling'.[1] FP&A professionals continuously make decisions which impact the future. They ask quantifiable questions related to corporate strategy and give leaders the information necessary to gain perspective and confidently move the organization forward. This largely involves determining **outcomes** of different business improvements, to help decide where priorities should lie. Which investments should be prioritized? Should the organization grow organically or by acquisition? This can be thought of as pulling levers to assess the impact of different actions. Which lever optimizes financial performance? Which brings in the most cash in the months and years ahead?

As I was starting my career as a management consultant over 20 years ago, one of my early projects was for an automotive distributor. My colleagues and I had just written a report about the future of automotive retail for the *Financial Times*, and on the back of this we were brought in to devise strategy for the business at a time when numerous trends such as the emergence of the internet and ecommerce were having a huge impact on the sector. Shortly after we arrived, we were in full flow discussing how they could exploit these trends. Mid-conversation, my colleague glanced outside the boardroom and stopped us in our tracks. We were astonished by the sheer number of cars parked outside. We asked them how many cars there were, and how many they were selling, and a quick calculation told us they had nearly two years' worth of cars right there. When we dug a little deeper, we found that the business was in crisis and haemorrhaging cash. Basic mistakes had been made, much of their **working capital** was tied up in stock, and they were reliant on simplistic models around their pricing which were based solely on **profit margin** – not **cash flow**. What was initially intended as a strategy project quickly became a rescue mission. This mission had two stages:

1 The stock needed to be shipped quickly to get cash in the door. As will become evident in this chapter, how cash flows in and out of a business is just as important as profit margin. It's all about turning stock quickly and not having inventory sitting idly in a warehouse. Think of it like having money in your bank account but not having a debit card. You must pay

the bank fees but can neither use the money nor move it elsewhere. Languishing stock has both a genuine cost and an opportunity cost, as if you deployed that cash elsewhere you'd probably get a better return.

2 The next stage was to create a break-even business plan. The business didn't need to make money, but it had to wash its face. To break even you use the following formula:

$$(price - direct\ variable\ cost) \times quantity\ sold - indirect\ cost = 0$$

Subtracting direct variable cost from the price gives you the margin, and once you've multiplied this by the quantity of cars being sold, that needs to equal your **indirect costs**. To break even and get the business back to health, the margin needed to be increased. This could be done by increasing the price, reducing the direct variable cost or increasing demand. I set to work and built a model based on price sensitivity and volume to find the optimal price that would shift stock as quickly as possible. I built **assumptions** around how much demand could be expected to increase if the price dropped by x amount, using **sensitivity analysis** and changing those assumptions by 5 or 10 per cent to assess what the impact would be. It also turned out that, as with most organizations, there were many **direct costs** which could be cut back, such as pet projects or sponsorships.

The important thing when faced with a situation like this is to isolate the information you can be sure about. This is what we knew:

- We had limited control over variable costs in the short term, which amounted to only a small number of percentage points.
- Price and quantity sold had an inverse relationship. If we increased the price, we'd sell fewer cars; if we reduced it, we'd sell more.
- The indirect costs were more in our control. For a given quantity and margin, the indirect cost is known, so we had a target that we needed to reach to break even. We were realistic about the price and the quantity that we would be able to shift. In the end we were able to take 50 per cent of the indirect cost out to improve the margin. This follows what is known as zero-based budgeting, where you start at zero and build up from first principles.

Once this was understood, we were able to get the business to a point where it had cash coming in and was solvent again. It all came down to understanding and forecasting the flow of cash in and out of the business. Difficulties had arisen because the need to balance a positive cash flow with maintaining a profit had been completely missed. There was no one in the organization with the necessary heads-up mindset I discussed in Chapter 1.1 to be able to scan the space and see what was coming. Neither was there anyone with the skills or tools to perform future-focused financial analysis, budgeting, planning and forecasting and see that having two years' worth of stock sitting in the warehouse was not going to benefit the business in the long run, no matter how much they leveraged the internet and ecommerce. I have used this case study to illustrate the kind of thinking necessary for good FP&A. It's important to understand capital, margin, the difference between direct and indirect costs and profit and loss, and cash flow. If the terms and concepts discussed within it are unfamiliar to you, do not worry – they will be explained throughout the course of this chapter.

The mistakes made by this organization are not unusual. Businesses everywhere can fall victim to these kinds of pitfalls if they fail to invest in an effective FP&A capability to plan and manage an organization's assets and fund and resource organizational strategy. As my former Chairman and mentor Richard Thompson used to tell me, formulating strategy is easy, it's getting the timing and tactics right that is the hard part. Strategy can only be effective if it is executed as intended so that the organization stays on track to meet its objectives.

The role of FP&A is to take the strategy and transform it into an action plan by assigning and managing resources on an ongoing basis. An FP&A professional uses their influence to ensure that the right strategic and investment choices are made based on **financial modelling** and insight from across the business. As there is unlimited demand for cash, there is a need to make continual trade-off decisions within a business's financial constraint. For example, if an organization intends to grow into new markets, decisions must be made about which geographies to invest in first, when, and how. Should growth be achieved through acquisition or organically? Should the business take on debt? Does equity need to be raised before investing? How should risk between the two be balanced? How profitable does the business need to be? Should the focus be on growing the top line (the revenue – see later in the chapter) or the bottom line (the net income)? It's not unusual to shoulder an initial loss to allow for greater growth and a higher profit further down the line (it reportedly took Jeff Bezos nine years to turn a profit with Amazon[2]). These are the type of trade-off decisions which are quantified, modelled and managed by FP&A professionals. For the failing automotive business I described above, FP&A thinking wasn't only needed to get the business out of the immediate mess it was in. It was needed from that point on to manage the cash flow and balance sheet against the profit and loss account and plan and model future scenarios to keep the business afloat and then thrive in the long term. The rest of this chapter looks at these key FP&A activities. I'll start by giving an overview of the three main financial statements used by FP&A to understand the overall financial health of the business, before progressing to look at the planning, budgeting, monitoring and modelling activities which are so central to the capability.

Management and performance reporting

Throughout this section and the one that follows, I use a fictional financial model of a toll bridge to illustrate the concepts discussed and help bring them to life. Specifically, I use it to walk you through what a profit and loss statement looks like and certain key concepts, before using it to illustrate how to perform financial modelling. I'll be clear from the off that toll bridges are not my specialism. At no point in my career have I spent time in the industry, and I know close to nothing about building bridges. I've merely selected it as an example that should make sense to people and help you to apply financial concepts to a real-life scenario. If you *do* have experience of building toll bridges, you may find that many of my guesstimates are wildly inaccurate, and if this is the case, I apologise!

The FP&A function is responsible for presenting financial reports to the business on a monthly or quarterly basis. Three financial statements are commonly reported:

1 profit and loss statement (sometimes referred to as the income statement)
2 cash flow statement
3 balance sheet

Profit and loss statement

A **profit and loss statement** (sometimes abbreviated to P&L) does what it says – it shows you whether you have made a profit or a loss over a specified period, which is usually a month, fiscal quarter or year. The statement outlines a company's **revenue** (the money your organization has brought in from its operations) and costs (which are divided into direct and indirect costs). Various profitability margins can be shown: your **gross profit**, a metric known as **EBITDA** (more on that below) and net profit, which is often referred to as the 'bottom line'. The bottom line shows the profit remaining once all costs, including interest and taxes, have been subtracted from the revenue.

DIRECT AND INDIRECT COSTS

There is a cost attached to generating revenue. This cost is known as the direct cost, and it is sometimes referred to as the cost of goods sold or the total operating cost. Direct costs include anything that can be directly attributed to producing the service or product that brings in your income. If the revenue increases, so (typically) do the direct costs. Direct costs differ depending on the industry. In the Software as a Service (SaaS) business they could include hosting costs or the cost of employing developers and customer support agents. In manufacturing, such as in the automobile industry, they could include direct materials, manufacturing supplies and labour.

Figure 1.3.1 shows the profit and loss statement for the toll bridge example mentioned above. In addition, the key assumptions for the bridge and the associated outcomes are shown in Figure 1.3.2. This profit and loss statement forms part of a financial model used to understand how long it will take to recoup the cost of the bridge through toll collection and return a profit in different scenarios, which I will return to later in the chapter. The capital cost of building the bridge ($100 million) is shown in Figure 1.3.2 as a key assumption. This would cover labour, materials and equipment. It's worth mentioning at this point that, while this is an example of a capital-intensive project, the financial model for a SaaS company such as Hokupaa wouldn't be entirely dissimilar. A product is built which customers pay a subscription to use, and the cost of developing the product is recouped over time.

The direct costs associated with maintaining the bridge over time are listed as maintenance and toll costs. This includes the cost of employing people to collect the tolls (or maintaining machines to do the job instead), the cost of supplies (such as oil or replacement parts) and services needed to maintain the bridge (such as electricity and petrol). As explained in the automotive distributor case study above, subtracting direct costs from total revenue gives the operating margin (sometimes referred to as the gross profit). In Figure 1.3.1, the operating margin is high at 98 per cent in year 1 and 99 per cent thereafter. Many industries (such as manufacturing outfits) have much higher direct costs and won't come anywhere close to such a high operating margin.

Indirect costs are the same as operating expenses, and are sometimes referred to as Selling, General and Administrative (SG&A) costs. This is money you need to spend to keep your business operating, but not as a direct result of producing your product or service. Indirect costs could be sales and marketing, insurance, maintenance, office supplies, rent, salaries or utilities. Figure 1.3.1 shows a very simple example of management, legal costs, accounting costs and the cost to run the office.

Non-cash expenses such as **depreciation**, **amortization** and tax are also included in indirect costs. Depreciation and amortization are similar, as they both calculate the reduction in the value of an organization's assets over time, and in so doing, help to reduce organizations' tax liability. They both relate to capital investments, which I look at in more detail in the discussion about the balance sheet below. If you capitalize a cost, it means that you can record it on the balance sheet as an asset, which in turn means that you can choose to depreciate or amortize the cost each year. Depreciation relates to **tangible assets** that decrease in value due to wear and tear. Returning to the example of the toll bridge, one of the key assumptions is that the bridge will cost $100 million to build, and that cost could be recorded as a capital expense on the balance sheet. Figure 1.3.1 is a stylized example and shows the bridge depreciating by $20 million per year over a five-year period. In real life, a bridge is more likely to depreciate over 20 or 30 years. Say it was 20 years, a $100 million bridge could be expected to depreciate by $5 million per year. In this figure and the related figures which follow, the key assumptions are shown with yellow highlighting.

Amortization refers to the **intangible assets** a company owns, such as copyrights, patents, or brand recognition. If, for example, an organization acquired another organization for its brand value, this intangible asset could be written off over time. As these are all assets that are used in the creation and promotion of products and services, amortization is a way of attributing the cost of their use. As there are no intangible assets associated with building the toll bridge, amortization is not shown in Figure 1.3.1.

EARNINGS BEFORE INTEREST, TAXES, DEPRECIATION AND AMORTIZATION

Subtracting indirect costs from the operating margin gives you your Earnings Before Interest, Taxes, Depreciation and Amortization (EBITDA). In Figure 1.3.1, EBITDA is shown as $23,009,420 for year 1. It can be useful for organizations (as well as lenders and investors) to understand an organization's profitability before it pays interest and taxes, and before depreciation

FIGURE 1.3.1 The profit and loss statement for a toll bridge

Year		1	2	3	4	5
Revenue						
Toll		$ 2.50	$ 2.50	$ 2.63	$ 2.63	$ 2.63
Number of Cars per day		26,800	29,480	32,428	35,671	39,238
Cars per year		9,782,000	10,760,200	11,836,220	13,019,842	14,321,826
Total Revenue		$ 24,455,000	$ 26,900,500	$ 31,070,078	$ 34,177,085	$ 37,594,794
Direct Costs						
Maintenance		$ 300,000	$ 300,000	$ 300,000	$ 300,000	$ 300,000
Toll-Cost		$ 100,000	$ 100,000	$ 100,000	$ 100,000	$ 100,000
Total Direct Costs		$ 400,000	$ 400,000	$ 400,000	$ 400,000	$ 400,000
Operating Margin		$ 24,055,000	$ 26,500,500	$ 30,670,078	$ 33,777,085	$ 37,194,794
		98%	99%	99%	99%	99%
Indirect Costs						
Mgmt		$ 500,000	$ 500,000	$ 500,000	$ 500,000	$ 500,000
Legal		$ 220,000	$ 220,000	$ 220,000	$ 220,000	$ 220,000
Accounting		$ 189,200	$ 189,200	$ 189,200	$ 189,200	$ 189,200
Office		$ 136,380	$ 136,380	$ 136,380	$ 136,380	$ 136,380
Total Indirect Costs		$ 1,045,580	$ 1,045,580	$ 1,045,580	$ 1,045,580	$ 1,045,580
EBITDA		$ 23,009,420	$ 25,454,920	$ 29,624,498	$ 32,731,505	$ 36,149,214
Depreciation		$ 20,000,000	$ 20,000,000	$ 20,000,000	$ 20,000,000	$ 20,000,000
EBT		$ 3,009,420	$ 5,454,920	$ 9,624,498	$ 12,731,505	$ 16,149,214
Cash	-£ 100,000,000	$ 23,009,420	$ 25,454,920	$ 29,624,498	$ 32,731,505	$ 36,149,214
Cumlative Cash		$ -76,990,580	$ -51,535,660	$ -21,911,163	$ 10,820,343	$ 46,969,557
Breakeven Year	4					

FIGURE 1.3.2 Key assumptions and outcomes

Key Assumptions	
Cost to Build	£ 100,000,000
Number of Years	5
Peak Cars per hour	2,000
Growth in demand	10%
Starting Price	$ 2.50
Increase in price Y3	5%
Reduction in Fixed Cost in Y3	25%
WACC	8%

Key Outcomes	Outcome	Baseline
NPV	$ 14,172,752	$ 14,172,752
Total Profit	$ 46,969,557	$ 46,969,557
Payback Years	4	4
IRR	13%	13%
Cost per year	$ 20,000,000	
Per Minute	33	
Cars through lane per min	10	
Lanes	3	

and amortization are subtracted. The metric gives an understanding of an organization's growth and its *potential* to generate cash (EBITDA is often seen as a proxy for cash generation ability), as opposed to its true profitability. An organization's true profitability is shown by the net profit, or bottom line, which is the figure arrived at *after* interest, taxes, depreciation and amortization have been taken into account. For simplicity, Figure 1.3.1 shows both the EBITDA figure and the EBT (Earnings Before Taxes, which, in this example, is the result of subtracting depreciation from EBITDA) but does not show the amount of tax and interest. Subtracting these from EBITDA would give you the net profit.

EBITDA is sometimes misunderstood to be the equivalent of free cash flow, but there is a difference. While the metrics on the profit and loss statement are all about profitability, cash flow is all about liquidity: in other words, how much *cash* a business has, and how that cash flows in and out. This not only comes down to payment terms (which I return to below; taxes and interest also have a huge impact on the amount of cash leaving a business. For this reason, cash flow is a far better way of understanding liquidity than EBITDA. For example, at the end of the financial year there might be a big outlay to pay tax, but there may not be any cash expected in until three months later. To understand this ebb and flow, the cash flow statement is needed. Note that in Figure 1.3.1, cash and EBITDA are one and the same. This is simply because I have provided a stylized example for simplicity's sake, and have not included interest and taxes.

Cash flow statement

The cash flow statement is important for understanding how well a business manages its cash and operating cost, by showing where cash is coming in from and how it is being spent. Unlike the profit and loss statement (which factors in money that might not have been received yet and expenses that might not have been paid), the cash flow statement only shows the cash a business has at any one time. The point of a cash flow statement is to show the availability of an organization's liquid assets and give insight into the ability of a company to fulfil its financial obligations, such as pay off its debts and pay its staff and suppliers. This is crucial to understand, as shown by the case study I described at the beginning of the chapter. That business had enormous amounts of stock (which can be thought of as cash sitting in big piles in the parking lot), it was quickly running out of cash, and it couldn't pay its staff.

Cash flow is categorized according to three different activities:

1 cash from operations – cash activities which are included in net income such as revenue generation or cash spent on SG&A

2 cash from financing – cash activities related to non-current liabilities and owners' equity

3 invested cash – cash activities relating to non-current assets, such as investments in equipment or property

How and when cash comes into a business through its operations is governed by payment terms, and these vary according to industry. For example, in the SaaS industry, most companies charge an annual subscription and take payment in advance of the system being used, whereas a company that delivers services might be paid on delivery or a specified number of days after delivery. A SaaS business can be loss making and cash generative at the same time, as revenues are recognized over the period of the contract, but cash is received at the beginning of the contract. If you are growing, cash generation will be greater than profit, but if you are declining, profit will be greater than your cash. It's crucial to understand the payment terms for your own industry and the associated impact on the flow of cash.

Balance sheet

The **balance sheet** is divided into two sections, one showing the total assets a business owns and the other showing its liabilities and the amount of shareholder equity (how much of the business is owned by the shareholders). As the name suggests, a balance sheet must be kept in balance, with the assets being equal to the liabilities and shareholder equity.

Assets are divided into **current** and **non-current assets**. For something to be counted as a current asset, it must either be cash or have the ability to be converted into cash within a year or less, such as stock or investments which could be sold off quickly. These are known as liquid assets. Non-current assets are such things as property, and anything held within property such as equipment like computers and printers.

The balance sheet is needed to understand your working capital, which is the money tied up in the ordinary course of running the business. Working capital is calculated by subtracting your current liabilities from your current assets. Imagine you have just gone into business selling diamond rings. You are new, so suppliers will only sell you stock for cash, and you buy 100 diamond rings at $5,000 each, spending a total of $500,000. You sell one ring per day at $10,000 per ring. To begin with, your working capital is $500,000. With no other costs and selling one ring per day at $10,000 per ring, it will take you 50 days to break even. After those 50 days, you still have 50 rings left in stock and your working capital will have reduced to $250,000. That money is still tied up in the business, but if you could sell those rings more quickly – say in 10 days rather than 50 – you will be able to release that capital more quickly to buy more stock, or pay staff, if you have them. This explains why payment terms are so crucial in industries like retailing. Once suppliers have been paid and stock is sitting on the shelf, cash is tied up. The success or failure of a business is not solely dependent on the margin you can make on a product, but how quickly you can turn it. Working capital has a time dimension that is crucial to understand. A growing, high-margin services business might only be able to invoice once a project is finished. If the project takes six months and the payment terms are 60 to 90 days, you might only receive the money for the project eight or nine months after starting it. With a lag like this, you need to know that you have enough cash to cover your liabilities, such as salaries, and a buffer in case debtors fail to pay on time.

Weighted Average Cost of Capital

When FP&A think about capital, many of the decisions made come down to equity and debt. A calculation called the **Weighted Average Cost of Capital** (or WACC) is used to understand and weigh the cost of capital depending on the amount of debt and equity used. Debt and equity come at a cost – the cost of debt is the amount of interest you're paying on your borrowings while the cost of equity is the required rate of return by equity shareholders. It's expressed as a percentage and provides a hurdle rate to inform investment decisions.

Debt is tax deductible and therefore carries a lower cost, which also reduces the burden on a business's profitability. Debt is always paid before equity (in bankruptcy/insolvency cases, equity is usually wiped, and debt is converted to equity). Debtors have a fixed return, and for this reason debt is often seen as less risky than equity. But there is a downside to debt – have too much of it, and you will be perceived as being at risk of default. The riskier you are, the more expensive the debt. If you can't keep up with your monthly payments, pay the debt back at the end of the term or incur other debt to replace it, the debt will be restructured into equity, wiping out much or all of the value that your shareholders have. Making decisions about debt versus equity comes down to a trade-off between risk and reward. Equity is riskier for those providing it, so it is more expensive. The decisions taken by an organization around how much risk to carry are captured in the WACC.

WACC can become more complicated than this as different types of debt and equity are factored in, but I won't go into that level of detail here. Most of the time, it isn't complicated, and sophisticated Finance functions often publish a standard WACC that is applied across the board. Many smaller enterprises don't even calculate WACC and would target thresholds in other ways.

It can be tricky to grasp how to calculate WACC, so I have provided two simplified examples to help. The basic method is to multiply the cost of each source of capital (debt and equity) by its proportional weight, and then to add those together to reach a total. Before demonstrating this in the context of the toll bridge, I'll give a non-financial example, using average temperatures across the four seasons (shown Figure 1.3.3). As you might know, I'm a New Zealander who lives in the UK. My goal in life is to maximize my number of summer days per year. The second column of Figure 1.3.3 shows the average temperatures in spring, summer, autumn and winter (which are about the same in the UK and New Zealand) and a simple average temperature for the year of 15.8 degrees Celsius. The third column shows the number of days I would ideally like to spend in each season (unfortunately it doesn't always work out like this, especially in times of global pandemic!). The proportion of time is shown in column four – I'd like to spend 25 per cent of my time in spring, 25 per cent in autumn, 41 per cent in summer and only 9 per cent of my time in winter. To work out what my average temperature over the 365 days of the year would be based on these percentages, I can calculate the weighted average. To do this, I multiply the proportion of my time in each season by the average temperature for that season. These calculations are shown in the fifth column. For example, I'm spending 25 per cent of my time in a spring temperature of 18 degrees, so 0.25 x 18 gives you 4.5. Adding these weighted figures together gives my personal average temperature for the year, which, rounded up, is 19 degrees Celsius. I'd take this over 15.8 degrees Celsius any day.

FIGURE 1.3.3 How to calculate a weighted average temperature

Season	Average temperature (°c)	Days spent	Proportion	Weighted Average Calculation
Spring	18	91	25%	4.5
Summer	25	150	41%	10.3
Autumn	15	91	25%	3.8
Winter	5	33	9%	0.4
Total	15.8	365	100%	19.0

Returning to the bridge example, this bridge needs to be funded, and the cost of that funding is calculated through the WACC. It has been estimated that the overall funding requirement, including some buffer, is $140,000,000. This will be achieved partly by raising equity, and partly by incurring debt: $93,800,000 is raised through equity (67 per cent of the overall funding) and $46,200,000 of debt is incurred (33 per cent of the overall funding). Equity is raised at an expected return, and therefore a cost, of 12 per cent, this being the minimum threshold hypothetical investors would accept for a venture with this risk profile. By comparison, debt is incurred at a cost of 6 per cent. You can work out the weighted average by multiplying the cost of equity and debt by the proportional weight of the debt. Sixty-seven per cent of 12 per cent is 8 per cent (this is the weighted cost of the equity) and 33 per cent of 6 per cent is 2 per cent (this is the weighted cost of the debt). Added together, this gives a total WACC of 10 per cent.

It does get more complicated once tax is factored in. As mentioned above, debt is tax deductible, meaning that the tax can be included as a cost on the balance sheet if you are making a profit. The 10 per cent WACC is the pre-tax figure, as shown in Figure 1.3.4. The post-tax WACC is 9.4 per cent. To calculate this, you apply the tax rate to the cost of the debt (in this example, the tax rate is 30 per cent and the cost of the debt is $2,772,000). The tax relief is therefore $831,600. Subtracting this from the cost of the debt gives you $1,940,400 – this is the true cost of the debt, and the figure that should be used to work out the post-tax WACC of 9.4 per cent.

Return on Investment

Before making any sort of investment, it is important to understand the return that you will get on it. This is known as the **Return on Investment** (ROI). There are various ways that this can be calculated, the simplest and

FIGURE 1.3.4 Calculating WACC for the toll bridge

		Cost	Funding %	WACC
Equity	$ 93,800,000	12%	67%	8.0%
Debt	$ 46,200,000	6%	33%	2.0%

	Cost	Tax Relief	True Cost	
Equity	$ 11,256,000	$ -	$ 11,256,000	12.0%
Debt	$ 2,772,000	$ 831,600	$ 1,940,400	4.2%

Weighted Average pre tax	10.0%			
Weighted Average post tax	9.4%			

Funding Requiremnt	$ 140,000,000			
Tax	30%			

most common of which is to express it as a percentage by dividing the net income by the initial cost of the investment and multiplying it by 100. A positive percentage indicates profitability while a negative one indicates a financial loss. Most organizations have hurdle rates which indicate the minimum ROI threshold that must be reached for an investment to be given the go-ahead.

Other methods can also be used to calculate ROI which give a better understanding of how an investment can be expected to perform over time, and how long it takes for the investment to break even. This is important as FP&A and OP&A professionals need a multi-year planning time horizon. In my stylized example of the toll bridge shown in Figure 1.3.1, likely financial performance is considered over a five-year period (as said above, in real life, this would need to be extended to 20 or 30 years). If the profit and loss account was done for a time horizon of one year, building the bridge would seem like a terrible idea. You'd spend $100,000,000, get $23,009,420 back and lose $76,990,580. There's no way the investment would be approved. For this reason, financial performance should be looked at over a multi-year time horizon, and metrics such as **payback period**, **Net Present Value** (NPV) and **Internal Rate of Return** (IRR) should be used to bring money back to today's value.

Payback period

The payback period is essentially the length of time it will take to recoup your investment costs or, for the bridge example, building costs plus debt. It is calculated by subtracting annual cash flow from the decreasing cost of an investment over time. Investment decisions are often made based on the payback period, as the quicker you can make your money back, the better.

The payback period is more relevant to some industries than others. For industries where it is necessary to invest a large amount of cash, either in stock or in a large capital investment, such as oil and gas or construction, the payback period is hyper-relevant. Returning to the toll bridge, the $100 million investment is a huge initial outlay, so it's important to understand how much cash will be received over time to recoup this investment and how long it will take before the investment starts to pay back. In my stylized example, the bridge pays back in year 4, and thereafter returns a profit. You can see that the amount of cash the business has each year reduces the capital investment cost steadily over the first three years, before cumulative revenue is equal to cumulative cost in the fourth year and a profit of $10,820,343 is returned. At this point, the bridge has 'broken even' (the definition of which is when revenue minus cost is equal to zero). The payback period is therefore four years. Later in the chapter I explain sensitivity analysis and how it could be used to model scenarios to understand the impact of different external forces on recouping costs.

Net Present Value

Net Present Value (NPV) is a way of calculating the time value of money, and therefore the present-day value of your investment. Figure 1.3.5 shows a part of the toll bridge financial model which demonstrates how much a dollar can be expected to be worth in today's money in one, two, three, four and five years' time. This is calculated based on the WACC. With a WACC of 8 per cent (shown in the key assumptions listed in Figure 1.3.2), in a year's time, one dollar is expected to be worth $0.93, in five years' time, it's expected to be worth $0.68 and in 10 years' time, $0.46. Each year, the value of the dollar decreases by a further 8 per cent. The total value over the 10-year period gives you your NPV.

This understanding is necessary to accurately predict when the investment will be returned. Without taking into account other criteria like the payback period, an investment will be worthwhile if the NPV is greater than zero – this will signify that you are likely to get a return. In the toll bridge example given in Figure 1.3.2, the NPV is $14,172,752, signifying that this is likely to be a worthwhile investment. I'll return to how NPV can be used in sensitivity analysis later in the chapter.

FIGURE 1.3.5 Understanding the value of the dollar over time in today's money

WACC	8%

NPV		1		2		3		4		5		6		7		8		9		10
$	0.93	$ 1.00	$	-	$	-	$	-	$	-	$	-	$	-	$	-	$	-	$	-
$	0.86	$ -	$	1.00	$	-	$	-	$	-	$	-	$	-	$	-	$	-	$	-
$	0.68	$ -	$	-	$	-	$	-	$ 1.00	$	-	$	-	$	-	$	-	$	-
$	0.46	$ -	$	-	$	-	$	-	$	-	$	-	$	-	$	-	$	-	$ 1.00
$	0.67	$ 0.10	$	0.10	$	0.10	$	0.10	$	0.10	$	0.10	$	0.10	$	0.10	$	0.10	$ 0.10

A $ today is worth $1	$	1.00
In one years time, it is worth	$	0.93
In 5 years time	$	0.68
In 10 years time	$	0.46
If got $0.1 at the end of each year	$	0.67

There may be times when you want to understand the lowest starting price you could charge for the bridge to achieve an NPV of zero, and just break even and pay for itself in today's money. This understanding can be gained in Excel by using 'goal seek' under 'What-If' analysis. You can change the value of NPV to zero and ask what the starting price would need to be to achieve this. By reducing the starting price from $2.50 shown in Figure 1.3.2 to $2.18, the NPV reduces from $14,172,752 to zero. This can form the backbone of pricing conversations. You know the minimum you need to charge to break even, but it would be sensible to include a buffer, so how high can you, or should you, go? I'll return to this in the section on sensitivity analysis later in the chapter.

Internal Rate of Return

Another method that those in Finance use to think through the impact of time on money is to calculate the Internal Rate of Return (IRR). IRR gives the rate at which a project breaks even using cash flow over time. It is called the *Internal* Rate of Return as it doesn't factor in external considerations which might impact that return such as inflation. In the toll bridge example it is the IRR percentage that would need to hit a hurdle rate for the capital expenditure to be approved. The IRR needs to be greater than the WACC, to cover the necessary financing. In Figure 1.3.2, it's all looking good, with an IRR of 13 per cent and a WACC of 8 per cent. If the price were reduced to $2.18, the IRR would reduce to 8 per cent. With the WACC and IRR both at 8 per cent, the NPV is zero, showing that the bridge is just breaking even. If IRR drops below the WACC, your NPV will be negative, making the project untenable.

I'll return to these concepts later in the chapter as they are crucial outcomes measured in the driver-based planning and modelling done by FP&A. First, I will look at a type of analysis commonly performed by FP&A and which is also leveraged by OP&A in relation to workforce planning: that of ratio analysis.

Ratio analysis

Ratio analysis is used in FP&A to assess an organization's performance. Some of the most common ratios used in financial analysis compare certain figures from the three financial statements to gain insight into such things as profitability and liquidity. These include:

- Cash Conversion Ratio (CCR) – This ratio is cash flows over net profit. If the ratio is above one, the company is in good health, but anything below one indicates that the liquidity of the company is poor. A negative number suggests that the company is making a loss.

- Quick ratio – The quick ratio is a measure of your capacity to pay liabilities. Think of it as your current assets over your current liabilities. Different definitions exist: some might say it's your cash and accounts receivable over your liabilities, while others might say it's your current assets minus your inventory over your current liabilities. There are different nuances but the basic idea is to measure a company's ability to meet its short-term obligations with its liquid assets.

- Current ratio – The current ratio is similar to the quick ratio, but it includes all of a company's current assets rather than just those that can be converted to cash in a very short period of time (your liquid assets). A current ratio above one is expected from healthy companies.

- Many industries use ratios specific to their own sector. For example, in retail, it's useful to understand the margin being generated per square metre of floor space, while in the restaurant business, it's good to understand the revenue or even the margin per cover. In the SaaS industry, the Lifetime Value (LTV) to Customer Acquisition Cost (CAC) ratio can be used to analyse growth. CAC helps you to understand how efficient you are at acquiring new revenue (which, in the SaaS industry, is expressed as Annual Recurring Revenue (ARR) – ARR is a metric used to understand subscription sales and shows the money that comes in every year over the life of a subscription). In the SaaS industry, you want to know how much it costs for you to acquire $1 of ARR. The LTV:CAC ratio helps you to understand how efficient you are at retaining acquired revenue, by looking at the Lifetime Value of a customer over the cost of acquiring that customer.

Future-focused planning, budgeting and monitoring

The continual feedback loop between financial planning, budgeting and monitoring forms the backbone of FP&A. Traditionally, planning and budgeting have been done on a static, annual basis where budgets were set at the beginning of the financial year and only looked at again 12 months later to assess where the year had landed against plan. There was no opportunity to revisit the budget throughout the year once things had inevitably gone awry. In contrast, organizations today are moving towards a rolling process where budgets and plans are revisited on a fixed cadence that makes sense for the organization and its industry. Budgets are monitored against the plan on the chosen cadence to see where the business is above or below expectation, and reforecasting is done where necessary so that the strategy can continue to be executed. It is also becoming increasingly common for organizations to budget using an entirely rolling forecast, meaning that as each month passes, a new month is automatically added to the plan so that you can continuously budget for 12 months into the future, with a lens that makes sense at that moment in time.

The monitoring performed by FP&A is done according to Key Performance Indicators (KPIs). Each industry has specific metrics that are particularly pertinent to the success or failure of businesses operating within the industry. There are a great number of KPIs that can be monitored at any one time, but each business should prioritize those that have the greatest impact. Commonly monitored metrics are profit margin, working capital, sales, expenditure and industry-specific ratios, which I have explained above. ARR is an example of a KPI which is of central importance to SaaS businesses.

Financial modelling

Financial modelling is central to FP&A and crucial for understanding likely future financial performance across a range of different scenarios. While no model can pinpoint the future with absolute precision (the phrase 'all models are wrong, but some are useful'[3] sums up financial modelling perfectly), the very process of putting it together can help enormously in getting your thinking straight, teasing out the right questions to ask about the business and deciding where trade-offs need to be made. In an ideal world, all OP&A professionals would be able to set up a basic financial model. The insight it gives you into the workings of a business is second to none, and there's no better way to learn about the mental processes necessary for good FP&A. For me, once I have modelled a business, I have understood it inside and out and have got to the bottom of what makes it tick.

Before setting up the model, it's useful to begin at a whiteboard, mapping out the business and getting your thinking straight. At this point you're asking yourself what the model needs to include, which KPIs should be monitored, which external forces could have the greatest impact on the financial performance of the business. Before leaping into the first version of the model, I also find it useful to build small parts of it initially so that I can zoom in on necessary detail and increase my understanding. I might also build a very simple overview model first to help me make sense of the telescopic, zoomed-out view.

Model building is an iterative process, and models are rarely perfect first time. They are also communication tools which can be used to challenge, persuade and get buy-in from decision makers, so getting the level of detail right is crucial. Too much detail could run the risk of overwhelming people, but too little might result in the model failing to get the key messages across to the audience. This is an example of the **Goldilocks Dilemma** (discussed in *Data-Driven Organization Design*). It relates to the art of getting things 'just right' – not doing too much, and not doing too little. It's common for the first version of a model to be too complex, as in learning about the business you are likely to have amassed a huge amount of detail, but from this point you can figure out what really needs to be incorporated for the model to do its job. And remember Colin Powell's 40/70 rule discussed in Chapter 1.1. Incorporating less than 40 per cent of the available information will make for an ineffective model, but more than 70 per cent will probably be too much. We all know the adage 'I didn't have time to write a short letter, so I wrote a long one instead.'[4] Building a succinct model which focuses on the right things takes time.

As communication tools, models must also be easy to navigate and structured in a logical way that makes sense to their audience. Data inputs should be in different-coloured fonts for assumptions, outcomes and KPIs (in the examples used here, I've highlighted only the assumptions as examples) and hyperlinks can be used so you can move around it easily. It's also useful for the most important outcomes and assumptions to be in one place (which I often put on a home page) for ease of interaction.

Sensitivity analysis

As Dwight Eisenhower famously said, 'Planning is everything. The plan is nothing.' In our continually disrupted world, the process of planning is far more valuable than the plan itself. As soon as plans are set in motion, they get knocked off course, and something that made sense in January might not make any sense at all in June. But if you have invested time in the planning process, understanding the trade-offs and range of decisions which need to be made, as well as the different options that are available to you, then you will be more likely to be able to tweak your plan in response to disruption and stay in line with organizational goals.

The idea of a financial model is to create a living representation of a business which can be reshaped, modified and viewed from different perspectives. The model is mouldable, meaning that variables can be changed to answer 'What-If' questions, and financial performance can be understood across a range of possible future scenarios. This is known as sensitivity analysis.

Models contain **inputs** and outcomes. The inputs consist of raw data, metadata and assumptions – essentially the factors that you expect will affect your future performance. An outcome is a final calculation which varies according to the assumptions made. Sensitivity analysis is done by changing various assumptions by a certain percentage and assessing the effect the change has on the outcome (or how *sensitive* the outcome is to the change which has been made). Modelling is a fantastic way to build intuition as the aim is to understand why the changes being made are having the impact that you expect. As you are modelling you can ask yourself questions. Did I expect this change? Does this make sense? Is what I'm seeing here a new insight which we should take into consideration?

In our toll bridge example, the key assumptions and outcomes are listed on the right-hand side of the profit and loss statement. They are:

- how much it will cost to build the bridge
- the number of years the bridge is forecast to be used (remember that the model is stylized – in real life it wouldn't be five years!)
- the peak number of cars crossing the bridge per hour

- the growth in demand anticipated over the five-year period
- the price that can be charged to cross the bridge
- how much that price could be increased over the five-year period and at what point
- how much fixed costs will reduce and at what point
- the WACC

The key outcomes being measured are:

- NPV
- total profit
- payback years
- IRR

Using the volatility and impact category in sensitivity analysis

The outcomes shown in Figure 1.3.2 are based on expected assumptions, and, on the face of it, it all looks rosy. The payback is four years, the NPV is healthy, and it looks like a viable investment. But to proceed on this basis alone without first questioning the assumptions that have led you to these figures would be unwise. How likely to be true are the assumptions you've made, and how might they vary? Very often, once you dive a little deeper into the model, things can start to appear far less clear-cut.

To help answer these questions, as well as determine which assumptions are worthy of time and attention, I categorize them according to levels of volatility and impact. This concept is called the **Volatility and Impact Category (VIC)**. Volatility is a way of measuring the level of uncertainty attached to an assumption by looking at the range of possible outcomes, and impact looks at the material impact an assumption has on outcomes. Changing assumptions may have a high level of impact on a metric but a narrow range of possible outcomes (i.e. low volatility), or vice versa. The idea is to identify those assumptions with the highest levels of volatility (or uncertainty) *and* impact, as these are the ones which have the highest chance of derailing your outcomes. Directing your focus in this way allows for the most accurate forecasting of the best, worst and likely scenarios. Note that when doing sensitivity analysis, it is necessary to apply the economic principle of **ceteris paribus**, a Latin phrase meaning 'all other things being equal'. It is the same thinking that is applied in the design phase of D-DOD. To assess the impact and volatility of one assumption at a time, all other assumptions are held fixed.

An assumption may be very uncertain, but if it has no impact, the uncertainty isn't particularly relevant. Once identified, these critical assumptions become KPIs that are used to mitigate risk as far as possible. Failure to identify and categorize assumptions in this way can result in a huge list. In the past, I worked on a programme with over 900 assumptions, but once I categorized them according to impact and volatility, it became clear that only 40 of them really mattered.

Volatility is calculated by working out the minimum, expected and maximum assumptions. For example, it is expected that the bridge will cost $100,000,000 to build. Might it cost less than this, and if so, how much less? More worryingly, might it cost more, and if so, how much more? Figure 1.3.6 shows the minimum, expected and maximum figures for all assumptions in the model. As a minimum, the bridge could be expected to cost $98,000,000 to build, which is 2 per cent less than the expected cost. As a maximum, it might cost $130,000,000, which is 30 per cent more than the expected. The volatility percentage reflects the delta between the minimum and the maximum. In the case of the cost to build assumption, subtracting 30 per cent from –2 per cent gives a volatility score of –32 per cent.

Let's also look at peak cars per hour. This is the expected number of cars per hour over each 24-hour period. At the peak, 2,000 cars are expected to cross the bridge. This expected number might be based on current traffic levels, but how is that figure likely to change over the five-year period? Is the traffic likely to increase, or decrease? To answer this, you'd need to dig further into certain questions: is the city that the bridge leads to growing? Is tourism increasing or decreasing? Are there certain times of year when traffic over the bridge is likely to increase or decrease? What if the city falls out of favour? Or if a pandemic hits and traffic over the bridge drops off like a stone? The Covid-19 pandemic taught us that we need to consider the extremes. Getting sensitivity analysis right is all about asking the right questions. The model shows that the minimum and maximum peak cars over the bridge might vary by plus or minus 33 per cent, which gives a volatility score of –66 per cent, signifying that this is more volatile than the cost to build assumption.

FIGURE 1.3.6 Performing sensitivity analysis by calculating volatility and impact

| Key Assumptions | Scenario | | | | Outputs | | | | Volatility | NPV |
	Min	Expected	Max	Variable	Min	Expected	Max	Variable		Impact
Cost to Build	-2%	$ 100,000,000	30%		$ 98,000,000	$ 100,000,000	$ 130,000,000	$ 110,000,000	-32%	$ -9,259,259
Number of Years	0%	5	100%		5	5	10	5.5	-100%	$ 6,181,818
Peak Cars per hour	-33%	2,000	33%		1,340	2,000	2,660	2,200	-66%	$ 11,210,959
Growth in demand	-50%	10%	20%	10%	5%	10%	12%	11%	-70%	$ 2,124,716
Starting Price	-33%	$ 2.50	10%		$ 1.68	$ 2.50	$ 2.75	$ 2.75	-43%	$ 11,210,959
Increase in price Y3	-33%	5%	10%		3%	5%	6%	6%	-43%	$ 332,328
WACC	-5%	8%	15%		8%	8%	9%	9%	-20%	$ -2,477,833

So, from this analysis we see that the assumptions about 'peak cars per hour' and 'starting price toll' have notable volatility. We need to understand whether there would be a material impact on the key outcomes if these assumptions have been over- or underestimated. Sensitivity analysis suggests that there would be. Figure 1.3.7 shows the outcomes in a scenario where only the minimum values for these two assumptions materialize. In this scenario (1,340 cars per hour, each paying $1.68) the NPV would be –$61,783,593 and the total profit is also negative, indicating a projected loss of $84,978,218. The 'baseline' outcome values show the results when all assumptions meet their expected levels. The 'impact' is the difference between this baseline and our scenario outcomes. The importance of these two assumptions (the number of cars and the cost of the toll) when considering the economic viability of the bridge comes into sharp focus when it is seen that the impact of achieving the minimum values negatively impacts the NPV by $75,956,345, and the profit by $131,947,775.

FIGURE 1.3.7 Sensitivity analysis showing scenario outcomes for different assumptions

Key Assumptions		
Cost to Build	Exp	$ 100,000,000
Number of Years	Exp	5
Peak Cars per hour	Min	1,340
Growth in demand	Exp	10%
Starting Price	Min	$ 1.68
Increase in price Y3	Exp	5%
Reduction in Fixed Cost in Y3	Exp	25%
WACC	Exp	8%

Key Outcomes	Scenario Outcome		Baseline (Expected)	Impact
NPV	$ -61,783,593		$ 14,172,752	$ -75,956,345
Total Profit	$ -84,978,218		$ 46,969,557	$ -131,947,775
Payback Years	-4		4	-8
IRR	-26%		13%	-40%

Validating assumptions

Think back to the discussion in Chapter 1.1 about Real Option Pricing (ROP). ROP dictates that the greater the range of possible outcomes, the greater the level of uncertainty; and the greater the level of uncertainty, the greater the option value. Just asking the few questions outlined in this chapter shows that the toll bridge has great upside potential, but it also shows that it could be financially catastrophic. There is a huge amount of uncertainty associated with building it, and categorizing the assumptions shows where time and money would be best spent validating them so you can feel more confident about the investment. You might opt to spend $500,000 to learn more about the likely cost of building the bridge, the price you will be able to achieve and what the flow of cars is likely to be at different toll prices. This $500,000 would be the Real Option Price, and, set against the $100,000,000 investment, would seem like sensible money to spend.

Final thoughts

FP&A is all about leveraging the right tools and techniques to make informed decisions about how to optimize future financial performance. To do this, FP&A professionals rely upon a set of standards and a rigour of discipline which history has shown us works. The House of Medici, one of the wealthiest families ever and a driving force behind the Renaissance, was among the earliest businesses to use a double entry bookkeeping system to keep track of debits and credits. We now take this system for granted and it forms the fundamental backbone of modern-day accounting. For the Medici family, pioneering its use helped them to reach a level of sophistication that elevated them above everyone else.

Such regulation, control and discipline should not be underestimated and can teach many lessons to those outside FP&A. Financial statements like the profit and loss account, cash flow statement and balance sheet provide a common language, and a great FP&A professional will not only understand these statements but also the relationship and interplay between them. They will know about cash flow and working capital, and recognize that a business can go bankrupt even when the margin looks healthy. They will consider various metrics simultaneously, and weigh up how one affects another, isolating those which they have control over (such as variable costs) from those that they don't (such as fixed costs). This type of thinking is very similar to how an OP&A professional should think. In just the same way that variable costs are easier to influence than fixed, the number of FTEs performing variable roles influences outcomes in a way that fixed roles don't, because they are, by their nature, fixed. The chapters in Part Three look at top-down and bottom-up workforce planning, which is essentially a negotiation focused on the number of variable roles necessary to achieve strategic goals.

Time is a key dimension in FP&A. As we saw with the example of the toll bridge, decisions can't be based solely on a single financial year. To get a true picture, financial performance is assessed over appropriate time horizons to understand return on investment over time. Metrics such as NPV and WACC are used to understand the impact that time has on the value of money. We cannot know for certain how much revenue we might generate in five, 10 or 15 years' time, what our costs will look like, or what might happen to exchange rates, new technology, or new business models that might disrupt us. This is exactly why we need to model and plan for different scenarios, varying the inputs to show the best, worst and most likely outcomes over different time horizons.

As the toll bridge example showed, financial models do not need to be complex to drive useful insight. It's as much about the questions that you ask of the model as the model itself. What if the numbers of cars crossing the bridge turned out to be 10 per cent less than imagined? What if people are unwilling to pay $2.50 to cross the bridge and choose to drive around it instead? Might any future event impact the number of cars crossing the bridge? It's all about identifying the 'What-If' questions and maintaining a heads-up mindset: constantly scanning the space to see what's in front of you. As will become evident throughout the rest of this book, this is exactly the mindset needed for good OP&A.

REMEMBER THIS

1 To properly understand OP&A, it is fundamental to understand and learn from FP&A.

2 There are three main financial statements used by FP&A to gain insight into the financial health of a business: profit and loss, cash flow and the balance sheet.

3 Looking at profit margin alone is not enough – how cash flows in and out of the business is equally important.

4 Sensitivity analysis directs focus to assumptions that need the most attention.

5 Time is a key dimension in FP&A.

Notes

1 Gartner (2022) Gartner glossary: Financial planning and analysis (FP&A). www.gartner.com/en/finance/glossary/financial-planning-and-analysis-fp-a- (archived at https://perma.cc/UD79-NX5G)

2 Hendricks, D (2014) 5 successful companies that didn't make a dollar for 5 years, Inc. www.inc.com/drew-hendricks/5-successful-companies-that-didn-8217-t-make-a-dollar-for-5-years.html

3 This famous quote is often attributed to the British statistician George Box.

4 First thought to have been said by Mark Twain.

PART TWO

Making it Real

Transformation and optimization

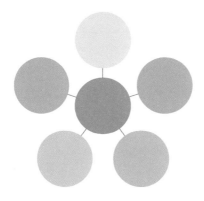

2.1

Introduction

What is Making it Real?

Peter Drucker, the founder of modern management, is thought to have said that good strategy is strategy that is executed. While this might sound obvious, it's amazing how management teams can spend months devising a strategic plan, but then fail to see that plan through or even think through how it might work beyond a high-level overview. The chapters that follow cover the 'Making it Real' phase of the organization design process. You'll remember that the work involved in strategically redesigning an organization can be divided into three phases:

1 macro operating design
2 micro detailed design
3 Making it Real

The work done in phases 1 and 2 involve developing models and blueprints by delving into schemas and applying frameworks to illustrate how strategy *should* be executed. How strategy *should* be executed rarely ends up being how it is executed in practice. The chapters that follow in Part Two explain how to take the plans laid out in the macro operating and micro detailed design and determine how they will work day to day, including the impact that those plans will have on every person in the organization.

In his book *Good to Great*, Jim Collins talks about the need to develop a culture of discipline to reach greatness. He discusses the difference between disciplined *thought* and disciplined *action*. Discipline runs through all three phases of the D-DOD process: macro operating and micro detailed design require disciplined thought while Making it Real requires disciplined action, defined by Collins as 'operating with freedom within a framework of responsibilities'.[1]

It's virtually impossible to think through every practical issue while in the territory of design. There will undoubtedly be some crucial aspects which have been overlooked. If one thing is sure, no matter how much thought was given to practicalities, you are likely to need to overrule assumptions made when making the plans real. The world may also have moved on if your design-making process is lengthy, so plans may need to be tweaked accordingly. The trick is to accept this and approach this stage with an open mind.

In a sense, this entire book could be called 'Making it Real'. The chapters all relate to the role played by the OP&A function in making organization designs a reality and optimizing the organization system to make gains in performance over time and through constant change. When most people hear the words 'organizational transformation' they think of large-scale, disruptive change brought about by a significant shift in strategy. They imagine the kind of wholesale change described in the macro operating design phase of my book *Data-Driven Organization Design*, when an organization needs to be transitioned from its current, **as-is** state to a target, **to-be** future state. This could be following a fundamental, strategy-led organization redesign, a post-merger integration or a reduction in workforce to adjust to changed market conditions. The chapters in this part have been written on the back of *Data-Driven Organization Design* and therefore largely address how to plan and implement (in other words, *make real*) this kind of extensive change. But it would be a mistake to think of transformation solely in these terms. The reality is that organizations are always transforming. When everything is 'business as usual', organizations are not standing still. They are continually changing in response to internal and external forces. Micro tweaks should regularly be made to the design to ensure that performance is continually optimized. Many of the tools and techniques discussed in relation to implementing large-scale change can also be applied to these micro tweaks. Whether you are working at the macro or micro level, always remember that the decisions you take can have far reaching consequences for the human beings involved.

The importance of a fair and well-governed process

There are many challenges implicit in making an organization's transformation a reality. It is both a change process and a mechanical one governed by employment law. Above all, it is a human process. Never lose sight of the fact that you are dealing with people – individuals with families, aspirations, responsibilities and a myriad of different pressures in their lives. There are obvious financial implications to losing your job, but for a great many people it goes deeper than this. For many, work isn't just a pay cheque but is central to their identity. Indeed, one of the first questions we tend to ask on meeting someone new is, 'What do you do?'

The people involved in this process deserve to be treated with sensitivity and respect, and this largely comes down to two things: ensuring that you run a fair and transparent process and *communicating* how you are doing it to those who are both directly and indirectly affected. This communication needs to happen with people at every level of the organization, not just those near the top.

If you communicate appropriately, you are more likely to win people's hearts and minds so that they willingly join you on the journey to make the transformation a success. This is difficult. People often feel confused, and, for many, the implications of the news will seem clear as mud. People become nervous about the unknown unknowns and what the news might mean for them. What do you really mean by change? How will it affect me? Is my job on the line? Should I get my CV out there? What do I tell my family and friends? It can give rise to overwhelmingly strong emotions which can make some people vote with their feet and demotivate others to the point of mental paralysis. The effect this news can have on people's mental health should never be underestimated.

The good news is that if the macro operating and micro detailed design have been done well, and the right communication strategies are employed, leaders can turn this negative perception of change around. Figure 2.1.1 highlights how leaders can move the workforce from being uncertain, full of fear and lacking intrinsic motivation to one of growing optimism, where everyone has a clear understanding of what will change and why, and feels fully motivated to get to where you want them to go. This last point is probably the most important. Be clear that you are not only talking about *organization* purpose, but also about *role* purpose. People need to know that they are not just a cog in the wheel. Show them that their individual competencies are recognized and demonstrate that you have thought through role accountabilities. This was highlighted while I was being interviewed about role design for the *Financial Times*. The interviewer stopped me and said that he had once quit his job because they had outsourced one of his accountabilities. In effect, they'd altered the purpose of his role, so he'd walked.

As Daniel Pink wrote in his book *Drive*, there are three things that make a role in the knowledge economy truly engaging: purpose, autonomy and mastery.[2] If to-be roles have been designed according to the properties advised in *Data-Driven Organization Design* (specifically by defining the purpose of the role, target accountabilities and competencies), you will be perfectly positioned to create an organization of highly motivated and engaged people, and it will be easy to communicate how these three things can be achieved. Remember that how you communicate is important not only to those people who are directly impacted by the change, but also to those who aren't. Everyone in the organization needs to be shown the upsides, and know that you are running a fair and well-governed process.

FIGURE 2.1.1 Position the change from one of uncertainty, fear and disengagement to optimism, transparency and motivation

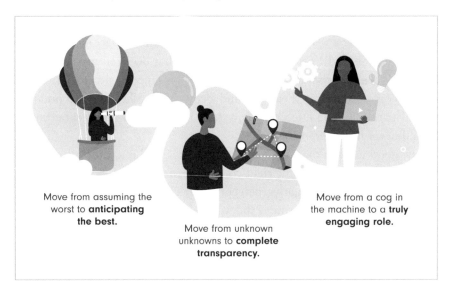

Move from assuming the worst to **anticipating the best.**

Move from unknown unknowns to **complete transparency.**

Move from a cog in the machine to a **truly engaging role.**

Structure and logic for Part Two

The chapters in this part of the book follow a four-stage process, as shown in Figure 2.1.2:

1 Prepare to execute (Chapter 2.2).

2 Assess impacts and plan communications (Chapter 2.3).

3 Manage talent transitions and consultation (Chapter 2.3).

4 Ongoing optimization (Chapter 2.4).

FIGURE 2.1.2 Making it Real follows four stages from planning for implementation through to ongoing optimization

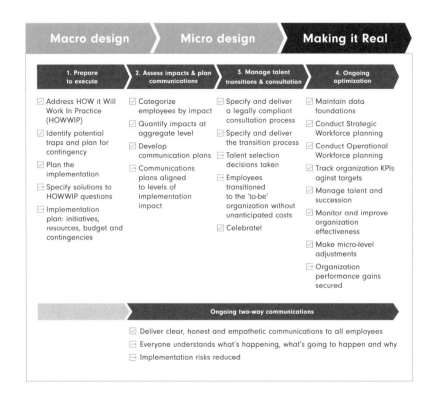

Executing plans is not a simple task, and if you don't prepare adequately it can go very wrong. Chapter 2.2 is all about preparing to execute the transformation. A piano player prepares their fingers by playing scales, a singer prepares their voice by doing warm-up exercises. Great preparation leads to great execution. At this point, you should prepare for how things will work in practice using certain tools and games that help to draw out issues you are likely to encounter. In this chapter I introduce HOWWIP, which stands for 'How it Will Work In Practice', and reiterate the importance of having a HOWWIP mindset and thinking through common – but avoidable – traps you could fall into along the way. My goal with Chapter 2.2 is to give you the tools and techniques to prepare sufficiently, identify what could go wrong before it does, and build in sufficient contingency so that the execution of the design can go as smoothly as possible.

Once you have prepared, it's time to action your implementation plan. At this point you enter the implementation phase. Implementation incorporates Stages 2 and 3 of Figure 2.1.2, both of which are covered in Chapter 2.3. First, you need to assess and quantify the impact that the planned changes will have on individuals in the organization. Employees can be categorized by impact and these impacts should then be quantified at an aggregate level. Once this is understood, it's time to start communicating the plans to the organization. Sadly, communication is all too often left as an afterthought, which can lead to an erosion of trust and a spiralling sense of unease.

Chapter 2.3 also covers Stage 3, explaining how to move the organization from its as-is state to the to-be design. This requires you to progress through an assessment and selection process in which people are slated into positions and then either selected or not selected. Those not selected will be asked to leave, and exit plans will be put into place. The ramifications of getting things wrong at this stage or not following due process can be enormous. It is very common to approach this stage with trepidation, and the work can feel overwhelming. The most important question to ask yourself is whether you are committed and brave enough to go for it. My advice is to structure the work into bite-size chunks so that it doesn't overwhelm you and I introduce the **Now, Next, Later** Kanban approach used in agile working to help you prioritize tasks. This will also allow you to achieve quick wins and build momentum as well as trust. This can be a difficult process, but to make it succeed you need to find a way to enjoy the journey and build in institutional resilience and excellence.

The last chapter in this part, Chapter 2.4, looks at the role of OP&A when it is 'business as usual' in ensuring that strategy is executed as it should be on an ongoing basis. Part of this comes down to workforce planning, the subject of the chapters in Part Three, but it is also about monitoring and improving organization effectiveness, making micro tweaks to the design to optimize outcomes, and putting talent management and succession plans into place to ensure that all talent is nurtured, and people are developed appropriately for future roles.

Notes

1 Collins, J (2001) *Good to Great: Why some companies make the leap… and others don't*, Random House Business.
2 Pink, D (2018) *Drive: The surprising truth about what motivates us*, Canongate Books, Edinburgh.

2.2

Preparing to execute

Introduction to Stage 1

Without proper preparation, flawless execution is difficult, if not impossible. Stage 1 of the Making it Real process is all about how to prepare for executing change. I don't just mean working out a plan. There is a difference between having a plan and *preparing* to both implement that plan and execute change on an ongoing basis. A plan is a list of set actions, sometimes in a sequence and usually with a beginning and an end. It lays out what should be done when, and might list dependencies, risks and 'mitigating actions'. But putting together a plan doesn't help you to prepare mentally and physically. It doesn't give you the tools to get everything ready, lay everything out and think everything through. It doesn't help you to get other people ready, so that they know what they need to do and why they need to do it. The tools and techniques I give you in this chapter will help you do just this – to prepare for how you are going to execute change in your organization, and to execute it on an ongoing basis.

While planning is passive, preparation is active. In my role as a junior rugby coach, we actively prepare before any game we play. We look at the weather conditions and modify the game plan accordingly. We run through a kit check to make sure we've got all the gear we need. The kids warm up, stretch and get their hands warm so they can catch and pass the second they're on the pitch. Preparation isn't only about preparing your body but also your mind, so we spend some time getting into the right mindset, ensuring that everyone feels calm and in the zone. We'll have a playbook, but we never go straight from the bus to the pitch without factoring in time to prepare.

By the end of this stage, you should feel fully prepared to implement change in your organization. You will already have an implementation plan which would have been worked out in the macro operating design phase when developing your business case. This will set out the necessary initiatives, the required resources and the budget. What's needed now is to take that plan and prepare the organization for it to be implemented, thinking through How it Will Work In Practice and how to avoid any potential traps along the way. You'll notice that the title for this chapter is 'Preparing to execute' rather than 'Preparing to implement'. Implementing the plan is only part of execution. Execution is ongoing, and you should prepare not only for implementing the plan, but also for ongoing micro tweaks. To a large degree, how you prepare will depend on how you have designed for the work to get done in different parts of the organization. Many organizations now use a mix of traditional and agile operating models, and for this reason, the chapter ends with the beginnings of a case study on how to prepare to make agile designs real.

Address HOWWIP questions

The HOWWIP acronym came up when doing a particularly complex and detailed project with a colleague and it has stuck with me ever since. I love it because it is a quick and easy reminder to think through how something will work in practice. It helps you to ensure that the theoretical is truly possible and that the detail has been worked out. Does everybody know what they are doing from day one of the change process through to two months down the line? HOWWIP questions will have been naturally popping up throughout the design process, but at that point they will only have been partially addressed. The reason for spelling them out as you prepare to execute is to head off any issues before they arise and uncover the answers to the questions that haven't yet been asked. It's a safe, low-stake way to think through any potential sticking points. As a junior rugby coach, I teach kids to play shadow rugby. They play without an opposition, running through scenarios and performing drills so they're free to make mistakes in a safe environment with no risk. The point is to help them *feel* what it's like to be in certain scenarios, so they are prepared when it comes to the real thing. Asking HOWWIP questions is really very similar, and below I run you through some HOWWIP games to play to make this process fun.

A large part of Making it Real is helping people to see what the design means to them personally. Furthermore, it draws out the process 'exceptions' that can drive most of the work. Part of this comes down to the interface design: how items of work (or the information needed to progress work tasks) will be handed from one team to another. It's also about making things tangible. In the design phase, accountability matrices would have been worked out. To see a matrix with a set of acronyms such as RAD (this stands for responsible, approve and do – for more information see *Data-Driven Organization Design*) is one thing; to understand what 'approve' or 'do' really means in the context of a specific output, task or decision is another. For example, 'approve' the recruiting plan might have the CFO and CPO marked as 'A' for approvers. When bringing the design to life in this way, the key is to think through the practicalities of delivering these processes and to focus on the detail, down to the level of the following sorts of questions:

- What should be done when actual performance is adrift from budget?
- What happens when there is an 'event' like a safety incident or an embarrassing PR incident?
- How are new positions approved?
- What happens if two approvers for a given decision can't agree?
- How should the Implementation Team hand over to the Ongoing Service Team?

Asking HOWWIP questions anticipates issues and deals with them. Questions about the approval process could be answered in the following way:

- Planned requisitions are detailed and circulated by the second Tuesday of every month and signed off in a meeting of approvers.
- All positions must be in the budget that is signed off annually, with a separate exception process that requires the CEO to approve.

Beyond this kind of detail, think what else would need to be thought through. What information needs to be produced and by whom? Does HR need to provide job specs and the expected hiring costs? Does the requester need to produce a business plan? If yes, what does that plan need to include?

HOWWIP is both a natural ongoing process through the design and preparation as well as a practical framework for structuring a set of exercises and games. When learning a skill, such as playing the piano or running, there are drills or small exercises that are repeated time and again, in a safe way, to improve the skill and build muscle memory. The same is true for commercial airline pilots. They spend hours in simulators preparing for multiple scenarios that may never happen, but they need to be able to make decisions in a matter of seconds. By gamifying HOWWIP you make it safe, and the process can be a lot of fun. In this section, I work through four exercises and games that I have found useful when preparing to execute change:

1 talk through the process with cards

2 interface ball game

3 the round robin interface conversations

4 Give and Get matrix

These are simply tools to help you think through exceptions and issues; to discover the sorts of things that will trip the design up so you can prepare effectively for the change to come. Before jumping into them, I will demonstrate how they fit into the bigger picture, and how they can be documented in a useful manner as part of the overall project.

HOWWIP outcomes

The point of the HOWWIP exercises and games below is to clarify answers to the question 'How will that work?' These answers are worth recording if they are going to be of ongoing use, as they are easily forgotten, and the same questions often pop up from numerous sources. It is also often the case that a question can't be answered immediately so by noting it down it gives you the time to think it over before fleshing out the detail. I am not suggesting you need to note down everything, and quite often it simply requires adding to existing documentation, but depending on the level of work, independent documentation can be invaluable. There are three documents you can produce:

1 HOWWIP log

Think of the HOWWIP log as a cross between a Frequently Asked Questions (FAQ) list and a list of things to 'park'. Questions and concerns will be raised that you won't have time to deal with immediately. So 'park' them and write them down in your HOWWIP log. A helpful way to structure the log is to link the questions to the Level 2 value chain and main activity they relate to. It is helpful to provide a priority rating so that you can manage the order in which questions need to be dealt with, together with an audit trail of when the question was raised, the forum it was raised in and by whom, and what the status of the question is. Document the issue, the issue type (by giving it a dimension), an explanation of the issue, and its status. As you answer the questions, make sure to document the outcome. Figure 2.2.1 shows a simple example log investigating the efficiency of a sales process for a Delivery and Support Team.

FIGURE 2.2.1 An example of a HOWWIP log

Item	Nearest current activity	Level 2 activity	Question	Priority	Dates		Who	Status	Outcomes	Comment
					Raised	Closed				
1	Solution design	Proposal	How to flag	M	Tuesday 03/05/2022		Rupert/ Peter	Open		Affects sales...
2	New client sole	Proposal	Why is it that..	H	Thursday 02/04/2022	Thursday 09/04/2022	Rupert	Closed	A level 2 activity...	n/a
3	Issue management	Issue triage	Why does support...	H	Thursday 02/04/2022		Michael	Open		For example...
4	Customer care	Monitor customer satisfaction	Customers who...	L	Thursday 02/04/2022		Michael	Open		The worry is that...
5	Solution design	Data integration	All too often	H	Tuesday 07/04/2022		Ben	Open		A bad data

2 Process descriptors

For those processes which are relatively simple, all you need is a quick one- or two-line descriptor for each activity in the activity taxonomy. The descriptor should give a little more detail so that what is meant by each step is obvious and unambiguous. If a question was raised in the HOWWIP log, it is also good to include the answer within this descriptor. For example, the process could be 'Conduct annual budget' and the descriptor 'How the annual budget is generated, reviewed, approved and managed in-year'.

3 Level 2 process swim-lane map

There will be instances where the detail is just too complex; where there are loops, branching of activities, and systems required to support the process. Where there is clear use for a subset of detailed workflows and the number of positions involved is three or more, then detail the Level 2 process swim-lane map described in *Data-Driven Organization Design*. As a reminder, most design only needs to be based on Level 0 and 1 maps. To recap, Level 0 is a summary value chain map used in designing the target operating model, while Level 1 is the activity taxonomy. Level 2 is a swim lane with owners and icons representing various actions such as: decision; activity; sub-process; and outputs. Figure 2.2.2 shows an example of how a support desk might deal with client issues.

Each row, or what looks like a swim lane, is a function or position. There is a clear start and end, so a sense of timing can be shown and the number of handoffs (interfaces) counted. A 'swim-lane Level 2 process map' details how a process should work. My experience is that these have their time and place, but should be used with caution. They are idealistic, can be confusing, and they take lots of time to generate. So don't try to define everything as a Level 2 process map. Only do it if the following apply:

- there are lots of handoffs
- there is a strict process that should be followed
- there are loops and complexities

Count the number of handoffs and ask whether it is going to be workable. The number of times that I have seen more than 15 handoffs within a single process is remarkable. I've seen processes take three months to execute when it should have been possible to do them in a week.

FIGURE 2.2.2 Level 2 process map example

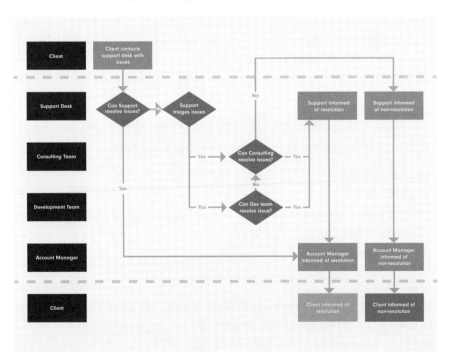

HOWWIP exercises and games

The four exercises and games that follow are intended as tools to draw out and answer any potentially problematic issues. Their purpose is to encourage people to discuss and visualize what is ahead of them; to understand their new role or the change in their role. They give people the opportunity to say that they feel confused or don't get how things are going to work and dig into issues further to solve them. Above all, they make the preparation process safe and fun.

Talk through the process with cards

Top sportspeople spend a lot of time visualizing how different scenarios will work and feel. This exercise aims to replicate that in a group setting. Take one sub-process that involves interaction at many points within the business – for example, recruitment, Learning and Development (L&D) or appraisals. For each step, print out the Match Attax-inspired process cards I describe in *Data-Driven Organization Design*. As a reminder, these cards can be used to create an activity taxonomy and process map when doing activity analysis and design. They are used to check for completeness and correct any inaccuracies. By dividing them into categories – for example, geographic location or sub-function – you can see if any activities are missing and then capture and document them in a Level 1 process map. Each card could include the following:

- the value chain component and the process and sub-process
- the activity and whether it is a **Decision, Output or Task (DOT)**
- how it fits within the taxonomy (and what the parent processes and value streams are)
- colour coding and icons for the key dimensions such as daily, weekly, monthly, annually
- who is responsible (if it has been defined)
- a succinct description on the back of the card

When using the cards for this HOWWIP exercise, lay them out in order on the table and use them to do the following:

- Define where the process starts and finishes.
- Identify the points where there are handoffs.

- Define the inputs, activities and outputs at each stage, plus any decisions.
- Test that the process will work and that it is clear:
  o List a set of questions concerning how the process will work.
  o Have a group stand up in a small circle with each person in the circle 'acting' one of the roles (or more, if there are more roles than people in the circle; but always being clear about the role each person is 'playing' at any moment in time). Start with the first step and then pass a ball to the person who acts next. The person with the ball is responsible at that point in time.
- At each step, ask: What will you need? What you will do? What will the outcome be? By walking through the process, each person talks over what they do and how they will do it.
- Write up any orphans (activities or decisions that don't have an owner), gaps, issues and questions on the HOWWIP log.
- Review after the completion of an area to understand the amount of workload that was missing from the original description.

Interface ball game

Building on the previous game, another good one to play is the interface ball game. This game addresses how the interfaces between people will work to understand who does what and how information and work are transferred between people. Another way to understand this is to use the Give and Get matrix, which I describe below. I'll pick up on the Hokupaa case study to explain how this game works. The Client Success Team at Hokupaa is responsible for technical support. The team consists of a Client Support Manager and a support desk consisting of a Support Desk Manager and First-line Support Administrator. The game below shows how the interfaces between people in the team can be discussed and agreed. It works in the following way:

1 A process is chosen.

2 Those involved in the process stand up (or someone acts as if they are one of the participants in the process).

3 The facilitator gives a context to a selected situation and then asks practical questions; for example, in the context of a client issue resolution process: 'What happens when the client contacts their sales rep with an issue?'

4 The person responsible for the first action (in this example, the Client Success Manager) raises their hand and catches a ball thrown by the facilitator. The person with the ball then talks through with the group:

o What they need (i.e. what they *get*): 'I need a detailed description of the issue from the client. I need to understand the context and the pain it is causing.'

o What they *do*: 'I'm going to find and understand the root cause, speak to the client if needed, work out where to take the issue and document it for internal purposes.'

o The outcomes they have generated (this is what they *give*): 'I will detail the issue and decide how to triage it depending on the type of issue it is. If it's a bug, I'll go to the Technical Support Team. If it's a capability issue, I'll work with the Enablement Team to either improve training materials and/or the Advisory Team to offer the client further support. If it's an implementation issue, I'll work with the Implementation Team to improve the process and verify that all work has been completed. I will communicate the outcome and/or plan to the client.'

5 The person who then needs to pick up the next action raises their hand and receives the ball from the first person. They repeat the three points (*get*, *do*, *give*).

6 This continues until the process is completed.

For the game to work, it needs to have enough pace; those with the ball need to be succinct and to the point. Short punchy sentences and humility are crucial. If people are unclear, have a brief discussion and try to resolve the issue. If it is too difficult to resolve, then capture it as an issue for the HOWWIP log and move on. This requires excellent facilitation and documentation skills. Ideally, there should be two different people facilitating and documenting. The documenter captures the details of what people say; what they get and from whom; how they do their work and any concerns and issues. For example, in the above case, good HOWWIP questions to ask could include:

• How would the issue be escalated to the Support Team?

• Do they call, email or enter information into a system? How does the issue get triaged?

- How will the Client Success Manager be informed of the plan and promised resolution date, etc.
- Who will then communicate this to the client?

The facilitator needs to keep the game going and maintain the playful aspect of it. Equally important is picking good processes to talk through. Start with the obvious and easy ones to get everyone familiar and comfortable with how to play.

The round robin interface conversations

Another good exercise is to get a group of people together who will be working cross-functionally and where there are lots of connection points. Everyone has a conversation with everyone else and a facilitator documents the conversations. Each conversation follows a pattern of both parties writing down:

- what they need (*get*) from the other person/role (each person is representing a role, but it is ideal for the person who will occupy that position to be preparing and participating in the conversation)
- things they are unsure about – for instance, who will be doing something or when something will be done

The first person then states what they need, and the second person seeks clarification or raises an issue if they believe that something shouldn't or can't be provided. For example, with the Client Success Manager, First-line Support Administrator and Support Desk Manager, the Client Success Manager could ask:

- 'How do I contact you?'
- 'What information do you need?'
- 'How will you keep me informed?'

The Support Desk Manager could then respond about what they would need to know in different scenarios: for example, if it's a bug, which use case and tenant instance of the platform. They would also need to know how urgent the issue is and understand the likely impact if it isn't resolved.

This is then repeated the other way around. Finally, there is a discussion about the lists of items both parties are unsure about, with a goal of resolving as many issues in the list as possible. Try to keep each conversation to between 15 and 30 minutes long. And bear in mind that if there are eight positions, then everyone will have seven conversations. So, with seven 30-minute conversations, scene setting and coffee breaks, that is a good half-day session. But, if done well, 56 detailed interface conversations have taken place in a focused and controlled way. This is far better than everyone scrabbling around independently trying to work it out. These conversations are important because they get into the detail. Commitments are made, which can be captured in the process charts as 'outcomes', Level 2 process maps, if needed, or the **Give and Get matrix**.

The Give and Get matrix

If you have read *Data-Driven Organization Design*, you will be familiar with the Give and Get matrix and you may well have high-level matrices in place. In Making it Real, you should return to these, to check that they make sense and delve into a further level of detail.

As a reminder, the Give and Get matrix visualizes the interfaces between roles and functions within the organization. It summarizes what each role or function gives to a list of other roles or functions, and what that role or function gets back in return. It is essential for understanding how roles and function interact, and what one enables another to do. My favourite way to do this is to create a large matrix on a wall and ask people performing certain roles to list what they will give to and get from other roles. For visual examples of Give and Get matrices, see Chapter 5.3, where I detail them in relation to the OP&A function.

HOWWIP is about how it will work, pure and simple. It aims to address the nitty-gritty. Embrace the HOWWIP. In my experience, it is only when you use games and exercises such as those outlined above that you get those 'Oh no!' and 'We really need to work that one out' moments as well as the 'Ah-ha' ones and 'Yes, I can finally see how this is actually going to work.' It is where it all starts to become real. Another significant part of preparing to execute change is thinking through potential traps you might be about to fall headlong into. These exist everywhere and a lot of the preparation done at this stage is concerned with identifying them and thinking through how to avoid them. I'll now detail some common ones to watch out for.

Identify potential traps and plan for contingency

When it comes to a redesign or transformation there is so much that can go wrong. In some respects, it would be a surprise if any execution went exactly as intended. In this section I begin by outlining some of the signs that indicate when things may be going off-track before highlighting some of the common traps you are likely to fall into. Much of dealing with these traps is mindset. With adequate preparation, you can begin to predict what's coming and recognize when things are going wrong, and the probability of execution success will greatly increase.

Knowing when and what things are going wrong

Common signs that could indicate that something's not right could include, but not be limited to:

- lots of one-to-one side meetings to share concerns and find out what's really going on...
- ... and, simultaneously, meeting mania where people are constantly in meetings with an excessive number of participants
- initiative fatigue with a feeling of achieving little while being too busy to change that fact
- a feeling that you are just shifting boxes around organization charts rather than implementing real, visible change on the ground
- challenges from people that jobs are being allocated based on personal connections rather than competencies
- an increase in absenteeism and attrition, with key talent leaving
- having a lack of clear priorities as to what needs to be done and why
- discussions and debates are becoming personal and are damaging relationships

The possible root cause factors that drive these problems are almost endless. It could be that communication has been ineffective, that the process hasn't been adhered to, that people are overwhelmed by too much to do, or that there is a lack of data integrity. There are almost countless examples, and I have included a sample as shown in Figure 2.2.3. The common traps are organized into six broad themes. This isn't a definitive list, as the number of things that could go wrong is endless. In fact, if you take some time to think about the many, many things that could go amiss, you may just want to give up. Why bother, if the chance of failure is so great? If the chance of success is small, the feeling of achieving success is even sweeter.

FIGURE 2.2.3 List of example traps

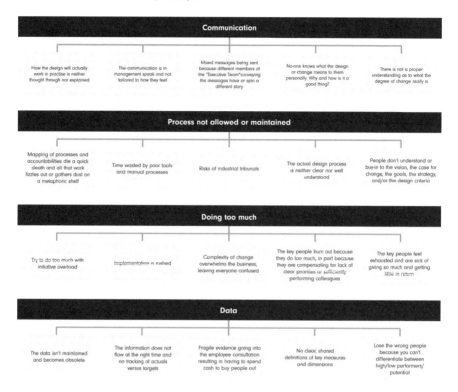

A great way to draw out what the traps might be, specific to your own situation, is to carry out a post-mortem analysis before you even begin. Gather your Implementation Team in a room and imagine you have just reached the point where the to-be organization is populated. Then, working backwards through the timeline, ask everyone to say 'what went wrong' and 'what the impact was'. This acts as a great way to uncover possible traps before you start and to document risks and priorities for the execution. I will now expand on seven generic traps which I believe can often be the main cause for derailment:

1 allocating insufficient resource

2 too many initiatives

3 forgetting the basics

4 allowing worry to trump fun

5 failure to establish a shared and common language

6 compromising the model

7 overestimating the effect of changing those at the top

The important thing to remember is that there are many, many things that can go wrong. The seven issues I highlight here by no means present an exhaustive list. I've simply chosen seven because, as you may remember from my advice on taxonomy building in *Data-Driven Organization Design*, seven is a magic number. Psychological experiments have shown that most people can only recall seven items on a list in one go. It took some work to narrow these traps down to seven, but I wanted to hit the magic number, so I persevered.

1. Allocating insufficient resource

Months and months can be spent doing the macro operating and micro detailed design phases of the work, and they often overrun, but despite this, implementation milestones are frequently expected to adhere to original timescales. As the design stages are theoretical, the impact of the delays is not as keenly felt as when making the design real. Having finalized the macro operating and micro detailed design and come up with an implementation plan, it is often assumed by management that the design will 'just happen'. All too often senior managers fail to prepare for executing change and steer clear of the detailed nature of it, preferring to leave it to junior resources. The result is that the execution is under-resourced and neither managed nor tracked properly.

Executing change well takes considerable effort. If anything, executive sponsorship needs to be more committed and public than in the design stages of the work. While the risk with macro operating and micro detailed design is going into too much detail, the risk within Making it Real is not going into enough. Making it Real is all about conscientious, thorough and dogmatic preparation and approach to delivery. You will need resilience and you will need to stick at it. There are no hard-and-fast rules in terms of the numbers of resources needed or the time required, but before you begin to execute the transformation it's vital that you have the following:

- a detailed plan with appropriate staffing
- significant contingency times in place as not everything will go to plan
- an appropriate budget – you can't afford not to

2. Too many initiatives

Too many high-level initiatives and too much change leads to inevitable failure. To get around this, prioritize based on your case for change and pick the most important initiatives to implement first. Be wise in that choice. Don't pick too many and ensure you see them through. When you think they are done, you are probably only halfway there. To make real and sustainable change takes a dogged and relentless commitment to a limited set of initiatives. Less is more. For example, having pulled the Reduce, Reallocate, Improve and Invest (RRII) levers to optimize processes (introduced in Chapter 1.2), you are likely to have a long list of potential changes. Prioritize these based on: ease of implementation; ROI; payback; scale of impact; and whether other initiatives are dependent on the change being made.

3. Forgetting the basics

When you look across disciplines such as sport, those who are at the top of their game emphasize the same point: they train until they can execute their basic skills to perfection without a moment's hesitation. When it comes to business, we struggle with the basics. We struggle to communicate effectively, sort our management information, be clear about who is doing what, and when, know the plan inside out and prepare to execute it with relentless focus, and fundamentally be clear about why we are doing what we are aiming to do in the first place. The truth is, it is much harder than playing a game. The feedback isn't as clear, and the sense of reward isn't as great either.

Getting the basics right requires an understanding of what is core to your organization and ensuring you are world-class at achieving that core. This approach is central to both good strategy and the execution of that strategy. To understand this, go back to your micro detailed design and define the core goals, objectives, processes and competencies. It might sound simple, but the process of defining the core elements within the micro detailed design is likely to cause a huge amount of debate amongst your Design Team. Try to keep it focused and principled. Once you are clear as to what is truly core, ensure you achieve those objectives and get the work done. The core elements from the macro operating design and micro detailed design that I would prioritize are as follows:

- macro operating design:
  - a clear vision, strategy, case for change and design criteria

- a clear target operating model that ties the structural design to the value chain through a high-level accountability matrix (RAD)
  - a clear and compelling business case
- micro detailed design:
  - a solid understanding of the as-is and to-be organizations, in terms of headcount and cost by position, including the detailing of reporting lines
  - a clear definition of the work required using the Level 1 process map and what each role is responsible for
  - clarity on the competencies required, the gaps and prioritization for closing them
  - a robust logic for determining the numbers of FTEs required in the to-be model

4. Allowing worry to trump fun

If you're not having fun, it's difficult to excel in what you're doing. Play is great. When you play a game, time disappears. You smile and laugh, and push yourself to your limits, often without realizing. You willingly give everything you've got, except your humility, humour and humanity. If the repercussions of failure are too great, this can zap confidence and fun, and consequently make it very difficult to achieve greatness. Worry takes the will to succeed away.

When coaching rugby, I love to see kids try stuff out, without worrying about what will happen if they fail. Kids who push a pass, take a chance, who then might fall but get up with a smile and give it another go. Far too often, corporate culture prioritizes risk avoidance over maximizing a return. Accept the risk, deal with it, and deal with failure. Be resilient enough, brave enough, perhaps even crazy enough to try it again and make it happen second time around.

In the film *See No Evil, Hear No Evil*, Gene Wilder's character obsessively worries about making a fool of himself. His blind friend, played by Richard Pryor, says he can fix that problem in ten seconds. He puts an ice cream cone upside down on Gene Wilder's head and tells him how silly he looks. Gene Wilder laughs. He looks silly, but no longer cares. He's realized that making a fool of yourself isn't such a big deal after all.[1] Life is short. It's gone in a flash, so enjoy it and find a way for others to enjoy it too. You owe it to yourself, and to them.

5. *Failure to establish a shared and common language*

It's rare to find a consistent language commonly applied across the same organization. Individual business units, geographies and functions often attach different meanings to the same terms or use different terms to mean the same thing. At the very least, this slows progress as clarification is repeatedly sought. Often, ambiguity can be a breeding ground for game-playing in the political context of organizational change.

To get around this, establish consistent terminology and apply it across the full scope of the organization to build a shared and common understanding. For example, how do you measure the size of the workforce? Do you use headcount, FTE contractors, or open/vacant positions? It's also key to clarify roles. It's common to find people with similar titles conducting very different work and people with different titles conducting very similar work.

This is amplified in the context of post-merger integration. When you integrate two companies, you're bringing together different roles and functions, and you need to work out which are performing the same work and therefore need to be merged into one. These roles and functions are unlikely to be called the same thing, so from a data management perspective you need to align them and get the terminology right across the board.

6. *Compromising the model*

It's important to ensure that the model is not compromised by establishing, documenting and repeatedly referencing the 'red lines' which can't be crossed. This will greatly reduce the chance of political game playing, which can derail design projects. The best strategy in the world is unlikely to succeed if the people delivering it don't see eye to eye. When people are aligned, relationships are strong, and designs have the best chance of being implemented as intended.

A lot of this comes down to aligning culture. Delving into the intricacies of culture clash is outside the scope of this book. Suffice to say that there's a lot of opportunity for cultures to clash in organizations: across functions, regions, geographies and in the context of acquisition and post-merger integration. Never underestimate the impact of bringing together large groups of people, especially if those groups are accustomed to significantly different organizational cultures. Establishing 'red lines' is particularly important in this context.

7. Overestimating the effect of changing those at the top

The tone of an organization is set at the top. People love shiny new things – the big stories and reputations, and the brands people come from. They get sucked into the allure, promise and hope. But hope isn't a strategy. Many people can spin a great story, but all too often it is just that – spin. The professional polish turns out to be vacuous fiction.

Again, this point is beyond the scope of this book, but I have fallen into this trap myself and want to point out the dangers. I've been sucked in by the silver bullet person – the big brand name and the stories. In retrospect, I would have been better developing someone I already knew in the organization. In Chapter 2.4 I introduce the internal **talent marketplace** and explain how it can be used for spotting talent and **career path mapping**. In most cases, it is usually far preferable to develop internal talent than recruit from the outside.

Preparing to execute agile ways of working

I'll end this chapter with some specific advice on how to prepare for making the agile organization real. Agile methodologies are increasingly being adopted in organizations to accelerate time to value. Agile working methods are a way for teams to self-manage how they get work done. They enable teams to itemize tasks, update them and pass them between people, as well as provide a process to monitor progress on a continual basis. Agile working is well documented, so I won't go into detail about the methods. This section will focus more on the structure of Agile Teams, and how the organization system is impacted by a shift to agile. It serves as a case study for what needs to be considered in organizations when undergoing this change. I return to it in Chapter 2.4 when I consider the importance of having a proper data model and planning capability when managing talent and deploying people to Agile Teams.

Contrary to what many people believe, agile working is not a new concept. Plenty of methods have been deployed over the past twenty years or so, and it was initially given a language and framework in software development because it is particularly suited to allowing new versions of code to be defined, tested and released in a relatively short amount of time. As an iterative methodology, it is based on the idea that releasing something quickly is better than releasing nothing at all, as the shorter feedback loops allow for constant improvement. A backlog of work in the form of new product features is broken into categories named '**epics**'. The backlog is also prioritized into **release trains**, and at the end of each release train new code is shipped to users.[2] Release trains are broken into shorter, time-boxed iterations known as '**sprints**', and Agile Scrum Teams sprint to develop new features to learn quickly from the feedback they get and improve at the next iteration. Sprints are usually around two weeks long. This is compared with the more traditional waterfall methodology, which is sequential in nature and doesn't chunk work to gain quick feedback. The feedback loops are much longer, and it takes a much longer time to create value.

While agile working has been popularized through software development, I believe its roots go far deeper than this. It has a lot in common with the way consulting firms have managed their Project Teams for decades. When I started out as a management consultant, I was assigned to Project Teams and I reported to an Engagement Manager for each team. That manager would give me an engagement review specific to the project, but I would also report to my line manager. I would work on projects for six weeks, nine months and everything in between. I would typically work on multiple projects with different clients at any given time. As will become evident below, this way of working has many similarities with what we now refer to as agile.

My colleagues and I have worked with many clients not in software development who have expanded agile into their business processes. One example is an agricultural machinery manufacturer who wanted to reduce defects and produce better results in less time. Specifically, they wanted to address missed delivery dates, quality issues and a lack of product ownership. They restructured so that they could use a release train agile scaling approach using cross-functional, co-located teams with a single product owner and a high-quality product backlog. The restructuring paid off and they saw improvements within six months. Another client in the bakery business wanted to support the growth of both in-store and digital sales with technology. They leveraged agile ways of working and ran a pilot with two projects focused on online orders before rolling out to the rest of the enterprise. They saw better alignment between technology and the business and a 25 per cent increase in digital sales. Finally, a toy production company wanted to redesign the customer experience. They implemented a scaled agile framework to take their company digital and change how customers engage with their product. Once implemented in one part of the organization, agile spread like wildfire to other parts of the business. In each of these examples, technology was part of the conversation, but each leveraged agile methodologies.

Preparing the data model in the shift to agile

In each of the examples given above, the companies needed a holistic view of how to transition teams to agile ways of working. The first thing people usually think about when they hear the words 'agile transformation' are the project management practices used in software development such as Scrum Teams and **Kanban** structuring of work. As explained above, scrums are a way of building creative, cross-functional teams to create value though time-boxed sprints. A Kanban board (Kanban means 'billboard' in Japanese) is a method developed by Taiichi Ohno to improve the flow of work across the production process. It visualizes workflows and limits work in progress. These are the types of methods you want to think about when considering the delivery or outcomes. But as you begin to architect Agile Teams across the enterprise, you find that strategy and planning are required across technology architecture, product strategy, operating model and resourcing. These things must be prepared for as part of the transformation process. How will the operating model differ depending on whether agile practices are being implemented? Before I delve into this in more detail, it is first necessary to understand the importance of preparing the data model, and linking Role, Position and People data when deploying people to Agile Teams.

LINKING ROLE, POSITION AND PEOPLE DATA IN THE CREATION OF AGILE TEAMS

In a traditional organization structure, people in hierarchical positions perform roles, and – beyond the most senior roles – there are multiple positions for the same role. One person is dedicated to one position, and stays in that position for an average of two to five years, although there is no specified end date. It is possible for some people to spend the remainder of their career in a single position, while others last only weeks. It is fluid and no set rules apply. This is shown at the top of Figure 2.2.4. In this image, you can see that both Ted and Jane spend 100 per cent of their time dedicated to their assigned positions.

Conversely, with Agile Team structures, people are assigned to agile positions within their role. One person performing a role can fill multiple positions across numerous Agile Teams. They stay in those positions for an average of three to 12 months, although it can vary greatly. Linking Role, Position and People data and specifying the start and end date for positions using data enables high-speed decisions to be made in terms of who should be assigned to which Mission Teams depending on their resourcing commitments. This is shown at the bottom of Figure 2.2.4. Ted spends 60 per cent of his time in Mission Team 1 and 40 per cent of his time in Mission Team 2. Imagine Ted is performing the role of a Campaign Manager. The campaign he's working on in Mission Team 1 might last three months while the campaign he's working on in Mission Team 2 might last six months. This means that when he comes to the end of the campaign for Mission Team 1, 60 per cent of his time will be freed up to dedicate to another Mission Team. If positions are defined with start and end date data, it should be relatively easy to fix him up with a new Mission Team. This illustration demonstrates why treating the organization as a system (as described in Chapter 1.2) is critical for managing Agile Teams at scale.

Performance is assessed differently in traditional and Agile Team structures. With traditional, it is done via an annual performance review with the line manager. With agile, people often have more than one manager – the manager(s) of their Mission Teams and their line manager. The manager(s) of the Mission Teams will report performance back to the line manager.

DESIGNING AGILE ORGANIZATIONAL MODELS

Figure 2.2.5 shows the difference in a human capital management company between a traditional organization chart at the top, and an Agile Team view at the bottom. Transitioning from traditional to agile structures requires deciding where people should go to support the new model. In the chart at the top, people are organized into chapters – communities of people who provide functional excellence and skills. Ted, a User Experience/User Interface (UX/UI) designer, reports to the head of UX/UI. In the agile view, people are organized into families (sometimes known as tribes). These families are collections of teams organized around a particular customer journey, in this case the home-buying customer journey. Within the family, there are three Mission Teams. These are multidisciplinary and have a common purpose, focused on a particular aspect of the customer journey, be that value proposition, eligibility or advice delivery. In the agile view, Ted sits in three teams and reports into three different product owners on a day-to-day basis, while also reporting into the head of UX/UI.

The highlighted boxes represent people in the traditional reporting structure who have been deployed into Agile Teams on the right. In the Agile Team structure, a time allocation is given to each person in brackets. Sally, a digital marketer, has been deployed full-time into the Value Proposition Team. Anna, a Product Manager in the traditional chart, now becomes a

FIGURE 2.2.4 Linking Role, Position and People data in traditional and agile structures

Traditional org view

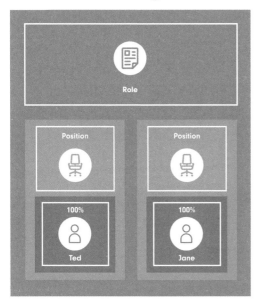

Agile team view

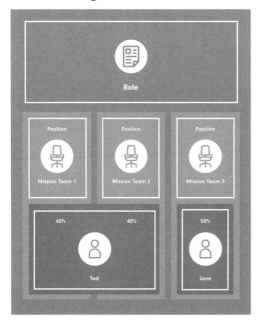

Role data: target activities, and competencies required

- - - - - - - - -

Position specification data:
→ FTE allocation
→ Start / end dates

- - - - - - - - -

People data:
→ Allocation to agile teams
→ Resourcing commitments
→ Performance record

FIGURE 2.2.5 The difference between a traditional organization and Agile Team view

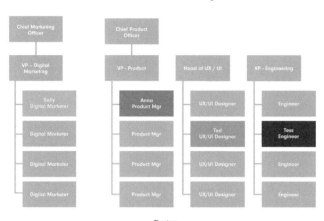

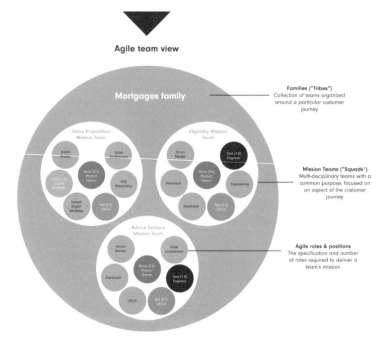

Product Owner and splits her time between the three teams. Tess, an Engineer, is deployed to both the Eligibility and the Advice Delivery Team.

This illustration raises questions that I will return to in Chapter 2.4, specifically around talent management and the importance of being able to view people's capacity to ensure that they are not over- or under-deployed. We can design the best structure of Agile Teams and roles, but if we don't have the people to fill those roles or we are burning the same people out, we will not achieve our strategy.

The important thing to highlight at this point is the need to prepare the data model and put a language to the new structures so that everyone is clear what things mean and how they will work. Playing the HOWWIP games and exercises highlighted in this chapter will help with the shift in mindset required when transitioning from traditional to agile organizational structures.

Final thoughts

Everything I've said in this chapter is just business basics. I started by explaining HOWWIP, which is about thinking through how things will work, pure and simple. The best way to do this is to use exercises and games to tease potential issues out and make the process fun. It is only when you have fun that you can fully immerse yourself in the preparation. These exercises and games provide a way for people to practise and mentally prepare, like getting your kit ready before a game or playing scales to warm up your hands before a piano performance. They encourage people to think through the detail, and role-playing scenarios is hands-down the best way to do this. So much of this comes down to the interface design within the organization. While interfaces will have been considered at a high level during the macro operating and micro detailed design, the detail will not have been thought through. To understand this detail, you need the right people in the room.

The chapter then progressed to consider some of the common traps that organizations fall into when executing change, and how to prepare yourself so that you stand the best chance of avoiding them. But no matter how well you prepare or how great your design process is, many things can and will go wrong. There can be an exodus of talent, lawsuits for discrimination and unfair dismissal, paralysis, company-wide confusion, culture clash and a breakdown of trust, to name but a few of the many consequences. These and other issues are caused by a range of bad management practices, and most are avoidable through great preparation. To a large extent, you can prepare for the unforeseeable by committing enough of the right resource, allowing enough time and, in the case of acquisition, ensuring that you think through proper post-merger integration strategies to ensure that the two companies you are bringing together properly align. There will still be many more traps, but if you manage not to fall into those covered in this chapter, you should have sufficient reserves to deal with any others that await.

I finished the chapter with some advice on some preparation strategies when implementing agile ways of working. The organization system and operating model are fundamentally impacted, and it's important to be aware of problems commonly encountered in agile such as data management and how you allocate people to Agile Teams without over- or under-deploying them. This is something I return to in Chapter 2.4.

REMEMBER THIS

- Encourage everyone to embrace the HOWWIP, so they can understand how the change is likely to affect them personally, and iron out any problems ahead of time.
- Record HOWWIP questions and answers so they are not forgotten.
- Learn how to recognize signs that things are going off track.
- Make sure you think through possible traps before executing change.
- Transitioning to agile ways of working involves a shift in data model and mindset. Understand what is required so you can help the organization prepare for this change.

Notes

1 *See No Evil, Hear No Evil* (1989) Directed by Arthur Hiller [feature film], TriStar Pictures.
2 'Release trains' is a term used in SAFe methodology. There are lots of other methodologies out there.

2.3

Implementation

Introduction

Once you have done your preparation, it's time to get going. As I stated in Chapter 2.1, this is a technical data-driven process, a mechanical one governed by law and a change process. Don't underestimate the latter. This is a human process, and if you fail to communicate empathetically and with total transparency you will also fail to win people's support. Things will go wrong at a rate of knots. Take care to follow the steps outlined in this chapter and follow them at the right time. Make sure you know the law and ensure you comply with it clearly. More than that, understand why the law is there. It's not just a box-ticking exercise.

What you will notice as you step through this chapter is that a great deal of the work required in making the change happen starts at the early macro operating and micro detailed design stages. Take care not to think of the macro operating design, micro detailed design and Making it Real phases as fully sequential. Although one follows another for the most part, this is not always the case. For example, the communication and consultation phases start way before you get to the implementation – they begin right at the beginning, and never stop.

There is a fine line between preparing to execute change, the subject of the previous chapter, and doing the implementation itself. In fact, you could argue that there isn't a distinct line. As you get closer to the implementation, you don't take your preparation hat off – there will still be many aspects that will need to be prepared for once you have started executing change. For this reason, some of the content of this chapter would have fitted equally well in Chapter 2.2, but this would have made for a very short Chapter 2.3! The actual *implementation* – deciding who gets what role in the new design – forms a very small part of this process. This chapter focuses on Stages 2 and 3 of the Making it Real process outlined in Chapter 2.1. Stage 2 involves assessing impact and planning communication, and in many ways falls more into the category of 'preparation' than 'implementation':

- Categorize employees by impact.
- Quantify impacts at aggregate level.
- Develop communication plans.

Stage 3 involves managing talent transitions and consultation and is comprised of the following:

- Specify and deliver a legally compliant consultation process.
- Select which employees get which position and articulate why.
- Inform people and roll out the communications.

The implementation is where all the work and documentation you have done come together. There is a lot to think about, process and manage. It can feel overwhelming, so it's a good idea to find a system to prioritize the work in front of you. A useful way to do this is to use the Now, Next, Later Kanban approach to prioritizing tasks, often used in agile working.

Prioritize work according to Now, Next, Later

'Kanban', meaning billboard in Japanese, is a method developed by an Industrial Engineer at Toyota named Taiichi Ohno. Its aim is to achieve 'just-in-time' manufacturing and eliminate waste. The system ensures that production is demand-led, with Kanbans alerting suppliers to produce and deliver a particular material based on consumption. The great thing about the process is the ease with which everyone can see the priorities at any point in time: the list of things everyone is working on, how long they have had it, the history of that work item and where it will go next. It is intuitive and brings together individual and team ways of working so they can see what they have achieved and what still needs to be done.

One of the most useful elements of Kanban is the Now, Next, Later approach taken to prioritizing work. Work listed under 'now' is of the highest priority and needs to be tackled immediately. Work listed under 'next' might need to be done by the end of the current quarter, while work under 'later' might not need to be done until beyond the quarter. Each week, there is a reiteration of what is happening now and next, allowing for constant reprioritization of tasks.

Breaking work down into chunks in this way makes the implementation seem surmountable. It is also a useful way to check, on a weekly basis, that no tasks have been overlooked. This is important as there are so many different elements to bring together. Start by getting your head around exactly what is going to change from every angle and the impact that the change will have on every person in the organization.

Stage 2: Assess impacts and plan communications

Impact assessment is all about understanding how every person in the organization will be affected by the implementation process. This needs to be understood at both an individual and an aggregate level before developing and actioning your communication plans. The assessment can't be a fair one unless you know that the data you are working from is accurate.

The importance of having an accurate baseline of data

You can't begin to understand and quantify change unless you have an accurate **baseline** of data to work from. Make sure you have been clear in your baseline and maintained strict rules surrounding your people and positions datasets. This is a moment when you must have the facts. If your data related to the as-is organization is out of whack, you'll risk making a myriad of mistakes. Inaccurate data could mean that:

- people are occupying different positions to the ones you think they are
- people may not report to the person that you think they do
- you may risk including people who no longer work in the organization
- you may leave people who do work for you out of the process

Don't use Excel for this. It is too easy to make mistakes and it's difficult and risky to share. Imagine the following scenario: the number of FTEs required for a given role is reduced, and therefore everyone who performs positions in that role should be classed as 'at risk'. But what happens if role titles are inconsistently defined? How would you know who should be put in the 'at risk' category? It would be very easy to miss some people out, which would result in an unfair process.

The ramifications of an inaccurate baseline can be enormous, and it can take a great deal of manual effort to get the facts straight. In a worst-case scenario, if the inaccuracies result in you conducting an unfair process, it can make the cost of an implementation skyrocket. The last thing you want is to be faced with an employment tribunal. Consistency is key. If you are unclear or inconsistent at any point, it will decrease your credibility as a management team and make people wonder what else you might be wrong about.

Understanding impact

I'll now take you through the process of how to understand who is impacted and in what way, first at an individual and then at an aggregate level. To measure the impact on people you first need to find a way to quantify it. Start by listing each possible impact area. At the most extreme, those individuals at risk of redundancy need to be flagged. But there are also those who will be affected more moderately. Roles, Positions and People might change:

- A role might change and be given new accountabilities and work. Different competencies might be needed to perform the role, or key deliverables identified in the objectives might have changed.
- The scope of a position might change (for example reporting line, location, team structures or the territory covered by a sales rep).
- A person might change because they've gone into a new position.

Even in the most fundamental organization redesigns, a significant proportion of people are unaffected, so if there is no change it is helpful to flag that there is no impact. Figure 2.3.1 shows an example for all the people reporting to a given manager, in this case Johnny Gomez. The first row shows that Scott Knowles is at risk while the fifth shows that Bailey Johnson has a significant change in his responsibilities and that he will need to relocate.

FIGURE 2.3.1 Manager's team impact table

Full Name	Role	As-Is Manager Name	FTE Impact	Role Change	Relocation
Scott Knowles	Recruitment Specialist	Johnny Gomez	-1		
Mohammed Sanderson	HR Manager	Johnny Gomez	0	✓	
Harvey Morris	Assistant Recruitment Specialist	Johnny Gomez	0		
Donna Lawrence	Assistant Recruitment Specialist	Johnny Gomez	0		
Bailey Johnson	Learning & Development Specialist	Johnny Gomez	0	✓	✓
Bryan Korn	Assistant Recruitment Specialist	Johnny Gomez	0		
Mia Tomlinson	Compensation Administrator	Johnny Gomez	-1		
Riley Norton	Assistant HR Manager - South	Johnny Gomez	0		

Once you have this individual analysis, it should be easy to aggregate the information. I suggest this is done at the role cluster level (see Chapter 1.2). You can then **slice and dice** the data, test it and ensure all bases are covered. Common questions include:

- the change in headcount and FTE figures
- the change in total employee cost. The total cost typically includes elements like base pay, pension, healthcare, car allowance and tax. It can include allocations for direct attributable costs such as IT, property (their desk) and telecommunications
- the cost of redundancy. This is often driven by tenure, salary and grade
- average depth and spans of control
- relocation costs

For each measure that you are aggregating, it helps to slice the data by each of the KODs: for example, by business unit, function, grade and geographic location.

QUANTIFYING THE IMPACT FOR ROLES

One of the hardest elements to understand is whether a person's role has changed, by which I mean that there is a substantive difference in account-abilities. Substantive could be defined as being a greater than 25 per cent impact (measured by time) on the time required to do the work (the activities). If it is less than 25 per cent, then it isn't significant. Technically, the way to do this is to map employees into both the as-is and to-be role and activity taxonomies. By doing an Individual Activity Analysis (IAA – see Chapter 1.2), you know what each employee currently does. The same framework of activities is used to link the to-be accountabilities to specific roles (see *Data-Driven Organization Design* for more information on how to do this). If the activity taxonomy used for the IAA is the same as that used to define to-be roles, you will have a clear measure indicating which responsibilities have changed and in what proportion. Practically, you should triage based on these insights. Take out those unaffected and those completely changed (for example, outsourced *en bloc*, or eliminated due to automation).

In this way, you will be able to quantify the change of activities in each function for the to-be design according to the four RRII levers described in Chapter 1.2: Reduce; Reallocate; Improve; and Invest. Assuming the IAA has been done, you can then see the number of employees impacted by the changes. Note that much of that change could be people just not doing what they should be doing, largely because it simply wasn't defined.

QUANTIFYING IMPACT ACROSS DIMENSIONS

As noted above, there are several ways in which each employee can be impacted. Figure 2.3.2 gives an example of how these can be aggregated by location. Defining impact at the individual level enables this type of aggregation.

This example has a total headcount of 600 (the second column) and it is planned that this number is going to reduce to 532 in the to-be organization. However, the aggregate numbers don't reflect the true nature of the change: the total number of exits is 102 as there are 34 new positions in the to-be organization. We see the Beeston headcount increasing from 20 to 42, but looking beyond these overall counts we see a greater degree of change: 10 employees are scheduled to exit (their positions are closing), 12 new positions are opening and 20 employees are being relocated from Ardleigh to Beeston. Across all sites we can also see that 10 per cent of employees are planned to have a change in manager, and 15 per cent are in roles which have changing accountabilities. Each of these changes will need to be managed effectively for the to-be organization to operate as designed.

FIGURE 2.3.2 Aggregate impact numbers by impact type by site

Location	As-Is	To-Be	Exits	New position	Reallocate from	Reallocate to	Manager change	Accountability change
Ardleigh	40	0	20	0	20	0	3	5
Beeston	20	42	10	12	0	20	5	9
Carlisle	100	90	13	3	0	0	4	45
Dunston	30	20	17	7	0	0	7	5
East Lancs	160	144	20	4	0	0	25	15
Foxfields	250	236	22	8	0	0	16	12
Total	600	532	102	34	20	20	60	91
Percentage Change		-11%	17%	6%	3%	3%	10%	15%

Now that you know exactly who is going to be impacted, and in what way, it's time to devise a communication plan and align those plans to the level of impact through a communication map.

Preparing and planning communication

Getting communication right is difficult. I have messed it up on many occasions. I have spent hours thinking it all through only to miss fundamental points and get it wrong. I have tried lots of different approaches in different circumstances and what seems good in theory can often turn out to be disappointing and sometimes even the cause of significant issues. I missed the mark completely the very first time I ran a redundancy programme. My company's growth had stalled after 24 months of spectacular expansion. We'd had a particularly bad sales quarter, cash was tight, a big account broke their contract and another fixed priced project was severely over-running. A range of things came together to create a perfect storm. Drastic cuts weren't necessary, but corrective ones were. After management discussions and negotiations, we established where we needed to get our cost base down, the roles that needed to be reduced, our selection criteria and finally the names. The key communication messages were then agreed:

- We needed to make reductions because of the situation.
- We needed to give reassurance that the business was still strong: we had a great reputation; loyal clients; a committed team; a strong balance sheet; and the backing of investors.
- My plan was:
  o to tell everyone at once on a Tuesday afternoon at 3.00 pm
  o for the managers to follow up with their teams and conduct one-to-ones with people who were worried

In theory this sounded like a good plan, but it didn't have the effect I wanted. Trust was quickly eroded and there was an almost immediate sense of distance between people within the organization. What went wrong? The main problem was my speech. It was not so much what I said, but how I said it. I rehearsed the whole thing and wrote down exactly what I was going to say. During the rehearsals, I was coached by a couple of members of my senior team. But when I spoke the words, I wasn't authentic or true to myself. I didn't talk to the team the way I usually would and there was a sense of awkwardness. I didn't look people in the eye enough, adequately explain the situation we found ourselves in or spell out why and how we were going to get out of it. In short, I spoke from the head, not the heart. The words came out, but the delivery failed to build empathy. I also didn't drive the message home. I didn't follow up with smaller groups and repeat the key points. My team had follow-up meetings, but it wasn't enough; I should have been more present. Everyone radiated fear and frustration. After the process I also didn't sufficiently talk through what we did wrong or what we would do to avoid being in this situation again. What had I learnt? What was the plan moving forward? How were we going to regroup? Having gone through complex and straining processes, you need time to reflect and learn. In many ways, the medicine was worse than the disease.

It is easy to communicate when times are good. When times are tough, it is just as easy to fall into silence or handle things in a ham-fisted way. From what I've seen and heard, many leaders struggle to get communication right. Mistakes can range from clumsy blunders to being secretive for too long and too selective with the truth. This can give an appearance of dishonesty. Before moving on to my top tips for how to communicate throughout the transition management process, I'll take a brief look at some horror stories I have heard of when transformation goes terribly wrong.

HORROR STORIES

I have heard many horror stories from people about bodged transition management and leaders failing to take the time and effort required to get the process right, often with dire consequences. Many of these stories have been told to me at conferences, where I am often asked to present on the topic of transition management. When asked to do this, I am always keen to emphasize, above all else, that organizations not only have a fiducial duty, but a moral one to get the process right and communicate the organization's situation and plans to the people who work there with sensitivity and respect. While I advocate a data-driven approach, the people behind the data should always be at the forefront of your mind. Data isn't really anything, it's what it represents that counts. The node called Adam, with a date of birth and a gender, is also somebody's son, perhaps a father, perhaps a coach and mentor. He brings years of learning, energy, hopes and dreams, but also scars from a life already lived. Data is a simplification of reality, but it doesn't infer cold and harsh decision-making. We try to describe through data, and we give it semantic meaning. This is why competency data is so important as it brings the person behind the node to life. Data is there to help us think and to *inform* our judgement and decisions, rather than lead them. Algorithms have their place, a human writes the rules and the logic that drives them, but decision-making should never be based on algorithms alone.

As I said in Chapter 2.1, we are dealing with people who have lives, families to provide for and mortgages to pay. But the financial component aside, most of us enjoy our work and feel invested in the organizations we work for. It forms a large part of our identity and self-esteem. Our position within a company is often something we have worked towards for years and when it is under threat our ego and self-esteem can take a huge knock. I have found that this is particularly true for those in high-pressure jobs who work long hours. When our working identity is threatened it can feel devastating and panic-inducing, and in extreme situations people can lose all hope. In December 2019, *The New York Times* reported that the former Chief Executive of France Telecom and two of his subordinates were convicted of 'institutional moral harassment' and creating an anxious atmosphere full of fear during a scrambled restructure. Their actions, which included creating unpleasant working conditions in the hope it would force people to leave, were ruled to have led to the suicides of 35 employees.[1] This might sound extreme, but sadly it isn't a one-off. Some of the stories people have told me have been equally upsetting. I've been told about a man who, after being let go at work, killed his family before turning on himself, and another who went home to get his gun and returned to work to murder his colleagues. Transition management is not a process to be taken lightly. But the point is that, while nobody wants to receive the news that their job is under threat, the Leadership Team can make it so much more palatable for people by being open and honest and explaining the reasons behind decisions that have been made. There can be no doubt in anyone's mind that it has been a fair process. This is important for those who are affected by the change but also for those who aren't, as people need to feel that their colleagues have been treated well.

Communication is clearly a huge topic: one far too large for a sub-chapter in a book. Hundreds if not thousands of books must have been written on the subject. What follows are my top tips and perspectives that are relevant for implementing organizational change.

BUILD REAL EMPATHY

Of the tips, this first one is by far the most important and most certainly the hardest. As Stephen Covey says in his book *The 7 Habits of Highly Effective People*, one of the habits is to 'seek first to understand, then be understood'.[2] You need to aim to feel what it is like from your employees' perspective, not yours. A useful framework for this is **WAMI and WIFM analysis**. WAMI stands for 'What is Against My Interest?' WIFM stands for 'What's In it For Me?' These frameworks are about understanding how it feels to be in someone else's position. We use all our senses to gather this information. It's not just about what we read or hear.

Asking these questions across the board helps to articulate how your audience will feel and probably react. The WAMI is easier to investigate because most of the time people look at the downsides and the negatives. If you know what people are interested in and expecting before you start the communication process it's much easier to frame and articulate the messages in the right way.

LISTEN

Remember that good communication is two-way. You have two ears and one mouth for a reason (as many of our grandparents will have taught us). But organization-wide listening isn't easy. It requires the creation of listening tools such as fast-feedback surveys (for example, five simple questions that take two minutes to complete where the analysis is automatically generated so that action can be immediate). It requires giving the person receiving the message time to receive, reflect and then respond with questions, comments, ideas or simply a burst of emotion. Like all these obvious points, it is about having the discipline to follow through with the action. Simply said, and hard to do well.

In Tom Peter's book, *A Passion for Excellence*, he discusses a framework called Management By Walking Around (MBWA).[3] I learn the most by walking around and talking to people – learning about what they are working on and how they feel about their work. The remote working that came with the Covid-19 pandemic took this away from me at a significant cost that is truly hard to quantify.

Similarly, I only really get to know a client when I physically spend time with them, and I only really understand a process when I walk it and see it in progress. It was only by going two kilometres down a mineshaft several times in South Africa that I began to understand rock support and blasting. Listening takes time and investment, and it isn't just about the words that people speak; it's about seeing and feeling the environment. It is hard to put yourself in someone's shoes if you have never spent time with them in their day-to-day reality.

CREATE A MESSAGE HOUSE

Much of this section on communication is inspired by talking to those in the communications business: advertising, PR and branding. The industry often uses a tool called the Message House to ensure that key messaging is clear and consistent. Figure 2.3.3 shows an example of a Message House. At the top is the key message – one short sentence that you want everyone to hear and remember. Use the FAQs documented in the HOWWIP log (Chapter 2.2) to guide you in what the single key message should be. Below that are the three main whys – the main takeaways that you want everyone to understand. Below these three points, there can be a maximum of seven follow-ups. This further detail should only be expressed as and when it is needed. The Message House helps you zoom in on appropriate words to use, set the tone for your communication and check that the structure of your story makes sense.

FIGURE 2.3.3 A Message House used for communicating a key message

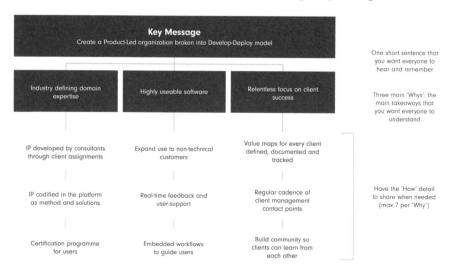

ACKNOWLEDGE AND PLAN FOR THE COMMUNICATION CHALLENGE FROM THE START

Accept that communication starts from the first moment a project is mentioned. As soon as a decision is made to do something, and is discussed between two people, communication has started. From the first second of your design process, start by thinking and planning through who is told what, and when. Don't forget that we humans are experts at reading body language and picking up on a vibe that something is up. Assume that after more than a handful of people know, word will get out and soon everyone will know. As much as you try to lead and influence the process, recognize that it is not one you can fully control.

If there are going to be redundancies, be sure to think through the consultation process. The mechanics of this are discussed in more detail below. Don't wait until the end to signal that this is a possibility if you need to take unions and/or your works council with you. Start early, even if off the record, to build trust. Trust is hard to earn and easy to lose. Consider how you are going to leverage and build on your case for change arrived at in the macro operating design as well as how you link the design to the design criteria that follow from that.

THE DESIGN PROCESS IS A COMMUNICATION PROCESS

By its very nature, you will need to engage with people who are going to be affected by the design. The more professional, open (in terms of being open to the ideas of those involved in the process) and logical/fact-driven the process is, the better. Be serious and take care to reach the right answers for the right reasons. The number of times decisions are made on a whim or through political horse-trading between power brokers is hard to believe. It feels terrible to be a pawn in the political moves of the powerful, especially when the power plays are evidently designed to maximize players' personal goals rather than the organization's. If the design criteria say 'what' is most important, deciding 'who' is to be involved is a way of you saying who you think is important. Choose wisely.

MAKE IT AS FACT- AND REASON-BASED AS POSSIBLE

Don't dumb things down too much. If those affected can understand why, then they will be far better equipped to deal with it. To achieve this, it can be very helpful to run 'Ask me anything' sessions, where small groups are invited to have a discussion and ask about anything that is concerning them in an open forum. I have had to let quite a few people go over the years for various reasons, be it redundancy or performance. When the reasons behind the decision were logically robust, properly considered and clearly explained, the person was almost always able to deal with the news effectively. To make sure that your messages are as reason-based as possible, consider the following:

- What are the design criteria and how did they translate into the design?
- What is the business case? How does it enable the strategy of the business?
- If employees are going to be put at risk, what are the objective selection criteria? What are you doing to provide other opportunities or support?

The worst thing is a lingering death. When you make the final decisions, make them clearly and move quickly. Be generous in the payout and support. If you are quick and fair, speed will pay for your generosity. If the process is fact-based, you will also do a much better job of retaining the good people who are often let go during a redundancy process. It is often simply too complicated to assemble all the information and make fact-based decisions across thousands of people. As a result, many companies have been through the experience of wholesale redundancy packages followed by hiring back experienced people as contractors or consultants because they had specific knowledge that was needed. A data-driven approach, particularly when it comes to historical performance and competency data, will give you the best chance of reducing or eliminating this problem. You'll retain the best people and face a much reduced rehire cost.

COMMUNICATION MAP AND TRACKER

A communication map lists who is being communicated to, how and when. I advise making it visual and reviewing it from various perspectives. Use your impact assessment to segment the workforce by the nature of their impact. For each impact, think through the communication approach, message and necessary support. By detailing how each employee is impacted, you can tailor your communication to him or her. For example:

- Those who have a change in reporting lines will need to know who their new manager is.

- Those who are being transitioned to agile ways of working will need to know how they will be deployed to Mission Teams and will need reassurance that their time will be properly managed. How will their performance be judged when working for lots of different managers at the same time and in quick succession?

- Those with changes in accountabilities may be losing elements of their work that they love. They will need to understand why and how this will help their career development.

- Those at risk of redundancy will have thousands of thoughts: 'How am I going to find another job?' 'What kind of package am I likely to get?' 'How am I going to pay my rent or mortgage?' 'What are my family and friends going to say?' They are likely to need lots of support through the process.

- Some may just be confused, even though the change doesn't affect them directly. Explain the business case and what it will mean for them.

It is good to know who has been communicated with, and whether there were any escalated issues resulting from the process. Implement a tracker so you can monitor the execution of your communication plan. For example, for each segment or group of employees, define the type of communication method, type of message, timing and responsibility for delivery. As the plan is delivered, each person responsible can then update his or her progress together with any issues requiring escalation. The key is to define the messages, who gives them, when and how. For each segment, think through the best mix of communication channels. Example channels include town hall presentations; team meetings; one-to-one meetings; breakfast or lunch Q&A meetings; video; short emails that emphasize key points; posters; intranet. For in-person communication, it is useful to create speaking briefs of the key points.

Stage 3: Manage talent transitions and consultation

Transition management is the process of determining which employees get which positions in the new organization and the physical process of making that happen. It's about populating the positions in the future, to-be photographic snapshot of the organization with the right people to do the work. For many positions, it is common practice that employees enter a selection process to determine which positions they will hold. For this, a workflow is needed (see the six-stage transition management process, below). Sometimes, those without a future position will need to have an exit plan put into place, and at other times there may not be a satisfactory internal candidate to fill a position so you will need to hire externally.

Transition management is a complex, high-risk process which typically occurs in time-pressured contexts such as downsizing, post-merger integration, restructuring or expansion. The risk can be categorized into three areas:

1 failure to meet committed targets and timelines

2 an operational risk if critical positions are not resourced

3 a litigation risk if due process cannot be demonstrated

By following a data-driven approach and leveraging the right technology, these risks can be reduced. In Chapter 1.2 I explained how the components of the organization system can be connected with data to bring control over complexity. The two components of the organization system in question in the transition management process are people and positions. Refer back to Figure 1.2.2, where I described the difficulties of many-to-many relationships with reference to succession planning. The same challenges occur with talent transition management: a single employee may be a candidate for many positions. Simultaneously, many employees may be candidates for the same position. Replicating this pattern across even a relatively small organization of just a few hundred employees provides a data management challenge which can't be managed effectively using Excel and PowerPoint. The risk of people falling through the cracks is uncomfortably high. With a data-driven process enabled by technology, you can know the status of every person and position in the company at any given time. The potential costly risk of missing transition candidates, treating people inconsistently, or not being able to demonstrate an audit trail of decisions can be alleviated. The last thing you want is for one person to be allocated to two positions, or to accidentally miss someone out of the process entirely, so they are, by default and unbeknown to anyone, at risk of redundancy.

A six-stage transition management process

The six stages of the transition management process are shown in Figure 2.3.4. Closely following this process and consistently categorizing positions and people mitigates all three areas of risk. Critical positions which need to be resourced can be flagged, and an audit trail to demonstrate why decisions have been made provided. I will now look at this process in detail.

In Stage 1 you need to determine which positions and which people are not included in the transition process (thereby being categorized as 'out of scope'). This is a simple matter of transferring those employees whose positions are not at risk to the new structure. Examples of people and positions that are likely to be out of scope are the CEO or the CFO. There might also be certain parts of the organization that are out of scope of the redesign: for example, the front end of the sales force might be in scope but the back end out of scope. The goal is to narrow down the entire population of the organization by 'automatically matching' unaffected people to to-be positions. This allows you to focus on those people and positions who are impacted by the transition to the to-be organization.

Stage 2 is the creation of pools of similar impacted positions and people. A position marked as 'pooled' means that it is included in a position pool. If a person is marked as 'pooled' it means that they have been included in a talent pool. Once you have the talent pools in place, you can start to make decisions about who should be considered for which positions in which pools. This is the beginning of Stages 3 to 5, the assessment and selection process, which I cover in more detail below.

ASSESSMENT AND SELECTION PROCESS

When assessing candidates, the first step is to define the inputs to the process: the assessment mechanism; the HR consultation policies; processes; and precedents. Then you need to think about what your selection rules will be and how the general and individual consultation processes will work (I go into this in more detail later in the chapter).

When selecting candidates, you can either use a select-in or select-out process. If there are large numbers of people competing for comparatively few positions, for example 60 people vying for 30 positions, a select-in process is best, where all 60 people are put into the assessment process for the 30 positions. If the change is more minimal and there are only a small number of people at risk, for example 22 people vying for 20 positions, you can transfer everybody across and determine which two of the 22 people should be selected out.

The biggest decision to make is which assessment mechanism to use. You can use historical data and/or freshly generated data:

- Historical – It's extremely helpful to have historical performance and competency data including proficiency levels, as described in Chapter 1.2. Unfortunately, many organizations are unlikely to have good historical data in place (unless they have followed the steps in my book, *Data-Driven Organization Design*!). This is also likely to be irrelevant if the transition management is being done in the context of post-merger integration. I can't think of a single example where a client has had sufficient confidence in their performance management data to use it as a basis for assessment. This is mostly because of an inconsistent application of their performance management process. It is often too opinion-based and the data can't be trusted... but that is a topic for another book.

- Freshly generated – This data aims to collect competency data so that a judgement can be made about who is best placed to do each role. It can be used to calculate **role match scores**, which I explain below. As described in Chapter 1.2, competency data can be broken down into general behaviours, cognitive competencies, generic business skills and specialized functional skills. Mechanisms for collecting this data can include:
  - employee self-assessments
  - interviews
  - manager assessment and surveys of each of their team
  - committee reviews
  - third-party standardized tests
  - assessment centre testing

These mechanisms are not mutually exclusive. You may want employees to do a self-assessment so that you can see where there is alignment or risk of a large variation in perception. Whatever the method of collecting the assessment data, it is crucial to run a well-structured calibration process by a committee of well-informed managers to verify that each of the judgements is robust and consistent. Also remember the important point I made earlier in the chapter that data should be used to *inform* human judgement rather than be taken at face value to drive cold decision making. Decisions should *never* be driven by algorithms alone. Human judgement and reflection are key, as is rigorous discussion and debate, so multiple viewpoints can be aired. The people involved in doing this work should challenge themselves and each other and build in time to review and reflect on the decisions that have been made.

There should be two people – or more likely, two groups of people – involved in the calibration process:

1 recommender(s)

2 ratifier(s)

In the context of the RAD framework, the recommenders are **responsible** for making decisions and the ratifiers are the **approvers** of those decisions. The ratifiers should perform legal and compliance checks to ensure the process has been fair and they should feel able to challenge the recommenders. Building reflection time into the process enables the recommenders to explain and the ratifiers to ask questions. It should never be left to one person to both recommend and ratify. Segregating duties in this way not only protects those doing this work (both legally and psychologically) but it also ensures considered, robust decision-making and a more effective due process. This is particularly important in the context of post-merger integration when you have two organizations: the one acquiring and the one being acquired. When stepping through the assessment and selection process in this context, the acquiring organization can often, consciously or not, favour its own people because they know them and feel on safer ground. This is not only unfair, but can put the acquiring organization at risk of losing much-needed and sought-after talent. This is a very common problem and one that the recommenders and ratifiers need to bear in mind. Two decisions need to be made throughout the assessment process:

1 who from the talent pool should be assessed as a potential candidate for a position (or 'slated' for a position – you are likely to have several candidates slated for the same position or one candidate could be slated for more than one position)

2 who out of the slated candidates should be selected to fill a position

Once this is done, be prepared to articulate to employees how the decisions were reached. It's also very important to demonstrate to people who have not been selected that a genuine attempt has been made to find them other roles. You may decide to check that each employee agrees or at least has a chance to challenge the decisions that have been made. It's useful to decide

FIGURE 2.3.4 Classification of people and positions in the talent transition process

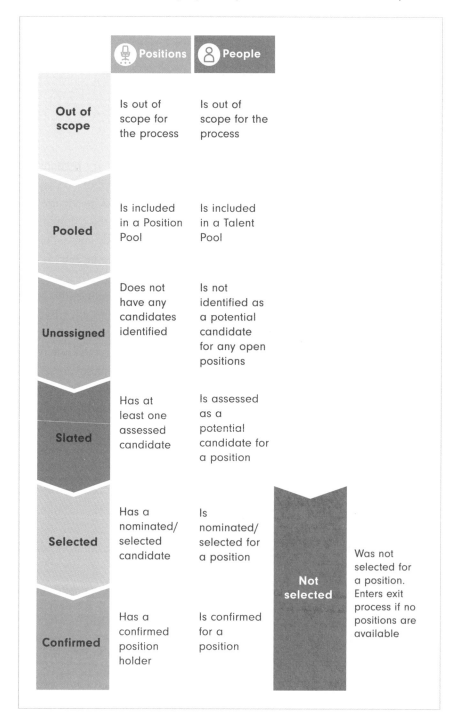

on your policy on this upfront, as well as on how much say employees should be given. For example, sometimes a person may be recommended for more than one role. Should they be asked for their preference? If someone has been put forward for an open position in a different location to the one they are currently working in, what degree of flexibility do they have? Must they accept it, or can they ask to be considered for positions elsewhere? An exception process can be run to deal with the most contentious issues.

Figure 2.3.5 shows how people and positions can be visualized at both individual and aggregate levels, providing transparency on the status of the transition management process. You can see that, at this point in the process, Jessica Talbot has been slated for two positions, HR Manager and HR Business Partner, but has not yet been selected for either. You can also see the status of certain positions, by seeing if anyone has been slated, selected or confirmed. In Figure 2.3.5, Ava Wilkins has been confirmed as CFO and Reece Harris, the other candidate, has not been selected. At an aggregate level, you can track the overall status of employees being assigned or exited. In this example, there are 108 candidates who have been confirmed for positions and a further 211 who have been selected for positions but not yet confirmed. There are 321 slated candidates and 628 candidates who are yet to be assigned to any open positions; 11 candidates are progressing through the exit process.

FIGURE 2.3.5   Categorizing people and positions provides transparency on the status of the transition process, individually and in aggregate

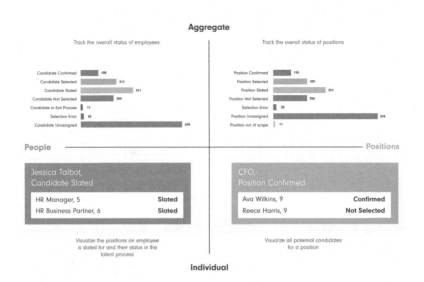

CALCULATING THE ROLE MATCH SCORE

In Chapter 1.2 I discussed how target and actual competency data can be used to calculate competency gaps and give people a 'current role fit' percentage score. These gaps can be viewed at both an individual and aggregate level to give insight into many things:

- whether the person in a particular role has all the competencies required for that role at the right proficiency level

- the competencies a person has which they are not currently using in their role and which they might be able to utilize elsewhere, in another role or on specific projects

This has obvious benefits when determining which candidates should be slated for which positions. The ability to aggregate this data in the context of the organization then becomes possible, as shown in the heat maps in Figures 2.3.6 and 2.3.7. Figure 2.3.6 indicates the people with the biggest gap when measured against their current role, while the matrix shown in Figure 2.3.7 shows which people in the organization have a fit for other roles. This can be referred to as the 'role match score' as differences exist in calculating the two types of role fit. The matrix shown in Figure 2.3.6 can

FIGURE 2.3.6 Analysing current role fit for the organization

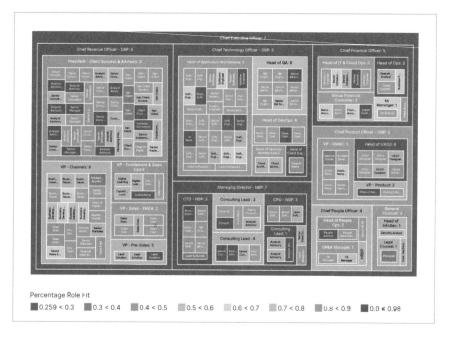

FIGURE 2.3.7 Analysing role match scores against a target set of roles

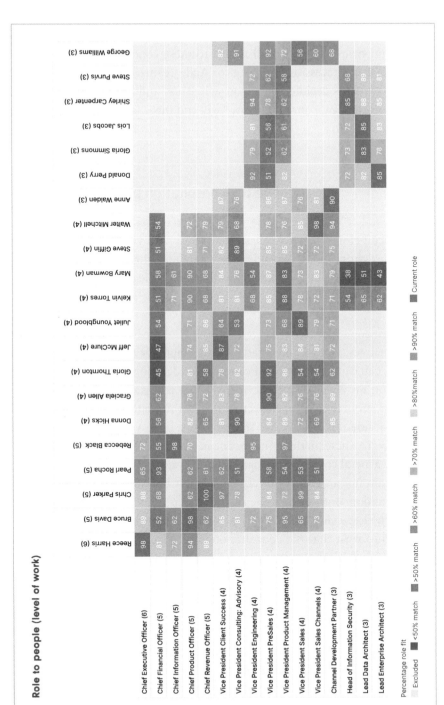

Role to people (level of work)

be used to assess whether the necessary competencies exist within the organization for all slated positions, because if not it may be necessary to recruit from outside. I will return to these concepts in Chapter 2.4 in the context of succession planning for Agile Teams.

As well as deciding how you will assess and select candidates, there are important legal considerations. I will end this chapter by looking at some of these.

Define the consultation process

It's vital to both define the consultation process in advance and get legal advice before you proceed so that you know you are planning a fair and watertight process. Depending on the context of your business, you may be required to get both general consultation and legal consultation.

General consultation

Sometimes, formal consultation with unions or works councils is required. This can cause anguish as it can be viewed as doing battle with the devil or a reason for people not to do many of the things deemed crucial by management. From the other perspective, that of those sitting on the works council or union side, it is all too often seen as paying lip service. They see a disingenuous management team that is not acting in their employees' best interests. I've seen how general consultations can spiral into acrimonious strikes.

I am not an industrial relations expert but have spoken with many who are, and on both sides of the fence. What is interesting is their views are very much the same. It boils down to trust. From the union's perspective they need to trust that the consultation is genuine. They want to know that it's not a done deal and that they have a genuine opportunity to influence the outcome. From the management's perspective, they need to trust that they can share thoughts and options without being held to ransom. They can have a personal relationship and rapport between the two parties, which can pay large dividends. There is an element of negotiation and give and take without either side fully devolving everything they hear. To gain trust you need to have an open mind, but equally not be easily intimidated. You must see arguments from both sides and represent various perspectives without blatantly pushing your own agenda. Once a relationship is broken it can be difficult, if not impossible, to fix.

Legal consultation

Getting your head around the legal requirements of redundancy can be a challenge but it is an area of great risk for organizations, so it is worth getting right. When putting together your consultation process I suggest you write it up and get legal input to make sure you are doing it properly for your jurisdiction. Figure 2.3.8 provides an example of an individual redundancy consultation process I received from Kathryn Dooks, employment law expert and Partner at Deloitte Legal UK. It gives some clear steps to follow when defining the implementation process in the context of individual redundancy. If you have redundancies across more than one jurisdiction, this can add significant complexity to the legal landscape you need to navigate. If you find yourself in this position, you may find the following sections helpful.

CONSIDERING VARIATION IN REDUNDANCY PROCESSES ACROSS JURISDICTIONS

When dealing with redundancy across jurisdictions, careful planning of the consultation in each jurisdiction is essential. According to Alison Dixon, a Partner at the International HR Services Group at Bird & Bird, the law that requires employers to consult collectively in the case of mass redundancies is likely to be similar across EU jurisdictions (as it derives from European Directives), but the way in which the law has been implemented in each country varies. For example, the threshold number of proposed redundancies that will trigger the obligation to consult on a collective basis differs from country to country. In Germany, the applicable threshold depends on the number of employees at the relevant establishment, while in France it is 10 or more redundancies within a 30-day period; in the UK the trigger is 20 or more over a 90-day period. There may also be additional obligations to consult with a European Works Council. The legal consequences of failure to comply with local duties to inform and consult range from financial penalties payable to the affected employees (UK) through to injunctions preventing the redundancies from being implemented (Germany) and criminal penalties (Belgium and France).

Strict requirements about when the duty to consult arises also vary across Europe, meaning that in some countries the duty will be triggered at an earlier stage in the process than in others. Management and HR need to be educated about these requirements at a very early stage in the planning process, to avoid inadvertently triggering a duty to commence consultations

FIGURE 2.3.8 Example of an individual redundancy consultation process

Redundancy consultation

Town Hall meeting
- ☑ Present current situation
- ☑ Present what you are doing about it
- ☑ Explain the implications, e.g:
  - → Select redundancies
  - → Sorts of numbers impacted
- ☑ Explain the process:
  - → Explain the process steps
  - → How long it will take
  - → What everyone should do
  - → The support you will provide

First consultation meeting
- ☑ Discuss with employees:
  - → Nature of the proposal
  - → Business reasons behind the proposal
  - → Impact on the employee's role
  - → Consultation process to be followed, including proposed selection procedure and criteria (if relevant)
  - → Whether there are any ways of avoiding or mitigating the impact
  - → Suitable alternative positions
  - → Redundancy package
- ☑ Allow the employee an opportunity to comment
- ☑ Respond to comments raised or agree on points to be taken away for consideration

Second consultation meeting
- ☑ Run through the matters discussed in the first meeting
- ☑ Provide feedback on points raised in the first meeting (if any)
- ☑ Take further feedback (if any)
- ☑ Encourage the employee to apply for any suitable
- alternative positions
- ☑ Allow the employee an opportunity to comment
- ☑ Respond to comments raised or agree on points to be taken away for consideration

Apply the selection criteria (if applicable)
- ☑ Apply objective criteria
- ☑ Gain feedback from more than one assessor
- ☑ Moderate scores
- ◇ Consider whether it is necessary to make reasonable adjustments for disabilities or to avoid other discrimination

Final consultation meeting
- ◇ Decide if there is an alternative position
- ◇ Decide whether to proceed
- ◇ Decide final terms

Gate to proceed
- ☑ If applicable: Communicate the employee's score
- ☑ If applicable: Allow them an opportunity to comment on the scoring
- ☑ If applicable: Respond to comments raised or agree on points to be taken away for consideration (if any)
- ☐ Confirm the outcome
- ☑ Provide support through the termination process

in any country before the business is ready to do so, or even undermining the validity of the consultations altogether. Communications with staff or their representative bodies need to be carefully coordinated across the affected jurisdictions to avoid this type of problem. A staff communication (or even an email between members of senior management) that is perfectly innocuous in one jurisdiction (such as the UK, which is one of the more permissive jurisdictions) may be a complete no-no in another (such as France, where the legal regime tends to be much more protective of employees).

Clearly, to devise the most effective plan, central management and HR need to fully understand the legal landscape in each country where redundancies are proposed, and both the legal and practical risks associated with non-compliance. For businesses unaccustomed to the regimes in mainland Europe, it can come as a shock to learn that non-compliance with consultation requirements can result not only in financial penalties but also in lengthy and costly delays to the process. It is much better for that realization to come during the planning stage than when those plans are being executed.

THREE COMMON LEGAL TRAPS TO AVOID

The process is one thing but, as we know, things rarely go as planned. I asked Kathryn Dooks to share her experiences and reflections on the traps you could find yourself falling into along the way:

1 *Coordinate your consultation process across the organization*
   In the context of a restructure, a decision might be made to close one function and refocus the business by growing a different function. A common error is to recruit for the growing function before starting to consult on the redundancies in the one being closed. This can lead to accusations that the consultation process is a sham and that the restructuring is a done deal. This frequently arises from a (sometimes erroneous) assumption that the redundant employee does not have the competencies to undertake the duties of the expanding function. Employers should make themselves aware of the employee's transferrable competencies as part of the consultation process and reasonable retraining should be offered. Give each employee a chance to express interest in all open roles, not just those in his or her area.

2 *Avoid grounds for constructive unfair dismissal claims*
   Employers can hire a new member of staff to slot into the structure over the head of an existing employee without first consulting the existing employee (particularly in a rapidly growing business). This can result in

a change of reporting line, team size, perceived status or responsibility for the existing employee. In a worst-case scenario, it may lead the existing employee to resign and claim constructive unfair dismissal. Scenarios such as these can be avoided if employers first take the time to consult with existing employees about their plans and the reasons behind them. It helps to build trust and demonstrates a level of respect for existing employees. This helps to strengthen relationships and increases the chance of them seeing the merit of new appointments.

3 *Ensure selection processes are fair*

If you are reducing the size of a function rather than eliminating it altogether, ensure you avoid discrimination issues arising from the selection process and criteria being applied. This most commonly occurs when an employee is disabled or has been on maternity leave during the period being assessed for the selection process. When employers score the employee as part of the selection process, they can fail to take account of the disadvantage to the employee arising from the disability or maternity leave. Apparent maternity discrimination (or other types) can arise inadvertently when, for example, it just so happens that a large proportion of those selected for redundancy are on maternity leave. Pull your numbers together by each group, consider the risk and consider how a situation would look in front of a tribunal judge. It's also important not to go too far the other way. Over-compensating for the impact on one group can lead to allegations from the other. It is always best to seek advice on the criteria used and any adjustments proposed in this context.

Final thoughts

The essence of this chapter is simple. Know what is going to change and make that change happen in a structured and fair way. Knowing what is going to change needs to happen at the individual level first and then be aggregated up. This is the impact assessment. Inversely, the communication and consultation processes need to start at the aggregate level and then be implemented at the individual employee level.

Many of the points in this chapter relate to the fourth point of the seven points of integration discussed in Chapter 1.1: high-level aggregation and individual level detail. Data is needed at an individual level to understand who should be slated for which positions and where individuals are in the assessment and selection process at any given point of the transition. It is also helpful to aggregate data to track the overall progress of the transition to understand the proportion of people who have been slated, selected, confirmed or not selected, and the number who are still unassigned.

The art of much of the implementation process isn't so much the how but the when. And the 'when' for a great number of the elements is right from the start of the macro design process. This is particularly true for when communication should begin. Don't make the mistake of thinking this starts at Making it Real. It doesn't. This is how preparation and implementation become blurred. In a sense, you are always preparing certain elements of the process, even once the implementation has begun. There is a catch-22. If you start too early with general consultation and don't have enough answers to specific questions you might send unfounded fear through the ranks. But if you wait until everything is worked out, you will at best break trust and at worst have missed an angle of thought that could have led to a far better outcome. No matter what, if you break trust, it is hard to get it back. So be thoughtful both in your timing and in developing strong relationships with those with whom you need to consult at the general level. For the individual consultation process, be fair and clear. Have a well-structured process that protects you legally and minimizes risk, but is also efficient so that you can move forward into getting the value from the to-be design.

When you come to the end of the implementation process, be sure to mark it in some way. In *Data-Driven Organization Design*, I wrote about the need to celebrate and rest after hitting a milestone. The word 'celebrate' doesn't sit right in a chapter that discusses how to conduct a redundancy process. Implementing a large-scale transformation can take its toll and it is likely to have been an emotional journey. Even if 'celebrating' feels too upbeat, it is important to find ways to acknowledge what has been achieved and give each other a well-deserved pat on the back. Once done, it is time to move on to managing the new 'business as usual' organization. That organization won't be static, and it needs ongoing management if you are going to achieve the goals you set yourself. This takes us to Stage 4 of Making it Real – ongoing optimization.

REMEMBER THIS

1 Build a comprehensive and detailed impact assessment at the aggregate and individual levels of the organization.

2 When communicating change, be as true to yourself as possible. If you don't, people won't believe in you or follow you on the journey.

3 Use all the hard work building your baseline to understand why things are changing and support your communication with the facts.

4 Be clear and fair about your assessment and selection criteria and consultation processes. Where necessary, bring in professional support to avoid legal traps.

5 Consistently categorize people and positions to enable a controlled and transparent transition process.

Notes

1 Nossiter, A (2019) 3 French executives convicted in suicides of 35 workers, *The New York Times*, December. www.nytimes.com/2019/12/20/world/europe/france-telecom-suicides.html (archived at https://perma.cc/Q2SL-ECXM)

2 Covey, S (2004) *The 7 Habits of Highly Effective People: Powerful lessons in personal change*, Simon & Schuster.

3 Peter, T (1989) *A Passion for Excellence: The leadership difference*, Grand Central Publishing.

2.4

Ongoing optimization

Introduction to Stage 4

In this chapter we reach Stage 4 of Making it Real: ongoing optimization. The to-be organization has been populated with the right people to perform the roles in the new organization. At this point, you're in the best possible place you can be in, but how do you sustain that position? How can you perpetually ensure that the right people with the right skills are doing the right work in the right place at the right time, so that gains in performance can be made over time? Remember the quote from General Electric's annual report in 2000 quoted in Chapter 1.1: 'We've long believed that when the rate of change inside an institution becomes slower than the rate of change outside, the end is in sight. The only question is when'.[1] If you're failing to keep up with outside change by making necessary micro-level tweaks to your organization design, then you're heading for trouble.

In September 2021 I completed my third Ironman race. Between April 2020 and February 2021 I lost 30 kilograms (66 pounds), got myself exceptionally fit and maintained a 'healthy' weight with 22 per cent body fat. After the Ironman, I picked up a small injury that made running painful, contracted Covid-19, travelled to the US twice in five weeks, celebrated Christmas and generally took it a bit easy. I stopped measuring my weight every day and reduced my exercise. The result? A 10 kilogram (22 pound) increase in weight. Will I get back to my target 'body composition' and fitness levels? Yes, but through consuming only 1,700 calories a day, no alcohol and sustained exercise. In other words, through work and consistent discipline. As mentioned in Chapter 2.1, Jim Collins calls this 'disciplined action'. He worked with 21 research associates for nearly five years to answer the question: what did it take for a set of companies (who weren't exceptional for a period of time) to become great over a sustained period of more than 15 years? They examined 1,435 Fortune 500 companies and found that the great companies outperformed returns by 6.9 times the stock market. They discovered that it wasn't a larger-than-life CEO that made the difference, nor the executive compensation process, nor mergers and acquisitions, nor having a well-defined strategy or a big transformation 'moment' or event. The great companies weren't, by and large, in 'great' industries. So what was it? In summary, what made the difference was discipline: disciplined people, disciplined thought and disciplined action. But, like getting fit, it takes *genuine* discipline. This isn't an earth-shattering insight, it's just common sense, and something we know intuitively to be true. To drive ongoing optimization of your organization and design requires consistently applied discipline and a need to not see it as a project that can be won and done. The key to it, again in the words of Jim Collins, is to cultivate 'a culture of discipline'.[2]

A very large part of ongoing optimization comes down to workforce planning, which is too large a topic to include as a subsection in a single chapter, so is therefore the subject of the chapters in Part Three. This chapter focuses on the remaining elements of Stage 4 set out in Figure 2.1.2:

- Track organization KPIs against targets.
- Manage talent and succession.
- Monitor and improve organization effectiveness.
- Make micro-level adjustments.

The advice in this chapter will help you to answer the following sorts of questions:

- Do we have the supply of talent to match our demand for skills?
- Where does L&D investment need to be prioritized?
- Who are the experts and role models across the organization?
- What competencies do those experts and role models possess, and can those competencies be used to predict outcomes?
- Where do individuals need to focus to grow into the next role?
- Who are the most suitable successors for critical roles?

Ongoing optimization involves a lot of tracking and monitoring to assess how close you are to achieving your goals and where you are falling short, and this, again, requires discipline. There's a lot to say about tracking and monitoring the performance of the organization, much of which I covered in my book

Data-Driven Organization Design. In this chapter I will therefore begin with some brief thoughts on the topic before moving on to talent management and the need to prioritize the development of internal talent over the acquisition of new talent. As part of this discussion, I introduce the internal talent market-place, and explain how it can be used for career path planning. It is also invaluable for Agile Team allocation, and I include a case study on building and allocating talent to Agile Teams demonstrating this to be the case. Next, I look at succession planning and development, with an emphasis on the need to prioritize development over planning and perform the process for all levels of the organization, not just those at the top. The chapter ends with a discussion of how to predict which competencies have the most significant impact on outcomes, which may lead to a need to make micro-level adjustments to target competency profiles to maximize performance.

The importance of tracking and monitoring

As mentioned above, I discuss the need to track and monitor the performance of the organization in depth in *Data-Driven Organization Design*. To recap, if the initial macro operating design is done well and the health of the organization is monitored on a continual basis, operating model redesigns should rarely be needed. This does not mean that organizations stand still. The role of management is to instigate change: to introduce new initiatives and put new goals into place to ensure the business constantly improves and thrives. These new initiatives often require small tweaks to the micro detailed design, for example the introduction of new roles or an increase or decrease in the number of positions performing certain roles. The aim is to ensure that the *right people*, with the *right skills*, are doing the *right work*, in the *right way* and in the *right numbers* with *real alignment*, to achieve *strategic objectives*, and for this to be the case on a continual, ongoing basis, not just for a moment in time when a macro operating redesign has just been implemented. This is progressive operating model design. Ongoing monitoring and resultant small, continuous tweaks to the operating model reduce the need for painful, demoralizing large-scale transformations.

This monitoring forms part of the **Analyse–Design–Plan–Monitor (ADPM) cycle**. Monitoring should happen in real time (or close to it) to ensure that the analysing, designing and planning are doing their job and enabling the organization to make continual gains in performance. Leading indicators can be tracked, and when things start to go off-plan (which they will), analysis can be undertaken to understand why. Jim Collins refers to this as confronting brutal facts (yet never losing faith).[3] As part of this, scenario modelling can be performed to understand the implications of the deviance from the plan. Once the crux of a problem is understood, small changes can be made to the design of the organization, such as altering roles and accountabilities, to improve performance based on the road ahead. When doing this, you are effectively pulling enhancement levers to assess the impact of changing certain variables.

A crucial aspect of the organization system to continually monitor and track is that of competency data. Organizations need a continual supply of the right people with the right competencies to execute future strategy. This monitoring will reveal gaps between actual and target competencies and the insight feeds into L&D to ensure that training and developing programmes are in place to meet the future needs of the organization. The remainder of this chapter focuses on talent management, career path planning and succession planning and development to explain why this monitoring is so crucial.

Talent management

Talent management is a significant talking point within organizations, which is no surprise given how crucial it is to an organization's success. Who you can attract and how you can best nurture and retain them over time are questions that many organizations struggle to answer. For Jim Collins, it's about getting the right people on the bus, the wrong people off the bus and the right people sitting in the right seats.[4] Thinking about organizations strategically means defining the 'seats' in the right numbers at the right level (this is workforce planning), and ensuring a flow of talent in the future capable of filling those seats. I hear 'the right people on the bus' quoted all the time, but it's rarely followed up with the need for those people to be in the right seats, or, in other words, the right roles and positions. It's simple, right?

In my view, organizations too often focus on acquiring talent from the outside to fill pivotal roles, rather than developing the talent pool already within the organization. Apart from anything else, the processes involved in developing talent – for example, tracking and planning career paths, identifying Learning and Development needs and providing training for people to move to the next level – cost far less than recruitment. And if you continually look externally to get great people but fail to look after them adequately once they are with you, it's likely they won't stick around anyway, and you'll be back to square one. Of course, there will be instances when you need to recruit from outside the organization if an entirely new skillset is required, but this should only be done if you are sure that nobody in the organization can be trained up to do that role.

Talent management is closely linked with the ideas of competency management and workforce planning. If competencies define the talent you currently need and have, then talent management is about managing and nurturing that talent for your future workforce. This section considers how OP&A can use the data model to understand who holds which competencies within the organization. I look specifically at how competency data can be used to create an internal talent marketplace, which, in turn, can be used to understand both the suitability of people to fulfil certain roles as well as help with mapping career paths. You'll notice throughout this section, and the one that follows on succession planning and development, that the processes, methods and tools used in transition management (discussed in Chapter 2.3) can also be deployed for talent management and succession planning. The difference is that talent management and succession planning are performed on an ongoing basis rather than as a one-off. Think of them like a soap opera rather than a movie, with a beginning and an end. In the transition management process, people enter a talent pool, are slated for positions and then are either selected or not selected, and those not selected leave the organization. This process has an end point – when the to-be organization is populated. With talent management and succession planning, there is no end point, and these tools are deployed on an ongoing basis. I'll start with a look at the internal talent marketplace, alongside a case study of how it can be used for Agile Team allocation.

The internal talent marketplace

In Chapter 2.3, I explained how, as part of the selection process, you can determine people's role match score to decide who should be slated for which positions. Figure 2.3.6 showed a matrix of roles and individuals, with a role match score assigned to each person for each applicable role. This figure is an example of an internal talent marketplace. It identifies those people who are sufficiently proficient in certain competencies to be considered for defined roles.

This data is not just useful for slating people for positions when transitioning to a to-be organization. Rather, it can be used continually to support career path planning and mapping, Learning and Development and succession planning and to identify people who can step into a role for a short period of time (otherwise known as 'emergency caretakers'). The talent marketplace can be used to ask where people can go to next. What's the plan for them, and what competencies do they need to progress to where they want to go? This isn't just about succession planning, which I come to later in the chapter and which focuses more on critical roles. While the processes and the data used in succession planning are the same as in broader talent management, career path mapping is for everyone, not just those who might be in line for critical roles. It's about understanding where else in the organization people could go to make the most of the talent pool and ensuring you are capitalizing on the full spectrum of competencies within the organization. In Chapter 2.3 I discussed competency gap management. If someone has a raft of competencies which they are not using in their current role, would they be more suited to a different role in the organization? What would the individual prefer? Would they rather use some of their competencies over others in the role that they do? The talent marketplace is particularly helpful for large organizations delivering a variety of professional services at scale where nobody can know everyone. It is also invaluable in the context of Agile Team allocation. I will now return to the agile case study introduced in Chapter 2.2 to illustrate how it can be deployed in this context.

CASE STUDY

BUILDING AGILE TEAMS

In Chapter 2.2 I introduced the concept of agile transformation. Before I get into the specifics of how the talent marketplace can be used for Agile Team allocation, I'll give a bit more background on the importance of using the right technology and data model to do this right, as well as how to build Agile Teams.

Many of the challenges in building and scaling Agile Team design are centred around accessibility to the right data. They can be broken down into three areas:

1 managing multiple hierarchies

2 lack of visibility into talent supply

3 inability to regularly manage capacity

Let me say from the off that if you try to do this work using data in disconnected silos and Excel spreadsheets you'll be doomed from the start.

The level of risk created by trying to execute Agile Team allocation in this way is huge. Take the problem of multiple hierarchies. As discussed in Chapter 2.2, people can exist in two or more places, which means that you need the ability to manage more than one hierarchy at once. Imagine the following scenario: Tess is an Engineer who belongs to the Product function. She is also deployed to the Eligibility Mission and Advice Delivery Teams, as shown in Figure 2.4.2. Her manager in the Product function is responsible for career path discussions as well as identifying any Learning and Development needs. They need to understand Tess's competencies and help to close any gaps that exist between the competencies that she currently holds and those prescribed to the roles she is deployed to or could be deployed to in the future. Without a clear view of team structures and where people report to versus where they are deployed, satisfactory career path planning discussions can't happen, and people's Learning and Development needs may not be met. It's vital to be able to visualize multiple hierarchies to understand both where someone resides in the reporting structure and where they get deployed in an agile context.

So how do you do this? The answer lies in linking Role, Position and People data and using an integrated data model, as described in Chapter 2.2, to construct and model Agile Teams. Connecting these datasets together allows you to do two things:

1   At the individual level, you can create a many-to-many relationship. One person can fill multiple positions and multiple people can fill the same agile position in cases where more than one person is needed to do the work.

2   At the team level, you can understand, in real time, what the implications are as you model, adjust, pivot and visualize.

Figure 2.4.1 shows one way to model and visualize part of an agile organization. When creating Agile Teams, the aim is to be able to organize roles and capabilities around a team design and assign target capacity and competencies to execute against the work. In the circle diagram in Figure 2.4.1, you can see the families (or tribes), the Mission Teams (or squads) and the agile roles and positions. At the top of the figure, you can see information related to the target and actual FTEs for each role and the gaps that exist. When you have this data in place, you can then zoom out so that you can visualize this across tens or hundreds of teams to analyse the size, mix and status of the teams being built across the company.

FIGURE 2.4.1 Constructing, modelling and visualizing Agile Teams

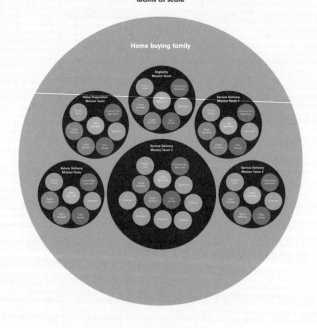

Visualize and manage cross-functional teams at scale

Value proposition mission team	
Target FTE(sum)	7.0
Total FTE(sum)	0.0
Gap FTE(sum)	7.0
Gap FTE(sum)	$0

Product owner	
Target FTE(sum)	1.0
Total FTE(sum)	0.0
Gap FTE(sum)	1.0
Gap FTE(sum)	$0

Digital marketing	
Target FTE(sum)	2.0
Total FTE(sum)	0.0
Gap FTE(sum)	2.0
Gap FTE(sum)	$0

Channel/Ops specialists	
Target FTE(sum)	1.0
Total FTE(sum)	0.0
Gap FTE(sum)	1.0
Gap FTE(sum)	$0

CRM specialists	
Target FTE(sum)	1.0
Total FTE(sum)	0.0
Gap FTE(sum)	1.0
Gap FTE(sum)	$0

Data analyst	
Target FTE(sum)	1.0
Total FTE(sum)	0.0
Gap FTE(sum)	1.0
Gap FTE(sum)	$0

Developer	
Target FTE(sum)	1.0
Total FTE(sum)	0.0
Gap FTE(sum)	1.0
Gap FTE(sum)	$0

Visualize and manage cross-functional teams at scale

I'll now move onto the second challenge: that of a lack of visibility into talent supply. In Chapter 2.2, Figure 2.2.5 showed how people could be transitioned from a traditional organizational structure. Figure 2.4.2 repeats the Agile Team structure for ease of reference. This figure illustrates a key problem in Agile Team allocation – that of people being over-deployed to Mission Teams. As can be seen from the expected time allocations, too much is expected of Anna and Tess. Anna has been deployed to three teams at 0.5 FTE each and is over capacity. Tess has been deployed to two teams each at 1.0 FTE and is also over capacity. There are clearly competing needs for someone with Tess's skillset, and with adequate visibility into the talent supply, the OP&A Team should be able to identify others who could do her job and take her place on one of the teams. As an aside, Ted has been deployed to three teams at 0.3 FTE which is reasonable for someone in his role.

FIGURE 2.4.2 Deploying people to Agile Team structures

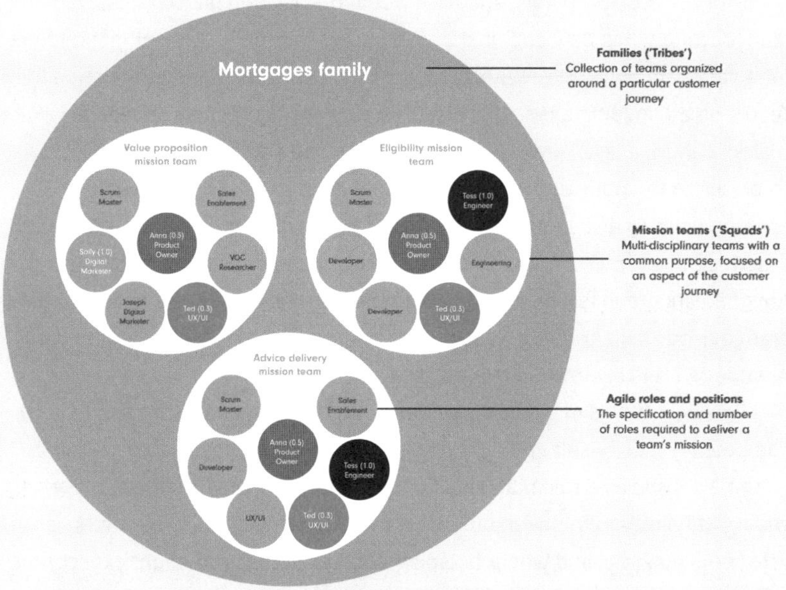

If you don't have a good oversight of the people in your business and the competencies that they hold, it is very difficult to properly build Agile Teams at scale. Figures 2.4.1 and 2.4.2 give insight into the amount of effort involved in equipping a single team to start operating in this way. Doing this at scale for 20,

50 or 100 teams becomes impossible without the right technology and data model. The task of slating talent into positions requires herculean manual effort and there is significant risk of certain people being favoured over others. Let's return to Tess. Tess has been in her organization for years and is very good at what she does. People know and trust her, and when a new Mission Team comes online, she is often the first Engineer people ask for. In the context of her organization, she can be thought of as 'Tried and Tested Tess'. When a new Engineer joins the organization (let's call him 'New and Unknown Nick') with the same, or even a higher, level of proficiency as Tess in the competencies required for an Engineer, he doesn't get deployed to a team because no one knows him. This is extremely demotivating for Nick, particularly as he is skilled in what he does. He starts to think of leaving, which would be an enormous loss to all concerned.

If the organization had a talent marketplace it would be possible to understand, at scale, who else had the requisite skills and knowledge to fill the needs of the Mission Teams, and Nick would quickly find himself deployed on a team despite being new and unknown. Figure 2.4.3 shows a talent marketplace for a variety of agile roles. With agile working, talent is mapped to Mission Teams on an ongoing basis. This effectively means that people should be 'slated' continually as new teams come online and are decommissioned. To be slated for a position in a team, people need to have the necessary competencies to deliver against the team's mission. As with the marketplace described in Chapter 2.3, colour coding helps to assess people's suitability. Anyone dark green is a pretty good match for a role, but anyone yellow to dark orange needs help, training, coaching and support to be effective and thrive. Anyone red is likely to be better deployed elsewhere.

I'll delve into this in a little more detail. Sometimes, understanding competency match isn't good enough when looking for specialized skillsets. Figure 2.4.4 shows a tree map view focused on identifying proficiency levels in coding. It helps you to understand where there are hotspots of strong skills across the business and where hotspots don't exist (but you might expect that they should). This tree map is helpful not only because it focuses attention on who is available to be deployed to Agile Teams, but also because it creates insight into where investment might be needed to upskill the workforce, or, if necessary, hire new talent.

FIGURE 2.4.3 The talent marketplace can be used to locate people with the necessary competencies for Agile Teams

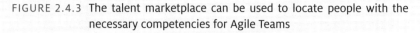
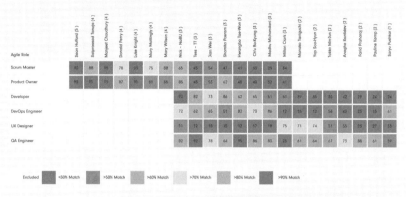

Excluded | <50% Match | >50% Match | >60% Match | >70% Match | >80% Match | >90% Match

FIGURE 2.4.4 Honing in on specific competencies and proficiency levels allows for deeper insight into talent supply

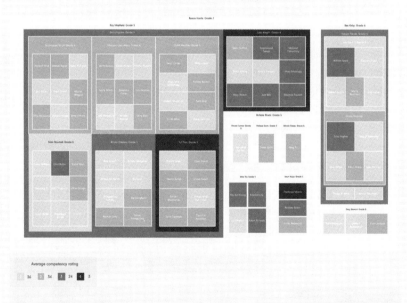

Average competency rating
36   34   24   5

Finally, the third challenge: an inability to manage capacity. This relates very closely to the second challenge, because without being able to visualize talent supply, it is also impossible to effectively manage capacity. It's important to be able to account for the movement of talent across the business and prevent issues occurring for people like Tess, Nick and Anna. For seamless deployment to Agile Teams, it is enormously helpful to be able to understand someone's current capacity as well as their capacity over a specified time horizon so that they can be slated to future Mission Teams ahead of time. Figure 2.4.5 shows how people (in this case, Anna) can be mapped into the agile structure so that their capacity constraints can be understood in real time.

You'll remember from Figure 2.4.2 that Anna had been over-deployed as Product Owner in three different Mission Teams within the Home Ownership family. Her FTE allocation was 0.5 to each team, so this clearly wasn't going to work. Figure 2.4.5 shows a much better allocation for Anna. She still sits within the Product function and is now assigned to two agile positions – Product Owner and the Scrum Master on the Value Proposition Mission Team. The left-hand chart shows Anna's statistics: the roles she has been allocated to and the start and end dates of her positions. The end dates clearly show when she will next be available to be redeployed.

The right-hand chart of Figure 2.4.5 shows that there are three roles within the Value Proposition Mission Team that are on target. Anna has been mapped into the two roles that were budgeted for 0.5 FTE. The Value Proposition Mission Team is looking in good shape. The Advice Delivery Team is more problematic. The Quality Assurance (QA) Engineer role has been filled, but it is filled by Tess, who appears to be over capacity. One of two things needs to be done – either reallocate Tess's time or find a different QA Engineer. The Developer role is also showing up orange to signify a gap. Six Developers are needed for this team, but only five people have been assigned, so one more person is needed to fill that role if that team is to achieve its deliverables. You can use the talent marketplace to find out who has the skills to perform that role, but how do you know who is available to do it?

FIGURE 2.4.5   Mapping people to the agile structure and understanding capacity constraints in real time

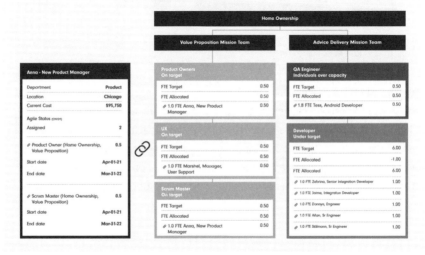

Figure 2.4.6 shows two versions of an icicle chart – one of the many visualizations that give a bird's eye view of the organization. The charts are useful for understanding pockets of people: those who are operating in an agile role and pockets of undeployed individuals. The top image shows an example of an IT organization. The colour coding makes it easy to see people's status. People coded as grey aren't assigned to any teams, those coded as green have been assigned as a full FTE, those marked as yellow are partially assigned and red people have been over-allocated. The bottom image zooms in on the Engineering Team. You can see that there are two people colour-coded as red, one of whom is Tess. You can also see that there are two people coded as yellow – Sarah and Georgia. Viewed from this perspective, there is very clear opportunity for Sarah and Georgia to take some of the pressure off Tess, thereby aligning 'demand' and 'supply'.

FIGURE 2.4.6   Zooming out to understand capacity and resource allocation across the business

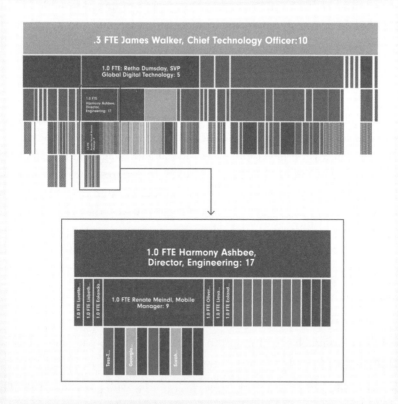

I hope this case study has given you a good grounding in how to build Agile Teams and map talent to those teams according to competency and capacity data. With agile working, you can't just design and map people to roles once – this is a temporal process that needs to be managed over time. Many people choose to do this on a quarterly basis, asking themselves questions which focus on the three Cs of cost, composition and capacity:

- Cost – How much does it cost to run teams? Ideally, you want to track cost by team and by functional unit where individuals are deployed into Agile Teams. This can then be used as a mechanism to begin tracking ROI.
- Composition – Is the construction of our teams working? What are the time zones and functional teams that they pull on, and what job grades make up the teams?
- Capacity – Do you understand at scale, as new teams come online or are decommissioned, where there are vacant roles, or where capacity challenges exist that need to be solved?

I'll now move on to another aspect of ongoing optimization which is very closely linked to talent management: succession planning and development.

Succession planning and development

Succession planning involves compiling shortlists of possible candidates who could replace those holding critical roles in the organization should the need arise. Succession development involves identifying possible candidates and developing them so that they are ready to progress into the identified role when the time comes. These are hot topics and high up the agenda for many leaders, but, like so many things in organizations, they are often talked about but not implemented; and when they are implemented, the execution often falls wide of the mark. There are three major problems with the way that most organizations approach succession planning and development:

1 There is not enough of a long-term focus.
2 The focus is primarily on *planning* rather than *development*.
3 There is too much attention given to the top of the organization and not enough throughout.

The first point for me is a no-brainer. If you take a longer view of the flow of talent over time, you will buy yourself time to develop that talent and help individuals fulfil their potential. This links with both the second and third points above: focus should be more on spotting talent throughout the organization and *developing* that talent so that people are able to step into critical roles, rather than seeing who's at the top already and trying to figure out who's going to be the next CEO. Succession planning shouldn't just be about the future stars, it should be on building the competence of your people – helping them improve and realize their innate potential and think through their career paths and possible next steps.

Too often, succession planning is seen as a one-off activity. You do your plan, have your list of candidates, and that's it. But what about those individuals who could be identified as brilliant successors for certain roles if they were given the right training? This links very much with the talent management discussion above. The focus is on improving existing talent to minimize the impact felt by the organization when key people leave. This is better not only for the organization but also for the people it employs. It's a win–win.

In my view, organizations are too obsessed with the top organizational tiers of management, i.e. the Top 150 in large multinationals. Who are the successors to the senior executives? Succession planning shouldn't just be about the next generation of leaders. While it makes sense to focus on critical roles, it needs to be much deeper and more far-reaching through the organization if there is any chance of developing talent in the long term. Remember that critical roles are found at every level of the organization, not just at the top.

I begin this section by highlighting the importance of succession planning, using the New Zealand All Blacks rugby team to illustrate my point. I then outline three critical aspects of succession planning. Throughout this section remember my point made above. Talent does not mean one type of talent, or a misguided focus on leadership, but a full range of focused skills and behaviours across the organization based on a particular role. The question is: given your set of roles today and your roles in the future, how do you spot talent suitable for those future roles throughout the organization?

The importance of succession planning

Organizations can become obsessed with succession. Does it deserve all the attention or is it all just hype? If someone leaves, why not just recruit from the outside? Does it really have a material impact on an organization's performance and is it really that important for optimizing organization performance over time? In my view, it is, and the hype is justified. When I was writing the first edition of *Data-Driven Organization Design*, New Zealand had won the 2011 Rugby World Cup for the first time since 1987. It had a highly capped and ageing team, and with the World Cup being its seemingly singular focus there was a big question about whether it could sustain its success. For a time, it did. Its win rate continued and in 2015 it won the World Cup again. After this the team was still unbeatable until 2019, when it lost the semi-finals of the World Cup to England. At the time of writing, the team has just had its first back-to-back defeat for 12 years. The team has lost some of its competitive advantage in recent years but its record over the past decades is nevertheless phenomenal and it is still the most successful team in the history of sport. The secret? In part, succession planning and development.

New Zealand faces an uphill struggle when it comes to achieving and sustaining success. It is a country with a population of only five million, which means that talent is at a premium in comparison to other top rugby nations, such as England and France. It also can't afford to pay as much as wealthy English and French clubs, and every year there is a huge exodus of talent. For this reason, New Zealand has had to put a real focus on attracting talent and putting talent and succession development plans into place. Its approach demonstrates three areas where organizations could significantly improve their succession planning and development processes:

1 *Have a long-term perspective.* New Zealand invested heavily in all stages of talent and succession development, introducing special non-contact forms of the game so that talent can be nurtured from as early as the age of three.

2 *Ensure structured development.* The talent system is not simply a plan, but a structured system focused on developing talent. Each age group is introduced to different forms of the game with a focus on certain skills and aspects of the game to stretch them. There are apprenticeship programmes for the national team to ease talent in gradually, with a focus on succession development.

3 *A focus beyond top talent.* Just as organizations shouldn't focus on the top level of management, New Zealand has built a system which goes beyond simply picking out the stars, by building talent which supports the whole team and the landscape of New Zealand rugby.

The thing that New Zealand has done so well is to execute a succession plan. The country's ability to foster and grow talent is not simply paying lip service but has become part of the culture through rigorous thinking and disciplined development. Organizations should take all these lessons on board if they are going to make a difference. The fact that the All Blacks' phenomenal record has tailed off slightly in recent years should also be a lesson to organizations. Despite the focus on talent and succession planning and development that served them so well for so many years, other teams can learn and catch up and erode their competitive advantage.

Finding the right people to nurture and develop has as much to do with their cultural fit in the organization as anything else. The right succession candidates need to align with the culture and ambition of the organization but, more importantly, with the role family and sub-role family they are part of. Different role families will have different cultures, and a successor to a critical role in sales and marketing is likely to look different to a successor for a role in research and development. Different behavioural competencies will be required (such as the ability to influence and sell ideas, to think innovatively, to plan and organize or build relationships with people) and the requirements for innate competencies such the ability to think and problem solve are likely to look different too.

The rest of this section sets out three aspects of succession planning that can be performed in every organization. I start by explaining how competency data and tools such as the talent marketplace can be used to assess who the successors to certain roles within role families should be. I then look at how to identify succession gaps and risks before progressing ways in which succession candidates can be tracked over time.

Approaches to succession planning

Succession planning can be thought of in terms of three key processes:

1 Identify succession candidates and succession readiness.
2 Identify succession gaps and risks.
3 Track the development of succession candidates.

I'll run through the first two points in detail.

IDENTIFYING SUCCESSION CANDIDATES AND SUCCESSION READINESS

You want to be able to determine who, according to your measures, is the closest fit and, therefore, the best candidate for succession. Identifying succession candidates is best done at a role family and sub-role family level. As I said above, different role families will require different competencies. As a reminder, competencies can be broken into skills (which in turn are broken into generic business skills and specialized functional skills), behaviours and cognitive processing. Skills and, to a certain extent, behaviours, require time and experience to develop, and gaps in these types of competencies can be filled by Learning and Development; you can provide training that builds knowledge as well as developing the ability to *apply* that knowledge. Innate skills like cognitive processing are much harder to develop through training. Someone's traits such as their ability to think through difficult problems, reason effectively and make difficult decisions tend to be something they are born with. So your starting point is to look at the underlying traits of those people who are senior in each role family. Think about the competencies that they have and split them into skills, behaviours and cognitive ability. Which competencies can be addressed through Learning and Development, and which are more innate? Once you have this information, look down through the role family and identify those people with the same competencies. Gaining insight on the innate competencies could signify who might be able to progress into critical roles in the future. For those who are potential successors, what are the things that they most need to work on? How are they progressing? Which skills are in the shortest supply? There is clearly a risk of unconscious bias. My hope is that this opens up the chances for everyone, and doesn't act as a mechanism to further enhance the chances of certain sub-groups of the population. To identify someone's succession readiness for various roles in the organization, go back to determining role match scores and the talent marketplace. Splashing colour on the marketplace as in Figures 2.3.6 and 2.4.3 helps you to visualize succession readiness. Any individuals colour coded dark green, with a score of 94 and above for a role, would be ready to progress into that role.

It's worth mentioning here that if there is a dearth of people with those innate competencies in the role family, then this is something to bear in mind with recruitment strategies. While it is best, where possible, to develop talent rather than recruit new talent, there is a need to be realistic about how far training can get you. If you don't have people in the role family with the required cognitive processing competencies, then you might need to think about recruiting from outside.

Diversity, Equity and Inclusion (DEI) considerations also come into play with succession planning. To get a more diverse workforce, help those groups which historically have been marginalized or underrepresented. The best speaker I have seen on DEI is Keith Wyche, the author of *Diversity Is Not Enough: A roadmap to recruit, develop and promote Black leaders in America*[5] and the Vice President of Walmart. According to Wyche, DEI efforts can focus too heavily on hiring diverse workers, often with not enough attention paid to equity and inclusion. Organizations have a responsibility to foster an inclusive culture where everyone feels valued and has equitable access to resources that will allow them to progress within the organization. For Wyche, DEI best practices include the following:[6]

- having structured programmes for 'high potentials' (although I believe that *all* employees deserve structured programmes, through which the true 'high potentials' will shine particularly brightly. And if you include all employees, you might just be surprised about who the true 'high potentials' are)

- recognizing the importance of 'bringing the outside in' and encouraging participation in external professional organizations. It's not enough to rely on learning from inside your organization alone

- providing a 'safe' environment for people to share ideas and learn effectively from one another. This ties in with the idea of achieving 'flow', written about extensively by Mihaly Csikszentmihalyi and as described in my book *Data-Driven Organization Design*. Achieving 'flow' is dependent upon meeting nine conditions, one of which is to feel safe in your work with no worry of failure[7]

- inspecting what you expect, and doing it regularly. In other words, measure continuously, and discuss your findings

- expecting accountability. Accountability isn't solely the responsibility of the organization or manager, it is every individual's responsibility to own their personal Learning and Development too

IDENTIFYING SUCCESSION GAPS AND RISKS

Succession planning is not a simple case of competency mapping. In the more immediate term, succession planning should also take a priority- and risk-based approach. You need to know where focus is required, which roles will be hardest to replace owing to key specialized functional skills or leadership, and whether any of those roles are at high risk of departure.

Start by segmenting the role family into critical roles (I explain role segmentation in *Data-Driven Organization Design*). In short, there are four key drivers for **role criticality**: scale of impact; Time To Productivity; growth; and prevalence. These four factors help you to determine which roles in the role family need to be prioritized in terms of succession planning. This is not just about senior leaders, as often critical roles can be at a low level.

Once you have this information, you can determine the **flight risk** for each of the roles. This can be investigated across all the critical roles regardless of the level at which they sit. Once you have this information, you'll be able to assess which critical roles with a high flight risk have a large set of potential successors in place with a high succession readiness score, and which don't. Any roles that don't have successors in place can be prioritized for succession planning.

Using competency data to predict performance outcomes

Aside from talent management and succession planning, a significant component of ongoing optimization is monitoring the organization and improving organizational effectiveness, as mentioned at the beginning of this chapter. There are many ways in which this can be done, and I delved into some of them at the end of *Data-Driven Organization Design* as part of a discussion about how to make perpetual gains in performance through monitoring the system to understand whether you are on track to hit your target objectives. In this section I focus on another way to monitor and improve performance – by assessing the outcomes that are being achieved and then tracking back to see if you can tell which competencies have the biggest impact on those outcomes. For example, by connecting competency and sales performance data, you can identify the most successful salespeople in your organization and work out whether they have a particular competency profile that should be used as a model. This is an idea which has been popularized through the incredibly influential book *The Challenger Sale* by Matthew Dixon and Brent Adamson.[8] In developing the methodology, Dixon and Adamson started with a pool of 700 sales reps but later expanded the study to include 6,000. They surveyed them and tested a range of attributes, which included:

- attitudes (including a willingness to risk disapproval and curiosity)
- skills (including communication, business acumen, teamwork and negotiation)
- activities (including sales, process adherence, preparation, administration and lead generation)
- knowledge (including both industry and product knowledge)

Based on the results of their survey and individual sales data, they segmented the sample into five different profiles:

1 the lone wolf

2 the relationship builder

3 the hard worker

4 the challenger

5 the reactive problem solver

Their analysis showed them that the challenger profile was by far the most successful. Someone fitting this profile loves to debate, isn't afraid to push and challenge their prospect and doesn't always say yes. This discovery broke a lot of myths and turned selling on its head. Whereas previously there had been an assumption that hard workers or relationship builders would be the ones to close the most sales, this research blew that idea out of the water. As a result of this work, many organizations now train their salespeople to develop and utilize the competencies in the challenger framework. I will return to the techniques used in this study in Chapter 4.2 when I look at segmentation and the importance of bringing different types of data together to reach deep insight.

   This kind of thinking can be applied to any roles in your organization depending on the outcome you want to understand and be able to predict. For example, you might want to understand the competency profile that makes someone great at quality assurance, relationship management or product development. You might not have as many as 6,000 data points, but bear in mind that Dixon and Adamson started with 700, and only after they realized they were onto something did they increase the number. A point that needs to be made is that we all need to think through the outcomes that need to be understood and the best way to understand them in the context of our own organizations. I have observed through many years of work with clients that people love to copy and paste. They like to take a tried and tested model that has worked in the context of one organization and apply it verbatim to their own. The Challenger Sales Model identified the challenger profile as the most effective in closing sales, but would this apply in all sales contexts? Selling in a B2B environment is very different to retail, or upselling wine as a waiter in a restaurant. Prospects are different, there are different sales processes, timeframes and levels of complexity. Do customers in restaurants want to be challenged by their waiters, or not? I know I do, but that might just be me.

One of the key takeaways of the Challenger Sales Model, for me, is to always question your assumptions. Until this landmark study, most people thought they knew what drove sales performance. Performance reviews would have focused on needing to work hard, and reps may have even been trained that the 'customer is always right'. We all have prejudices. We might think we know what drives performance, but do we really? These are questions that this book seeks to answer.

Final thoughts

A large part of securing continual gains in performance comes down to the people you employ. That means creating a culture of building a talent pipeline and ensuring succession planning becomes a core management process. This needs to be part of your culture. Talent is a big topic in HR circles and the idea that there is a war for talent is no longer new. But the common practice I see is to focus too narrowly and in too much of a subjective way. The starting point is to understand the type of talent you need. This is defined by the list of competencies required for each role (the demand). From there, it is about looking forward and working out the development needs of those people deemed to be critical successes. The importance of each role in terms of succession planning relates to the risk of those in that role leaving (the flight risk) and the impact that will have. The impact doesn't just relate to how close the role is to the CEO. Some roles may be senior and easy to replace while others more junior but almost impossible to replace. As this chapter has shown, the methods and processes you employ in talent management can also become a framework for executing agile ways of working.

I hope this chapter has also demonstrated the importance of disciplined action in achieving success, be that in accomplishing your outcomes and executing strategy, or ensuring that you have clear development plans in place for every employee so that people are equally equipped to close competency gaps and perform at their highest potential. In this way, every employee will have an equal chance to progress in the organization. Reflecting on DEI, this disciplined approach should help address the innate inequalities in society at large and therefore your part in helping to make progress against those goals too, as is so effectively laid out by Keith Wyche.

As mentioned at the beginning of this chapter, the advice given here only gives half the picture of how to optimize organizational performance on an ongoing basis. The rest comes down to workforce planning, a hugely significant topic, and the subject of the chapters in the next part of this book.

REMEMBER THIS

1 Ensure you have effectively mapped employee and role attributes to compare and see the gaps.

2 Prioritize and focus effort by assessing where high-impact staff are at high risk through analysing a range of data.

3 Create a long-term view by predicting individual success and facilitating development to fulfil potential where possible.

4 Invest in and take practical steps to ensure structured development.

5 Connect inputs in talent development such as training and recruitment with outputs such as performance and career progression to understand effective methods.

Notes

1 General Electric (2000) *Annual Report 2000*. www.annualreports.com/HostedData/AnnualReportArchive/g/NYSE_GE_2000.pdf (archived at https://perma.cc/BJ7X-7J4Y)

2 Collins, J (2001) *Good to Great: Why some companies make the leap... and others don't*, Random House Business.

3 Ibid.

4 Ibid.

5 Wyche, K (2021) *Diversity Is Not Enough: A roadmap to recruit, develop and promote Black leaders in America*, Kandelle Publishing.

6 I made these notes when listening to a lecture Keith Wyche gave in Atlanta in December 2021.

7 Csikszentmihalyi, M (1990) *Flow: The psychology of optimal experience*, Harper & Row.

8 Dixon, M and Adamson, B (2012) *The Challenger Sale: How to take control of the customer conversation*, Penguin.

PART THREE

Workforce planning

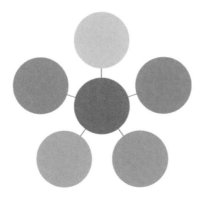

3.1

Introduction

How do you know you have the right people, with the right skills, doing the right work, in the right numbers, at the right time, and in the right place to execute organizational strategy? How do you manage this over time? What is your governance process for dealing with changes and how do you know whether you are on track to meet compensation and FTE budgets and targets? The answer lies in effective workforce planning. I use the word 'effective' because workforce planning is a difficult thing to get right, and most organizations struggle to perform it well, meaning that they are unable to answer these kinds of questions with any degree of certainty or efficiency. It is generally performed in Microsoft Excel and PowerPoint, which results in hundreds of separate files that are used to manually update finance and HR systems. It is often something that at best people feel inconvenienced by, and at worst people dread having to do. Too often, the goal is to get it done and get back to the day job as quickly as possible. Workforce planning is too important to be perceived in this way.

Workforce planning is about managing the demand for resources and the supply of workers (be they permanent or temporary, full-time or part-time, direct employees or indirect, contingent employees) required over specified time periods (which might be over a period of several years, a year, a month or a week). It sits squarely within the remit of the OP&A function, with separate teams responsible for planning over different **time horizons** and at different levels of aggregation. Consider the following definitions:

> Workforce planning and modeling includes tools that enable teams to plan and monitor the evolution of their organization by aligning talent supply and demand for various business scenarios.[1]

> Workforce planning is the process of balancing labor supply (skills) against the demand (numbers needed). It includes analyzing the current workforce,

determining future workforce needs, identifying the gap between the present and the future, and implementing solutions so that an organization can accomplish its mission, goals, and strategic plan.[2]

The term 'workforce planning' is used for a wide range of related activities, but the notion of aligning labour supply and demand to achieve business objectives is foundational to the concept. Getting terminology and concepts down is one of the key goals of D-DOD and OP&A. There are a few concepts which are important to understand before reading these chapters.

Workforce planning terminology

Too often, business speak is simply a jumble of meaningless terms thrown into verbal sparring matches to score points. There are several concepts to grasp with workforce planning, related to both content and process. Many relate to the seven points of integration discussed in Chapter 1.1. Different types of workforce planning involve different activities, but it's all connected. Below, I outline the following:

- demand and supply
- strategic, operational and tactical workforce planning
- top-down and bottom-up workforce planning

Demand and supply

The workforce plan contains the demand for workers into the future, the likely supply of workers and the gap between the two. How far into the future the plan goes depends on whether the planning is done with a strategic, operational or tactical focus (see below). OP&A is responsible for monitoring the supply of workers and making amendments where necessary to plug the gaps and stick to the planned demand. Gaps between demand and supply can exist for many reasons: it may be because the numbers of FTEs specified in the demand plan were not recruited, or start dates were delayed, or the churn rate may be higher than had been assumed in the planning process. It is only when you understand why gaps exist that you can do something about it. Plugging the gaps isn't just about headcount. It's also about competency and capability management. The fact that each role has a target set of competencies means that, at a people level, you can forecast how the demand for competencies is likely to evolve over time. This, in turn, gives insight into the gap between future competencies and the competencies your workforce has today. At an organizational level, the focus can be more on core organizational capabilities – what capabilities does your organization have today, compared to what might be needed in the future?

Strategic, operational and tactical workforce planning

There are three levels of workforce planning:

1 strategic

2 operational

3 tactical

All three types involve the planning and tracking of the supply and demand of the workforce over time, but, as Figure 3.1.1 shows, they are done over different time horizons, at different levels of detail (be that KOD, role cluster or the detailed people and position level) and are tracked at varying levels of granularity. In this book I look at the activities involved in strategic and operational workforce planning. **Tactical workforce planning**, often referred to as resourcing, falls outside the scope of this book (although I did consider this briefly in relation to operational agile workforce planning in Part Two).

FIGURE 3.1.1 Strategic, operational and tactical workforce planning

	Objective	Planning span	Tracking granularity	Planning level
1. Strategic	→ Ensure the workforce responds to the external environment and can achieve long-term strategic evolutions.	→ 2-20 years → Becoming more frequent with shorter time horizons	→ Quarterly to Annually	→ Key Organisational Dimensions (KODs e.g. Geography, Function, BU) → Role families → Role cluster

2. Operational	→ Ensure the workforce will be in place to deliver annual budgets and operational plans.	→ 12-18 months	→ Monthly
			→ Aligned to business reporting cycles
				→ KODs by:
				  → Roles and role Clusters
				  → Positions
				  → People

3. Tactical (Resourcing)	→ Ensure the individuals and teams are in place to fulfil immediate tasks	→ 4-8 weeks	→ Daily and weekly → Individual shifts	→ People

STRATEGIC WORKFORCE PLANNING

Those involved in **strategic workforce planning** have their eyes firmly set on future years. Their role is to determine how the workforce will need to evolve across a time span of anything between two and 20 years to ensure an organization's short- and long-term strategy can be executed. The length of time is very much dependent on the industry. It takes longer to build competence in some industries (for example, nuclear energy and mining) than others. This lengthens planning cycles. Over the time span being planned for, the strategic workforce planner asks where the right resources with the right competencies will be needed, whether the organization is likely to have the right people in place to execute the strategy, and if not, how they can make that happen, whether that's moving people around the organization or recruiting from the outside.

As shown in Chapter 1.1, organizations which aren't adept at adapting are going to the wall more quickly than they have in previous decades. To keep up, strategic workforce planning can be performed more frequently than it has been in the past. For many organizations, it's shifted from being an annual to a quarterly activity. One of the many benefits includes not having to wait a year to rectify a wrong decision. Advances in SaaS technology are facilitating these faster planning cycles, streamlining a previously cumbersome and daunting process which was generally performed in Excel and visualized in PowerPoint. This point about technology is not specific to strategic workforce planning – it is true for all types of planning.

Strategic workforce planners need a heads-up view of the world. They need to understand what is happening now, what could be around the corner and what impact it might have. Seeing the space ahead gives the gift of time. What forces could disrupt you? What impact could this have? Where would the impact be felt, and when? Business strategists predict megatrends such as digitalization or environmentalism. They keep track of geopolitical changes and spot new technologies. The role of the strategic workforce planner is to understand what is on the horizon and ensure that the long-term workforce plan factors in the changes that need to be made to be able to continually execute strategy.

Scenario modelling and horizon scanning form a large part of the strategic workforce planner's role. As well as helping to evaluate different options and shed light on opportunity, they can also help to highlight risk. According to Kaplan and Mikes, there are three categories of risk: preventable, strategic and external.[3] Strategic risk is the type of risk you need to take to get superior returns. While strategic risk is not necessarily a bad thing, you can also take action to reduce it. External risk comes down to factors which are outside your control. Horizon scanning and scenario modelling, as well as helping to evaluate different options, mitigate both strategic and external risk.

As it is performed so far into the future, strategic workforce planning cannot be done at the detailed positions and people level. It is therefore performed according to Key Organizational Dimensions, role families and role clusters. Relating back to FP&A in Chapter 1.3, there will be milestones you need to achieve in terms of outcomes. It's helpful to name them. For Hokupaa, a goal is to achieve global expansion and an ARR of a certain percentage in two years' time. What does the workforce need to look like over the next two years to achieve these things? The further into the future you look, the more abstract the goals become.

OPERATIONAL WORKFORCE PLANNING

Those responsible for **operational workforce planning** look at the medium-term view. They are tasked with planning 12 to 18 months into the future to ensure that the right number and type of people are in place to execute strategy within the annual budget. Operational workforce planners work to mitigate the preventable, controllable risks discussed by Kaplan and Mikes. If there is a mismatch between the number and type of people needed in the future and the actual number and type of people, then steps can be taken to address this. Operational workforce planning involves the management of an ever-shifting workforce against an agreed target line. Operational workforce planning is usually performed monthly, in alignment with business reporting cycles.

Another crucial difference between strategic and operational workforce planning is the level of granularity of the work. Whereas strategic workforce planning is done according to KODs, role families and role clusters, operational workforce planning is done at the level of Roles, Positions and People. As such, in operational workforce planning, supply and demand can be thought of as people and position planning, and it's crucial to understand the concept of positions lifecycle management. The number of planned positions creates a demand for people, and people provide the internal supply for positions. Roles, Positions and People are not static and the demand and supply of labour over time is a difficult thing to manage. Once the plan is finalized and agreed, it becomes the target; the role of the operational work-force planner is then to manage the supply of workers against this line and within the annual budget, asking such questions as:

- How many FTEs are needed each month and where?
- What is the change in the recruitment list?
- What does the pipeline look like for the next 12 months?

From small alterations in start dates to changes in business requirements, or from the budget being removed through hiring freezes, the only thing you know for certain is that the actuals will vary from the plan. But if resource supply (current FTE in each position) is linked with resource demand (demand for each position), you can then assess whether there is over- or under-supply, and plan additional resource, move people around the organization or work out whether redundancies are necessary.

Top-down and bottom-up workforce planning

Top-down and bottom-up planning relates to process – how workforce planning gets done in the organization. The process of reaching an approved demand plan requires a combination of top-down budgeting and bottom-up positions modelling, as shown in Figure 3.1.2. The terms top-down and bottom-up get used a lot in business. So much so that they have come to mean different things in different contexts. What do I mean when I use these terms in relation to workforce planning? And does top-down always precede bottom-up?

The chapters in this part are divided into top-down and bottom-up. Top-down demand plans can be pushed out to the business for bottom-up positions modelling to take place. Bottom-up positions modelling is done at the Role, Position and People levels and makes the top-down demand plan a reality. But top-down doesn't necessarily need to come first. Sometimes the bottom-up will be done first, and then sense-checked with a top-down focus. Often, they are done simultaneously. Each process tests the thinking of the other. You are effectively scaling up and down a hierarchical structure. The 'top' is the aggregate perspective – the sum. You drill down, through subsections, to the 'bottom'. Think of it like leaves of a tree.

The further you look into the future, the higher up the structural tree you go, to plan at a higher level of aggregation. Longer term, more aggregated and strategic planning is more assumption driven. On the supply side, you'll want to look at attrition, the average time and grade in position or retirement age. On the demand side, you'll want to use drivers and ratios. Top-down tends to be at a higher level of aggregation, longer term in focus (or can be more easily stretched into the future) and 'driven' more by assumptions. It is therefore more aligned with strategic workforce planning. Bottom-up tends to be aligned with operational workforce planning because it's done at a people and position level and is concerned with the in-year budget. Neither process is a starting or finishing point, and the term 'top' doesn't infer that top-down is more important than bottom-up. At the end of the day, it is a process of triangulating.

FIGURE 3.1.2   Target setting is an iterative process with top-down and bottom-up inputs

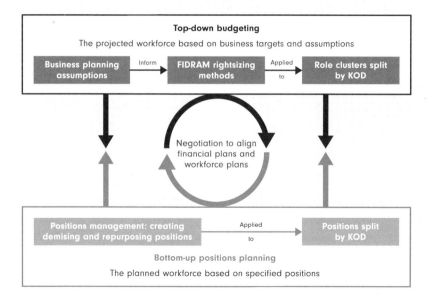

Structure and logic for Part Three

The chapters in this part of the book set out a process to follow for effective workforce planning. As Figure 3.1.3 shows, the process consists of six steps:

1 build the as-is baseline
2 top-down supply forecasting

3 top-down demand planning

4 bottom-up position planning

5 finalize budgets and targets

6 analyse and monitor

FIGURE 3.1.3 The six-step process for effective workforce planning

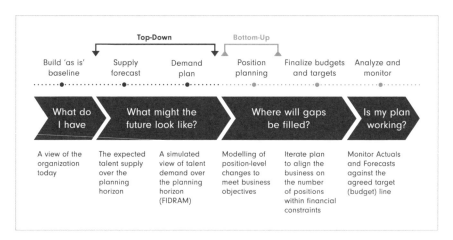

Steps 1 to 3 are covered in Chapter 3.2. The chapter begins by explaining how to set up a baseline of data and why one is needed. You can't confidently plan the supply of workers over time if you don't know your current situation. The baseline of data is crucial for a comprehensive understanding of what your organization looks like today. There are three factors to consider when building your baseline:

1 the time horizon you want to plan over

2 the Key Organizational Dimensions

3 the groups of people you want to plan over

This chapter recaps role families and role clusters, and explains the importance of segmenting role clusters into critical and non-critical categories.

The chapter then moves on to Step 2 and explains what should be considered when making supply projections over the planning horizon, such as current attrition levels, retirement age and dates when any people are due to leave, or new starters are scheduled to join. These supply projections are made with a top-down perspective and scenario modelling is often used.

It then moves on to Step 3: Top-down demand planning. This step translates business strategy into a top-down plan and is where scenario modelling is used to prepare the business for an array of different outcomes. The demand for each role cluster is planned by using a range of methods known as FIDRAM:

- Fixed roles
- Incremental percent
- Driver analysis
- Ratio analysis
- Activity analysis
- Mathematical modelling

These methods are the same as those used to rightsize the organization during the design phase (see *Data-Driven Organization Design*). The difference is that they are used to plan over time in a series of increments (e.g. monthly, quarterly and annually) rather than between two fixed points in time (the 'as-is' and 'to-be' states).

At the end of the steps in Chapter 3.2, the supply of workers can be compared to the top-down demand for the period you are planning over to gain visibility on any gaps between the ideal and actual workforce. The people best qualified to specify how these gaps can be filled may not sit within the OP&A Team, but are the team leaders within the business who manage the role clusters being planned for. There may also be others in the organization who can help, for example the HR Business Partner (HRBP – for an explanation of their role see Chapter 5.3). This is Step 4, bottom-up position planning, which is covered in Chapter 3.3.

Chapter 3.3 starts with bottom-up position planning and explains how the top-down demand plan is made a reality by specifying positions to fill the gaps identified in the previous part of the process. The goal is to model position-level changes to meet business objectives. Much of this chapter is concerned with governance and agreement of the final demand plan. The bottom-up position planning is where you hit reality and realize that not everything asked for in the top-down plan is going to work or can be afforded within budget constraints. The negotiation process is part of Step 5 when the budget and target are finalized. Chapter 3.3 ends with Step 6: Analyse and monitor, when the actual supply of workers over time is managed against the demand.

As these chapters will demonstrate, workforce planning is useful for many things. Not only for understanding and analysing your current workforce and closing the gaps between the two, but also for setting a headcount budget for the year to manage your costs in line with goals, and then monitoring your actual headcount and costs over time. It also provides a fantastic way to manage competencies in your workforce, comparing those of your workforce today with those needed in the future and working out how to fill the gaps. In short, workforce planning is a source of competitive advantage and differentiation and should be a core competence for all organizations. Organizations that fail to do it well suffer a lot of waste and risk losing out to a more streamlined competitor. If you don't scan the future and give yourself the luxury of time to deal with what you see coming, it becomes impossible to effectively manage risk. Following the six steps throughout these chapters breaks down what might first appear a daunting process into clear and comprehensible chunks of work. So let's begin at the beginning: with building the as-is data baseline.

Notes

1   Zuech, T (2020) 3 trends in the Gartner hype cycle for human capital management, Gartner. www.gartner.com/smarterwithgartner/3-trends-in-the-gartner-hype-cycle-for-human-capital-management-2020 (archived at https://perma.cc/4BQW-LP43)
2   CIPD (2021) Workforce planning. www.cipd.co.uk/knowledge/strategy/organisational-development/workforce-planning-factsheet#gref (archived at https://perma.cc/BQ6Z-QQT5)
3   Kaplan, R and Mikes, A (2012) Managing risks: A new framework, *Harvard Business Review*, June. https://hbr.org/2012/06/managing-risks-a-new-framework (archived at https://perma.cc/XVM9-FYUK)

3.2

Supply forecasting and top-down demand planning

Introduction

This chapter covers the first three steps in the workforce planning process:

1 build the as-is baseline

2 top-down supply forecasting

3 top-down demand planning

When you come to the end of these three steps you should have a clear idea of your organization's likely supply of workers over time versus a top-down view of the talent the organization will need in order to continue executing strategy effectively. The demand can be understood not only in terms of headcount numbers and cost but also in terms of the role-specific competencies that are likely to be needed over time. With strategic workforce planning, the focus might be more on core organizational capability areas than individual competencies. As we've seen, VUCA forces mean that things can take unpredictable turns and the needs of the organization will change. The question is *how* those needs will change and what that will mean for the future workforce. Having a heads-up mindset is important to perform these steps well. Horizon scanning and asking What-If questions form a large part of this process. The role of the workforce planner is to make predictions, model scenarios and provide various workforce plan options from which one will be selected for the bottom-up position planning (the subject of Chapter 3.3) to take place. Much of the work that top-down planners do involves encouraging leaders to think strategically about mitigating areas of strategic and external risk. It's not only about identifying that the risk exists but also figuring out if the risk is significant enough for something to be done about it. It is also about 'frontloading' the HR measures following the value chain (for example, adjusting recruiting policy like external hiring versus internal mobility). OP&A works out the detail to make the job of the decision makers easier.

If one thing is for sure, the forecasted supply and top-down demand will never be in alignment over time, and comparing the two will leave you with a gap to fill. There is likely to be an oversupply of workers in some areas and an undersupply in others. The OP&A top-down planners identify these gaps before pushing the plan out to the business to close them. Sometimes gaps can be closed, and sometimes they can't. The strategic workforce planner needs oversight on those that can't be filled so they can work out what to do about it. Can the business still execute strategy despite the gaps, or does something need to be done?

This chapter takes you through how to make top-down supply projections before doing top-down demand planning. This is performed in a very similar way to rightsizing, described briefly in Chapter 1.2 and in full in *Data-Driven Organization Design*. Using one or a selection of the six methods known by the acronym FIDRAM, role clusters can be sized to meet the needs of the future organization. The first step is to build a baseline of data. This involves specifying the scope and reporting periods: the Key Organizational Dimensions, role families and clusters that you want to plan for, and the time horizon you want to plan over.

Step 1: Building the as-is baseline

When setting up your baseline you are effectively building a picture of your current situation. The idea is to determine and structure the data you need to understand the existing supply and demand of workers. This means taking your current workforce, existing productivity ratios, and current assumptions around such things as attrition. You may have improvements planned which will impact your current assumptions, but these do not form part of your baseline.

With luck, and if you have followed the steps outlined in *Data-Driven Organization Design*, you will have sound **master data management** processes in place and your data will be in pretty good shape. If not, refer to the nine-step process in Chapter 4.2 for how to build a data model. The steps below assume that you are working with complete and clean data. They also assume that roles within the organization have been designed to include, at a minimum, the 'must have' data shown in Figure 3.2.1. This figure shows all the various types of data that can be used for role design, but it isn't all vital for workforce planning. The following data must be in place:

- people and position data (headcount FTE and cost per FTE), broken out by roles and KODs (e.g. geography, function, business unit or product)
- role data broken down by level, role family and role cluster

As will become clear later in the chapter, workforce planning is not only about variations in headcount over time. It's also about understanding the *cost* of the workforce at specified points in time, and how this aligns with the Finance function's understanding of cost. For this reason, pay benchmarking data is an example of data which you should have (but it's not 'a must'). It can be helpful when modelling role cost (alongside other costs such as those related to Learning and Development).

The 'good to have' category includes data which isn't necessary, but which can provide huge value. This includes data related to the purpose, objectives and accountabilities for roles, which helps you to understand the work. And as workforce planning is useful for ensuring that the right people are in place with the right *competencies* at the right time, target and actual competency data is extremely valuable to add to the baseline.

FIGURE 3.2.1 The role data needed for workforce planning

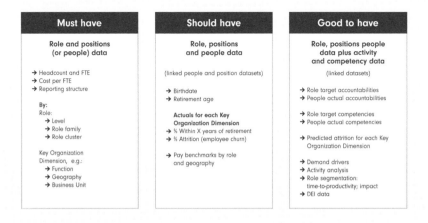

When building your baseline there are three factors to consider:

1 Time horizon
   As explained in Chapter 3.1, this book deals with two types of workforce planning: strategic and operational. Strategic workforce planning looks at supply and demand over a timeframe of multiple years while operational workforce planning focuses on the more immediate 12 to 18 months. The first thing to do is specify how many months or years you want to plan over. The second is to specify the planning cycle within that time frame. This might be monthly, quarterly or annually. The important thing to remember is that in operational workforce planning, the planning cycle should link to the business reporting cadence so that the OP&A function is able to directly feed into the planning and analysis performed by FP&A.

2 Key Organizational Dimensions
   I introduced Key Organizational Dimensions (KODs) in Chapter 1.2. It is essential to segment the organization into KODs and perform workforce planning against each one. This allows you to see such things as where there is oversupply or undersupply (for a particular product or geography, for example). It is also useful because the assumptions you make may not be applicable to the entire organization. For example, attrition may be far higher in London than in Sydney. In London it may be highest in one function, or for one product. Due to the many different variables and drivers in workforce planning it is necessary to segment the workforce and slice and dice the data to get to real insight.

3 Planning scope
   The scope of your planning refers to the KODs to be included in the planning cycles. Which geographies, functions or divisions do you want to include in the planning? Which role families or role clusters? As a reminder, role families are groupings of roles with similar skills, competencies and professional qualifications. Role families are then broken into clusters which are at similar levels on the role grid. Due to the sheer number of roles in most organizations, it is near impossible to perform top-down workforce planning at the role level. It is also difficult to do it at the role family level, due to the huge variation of levels within a single role family, and the fact that those at the top level(s) tend to be fixed and those lower down are variable. It is therefore best done at the role cluster level.

Take the example of a developer (engineer) role family. This role family may be broken into two sub-role families: 'front-end' and 'back-end'. Within the 'front-end' sub-role family, there might be four levels of developer by seven grades:

- Level 1 – Graduate; Engineer
- Level 2 – Senior Engineer; Team Leader
- Level 3 – Team Leader; Architect
- Level 4 – Vice President Engineering

The four roles within Levels 1 and 2 could form one cluster – 'FE Engineers'. The three roles within Levels 3 and 4 could form another – 'FE Engineering Architecture and Management'.

Once you've clarified the clusters you want to plan for, you can determine which ones are the most critical to the organization and therefore should be prioritized when ensuring the supply of resources.

Segmenting role clusters into critical and non-critical categories

Not all roles are created equal, and it is helpful to segment role clusters into those that are crucial to the operation of the business and those that are not. Without segmentation to prioritize role clusters, it's very difficult to know where to focus attention. Often, those who shout the loudest in planning meetings have their role or the roles of their team members prioritized, regardless of the best interests of the business. It's worth mentioning that, depending on the scale of your organization, you may need two workforce planners – someone to consider specific segments of the workforce and the other to look at the total workforce over all planning horizons (see Chapter 5.3).

So how do you objectively determine role criticality? The answer lies in segmenting role clusters according to two factors: **Time To Productivity (TTP)** and **scale of impact**. TTP refers to the average duration, in months, from a position opening to a new position-holder performing productively in the role. It factors in the time it takes to source, onboard and upskill someone so that they can perform effectively. The scale of impact has both positive and negative sides to it. The positive side of impact considers the financial benefit a role-holder could bring to the organization when performing well in their role. The negative side is concerned with the risk the organization would face if the role-holder failed to execute their responsibilities correctly. The critical role clusters are those that deliver high business impact and have high TTP. These roles can be seen in the upper right quadrant of Figure 3.2.2. These roles should be marked as critical and prioritized throughout the workforce planning process.

FIGURE 3.2.2   Segmenting roles by scale of impact and TTP reveals which roles should be prioritized

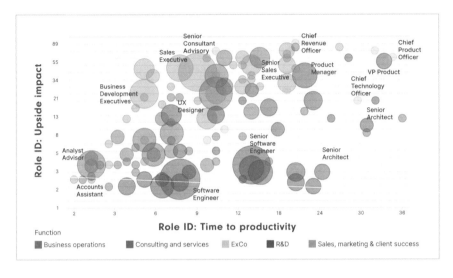

The importance of aligning with Finance

Once the data baseline is set, check for alignment with the Finance function. I've lost count of the number of times I've seen Finance and HR functions have a completely different understanding of headcount cost due to a lack of calibration. Check that any cost-related data aligns with Finance's method for applying a cost to people. Agree definitions and be crystal clear about what is included: is it just base salary, or base plus the expected bonus? How about healthcare, tax or, in the UK, National Insurance? What about an allocation for IT or training, or office costs? Should these be factored into headcount cost?

It's best to do this throughout the supply forecasting and top-down demand planning. Check that figures from Finance align with those being used in the plan, and if they don't, find out why. In Chapter 3.3 I discuss position management. Very often, you find positions which are open, and therefore budgeted for, but not filled by a position-holder. If Finance is including these open positions in their forecasting but HR isn't, there will be a mismatch. The same thing goes for temporary labour – should that be incorporated in forecasting and planning or not? What about how cost is worked out for people who are hired part way through the month? Say someone arrives on 15 April, the headcount cost on 1 April will be different to 31 April and the average cost across the month will be different again. If Finance works from the average figure in April but HR takes the figure from 1 April or 31 April, the numbers won't tally. This might sound like a lot of detail, but these things need to be thought through. Once the baseline data-set has been reviewed and checked with Finance, you're ready to move on to Step 2: supply forecasting.

Step 2: Top-down supply forecasting

Making supply projections is all about understanding how your current headcount (or your baseline) is likely to change over specified time periods, according to natural forces. A supply projection factors in such things as standard level of attrition based on historical data, retirement age, known hiring and the people known to be leaving open positions. The point is to only factor in natural forces that can be predicted by looking at past data. You want to know what the supply of your workforce would look like if nothing changed. More strategically focused supply projections will be done over a period of several years, while operational projections are done for the more immediate 12 to 18 months.

As with most things, there are varying degrees of complexity you can go to when performing this exercise. At the most basic level, it is a simple fact-gathering exercise which asks questions about the known headcount and current known changes to that headcount:

- When do contracts for temporary labour end?
- When are the new starters scheduled to join?
- What is the TTP for each role?
- What is the headcount and associated cost per role cluster?
- Using date of birth data and the known retirement age, what proportion of the workforce is heading towards retirement? How does this break down across KODs or role clusters?
- What do historical and current attrition rates look like and can these be used to predict future attrition?

This last point is where things start to get more complex. Future attrition is not a simple thing to predict. While, at the most basic level, it is possible to extrapolate future figures by looking at historical data, applying a blanket percentage will never give you an accurate view. Machine learning algorithms can be helpful when predicting attrition. They use conditional probability applied to various drivers, but they should be used with caution as they don't factor in external risk and they need to be used in combination with human thought (for more, see Chapter 4.3).

By looking at the data, you might be able to identify tipping points for positions when people are more likely to leave. For example, there may be time-in-grade thresholds whereby if someone has been in the same grade for a period without being promoted, they will leave, or a graduate might stay in a position for two to three years to gain experience before moving on to try something different. This understanding not only helps with calculating attrition levels but also with succession planning, which I looked at in Chapter 2.4. For most organizations, it doesn't make sense to have a single attrition figure for the entire business. Attrition is likely to be different over KODs, role clusters and business units so algorithms can be used to ascertain the different percentages which should be applied.

The above questions will help you to plan scenarios to understand the supply forecast by period, dimension and role family or cluster, as shown in Figure 3.2.3. The supply projections can then be put to one side while top-down demand planning takes place.

Step 3: Top-down demand planning

Top-down demand planning translates the business strategy into a top-down plan and is best done in close collaboration with FP&A. It plans the number and type of FTEs required over time in each area of the business so that strategy can be executed on an ongoing basis.

The point of top-down demand planning is to ensure the right number of people with the right competencies are doing the right work in the right place over time. You're determining the numbers needed over a specified period, who should go where, at what point, and when you might need to recruit new talent or move people around the organization. Unlike supply forecasting, you're no longer assuming that it will be 'business as usual'. Different assumptions are used to plan scenarios and prepare the business for a range of outcomes. The objective is to ensure that the workforce is in

FIGURE 3.2.3 Supply projections over time by product and function

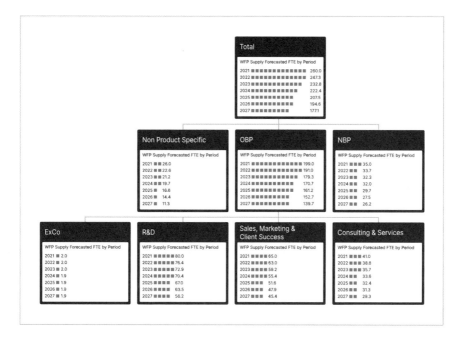

place to respond to the external environment to achieve long-term strategic evolutions. The type and number of resources is planned for by asking questions such as:

- What does a given scenario 'look like'?
- How big would the change be from the expected line?
- How does it compare with a different scenario or the current headcount?

Remember Eisenhower's quote in Chapter 1.3: 'Planning is everything. The plan is nothing.' At no point in recent memory has this been truer than when the Covid-19 pandemic hit. The extreme unpredictability of the year 2020 taught us the value of planning for different scenarios and how that planning helps you to adapt at a moment's notice to a seismic shock. At Hokupaa, three scenarios were planned for:

1 U shape – a scenario where financial performance would dip, things would get difficult, but business as usual would soon resume

2 W shape – a scenario which factored in a second wave. Financial performance would dip and rebound as in the U shape, but it would then dip again.

3 L shape – a worst-case scenario, in which financial performance would dip, and stay down for a long time.

Modelling these three scenarios gave a clear vision of possible futures, even though it was an unprecedented path characterized by external influences. The second scenario on the list, that of the W shape, reflected what was expected, but it would have been dangerous to plan on this alone. The U shape reflected the best-case scenario, and the L shape reflected the worst-case scenario. Assumption-based planning always needs to follow this logic, as discussed in Chapter 1.3. Take attrition – you might assume that it's going to be 15 per cent, but it could be as low as 10 per cent or as high as 30. It is important to test out different strategies for meeting a challenge. How deep and how long can a drop in the demand be before the business gets into trouble? What early indicators can be used to base decisions on about downsizing or cost-cutting?

The importance of agreeing a budget philosophy

It is extremely helpful, if not vital, for a budget philosophy to be agreed. This will usually come from the Executive Team, and in particular the CEO and CFO when determining priorities at the start of the financial year. As will become clear in Chapter 3.3, once bottom-up position plans are submitted for approval, there is often a negotiation to decide where priorities lie. It's where you meet reality and find that, very often, top-down plans cannot be executed as intended. Certain things will inevitably need to be held back for future years, depending on what is affordable, and very often trade-offs need to be made. Being clear about the business priorities from the start matters. Think back to Chapter 1.3 and the mindset needed to work in FP&A. These are the kind of questions which need to be asked for a budget philosophy to be agreed:

- Are you optimizing new growth or do you need to balance growth with profitability?
- Have you identified your must-wins that can't be compromised, no matter what?
- Where do you need to invest the most? Should you scale marketing, different regions or certain R&D investments? Reflect on the objectives devised in the design phase of the work. Which objective is the most important?

As part of this process, be clear about the governance structure and who has veto power on the trade-off decisions that need to be made. I'll explain this in more detail in Chapter 3.3. The rest of this chapter is concerned with the methodologies which can be used to devise a top-down demand plan. To do this we use FIDRAM: six data-driven methods for determining the optimal size for role clusters over time.

FIDRAM: Six methods for performing top-down demand planning

FIDRAM is an acronym for:

- Fixed roles
- Incremental percent
- Driver analysis
- Ratio analysis
- Activity analysis
- Mathematical modelling

You may be familiar with FIDRAM from *Data-Driven Organization Design*. The methods are used to rightsize the to-be organization during the design phase of work. Rightsizing, like the rest of organization design, is done for a fixed point in time. In workforce planning, the FIDRAM methods are used to plan demand over an array of time points. Scenario modelling is used to project an array of possible futures, and determine the type and size of the workforce needed to continue executing strategy in each one.

Each of the FIDRAM methods described below provides a robust way to plan workforce demand over time. You may want to use just one of the methods, or combine them. It depends on the role cluster you are planning for. The simplest way to plan the demand is to use the fixed roles and incremental percent methods, and these may be sufficient for many role clusters. For more advanced scenario modelling you will need an understanding of your internal business drivers, such as revenue and number of customers, and use the other methods such as driver and ratio analysis to model and simulate demand.

Workforce planning can get political. How functions and teams are resourced can be the subject of much dispute and tension within organizations, so I recommend that you take the time to engage stakeholders who are responsible for the bottom-up position planning up front before the plans are pushed down to them. If there are contentious points, explain the rationale behind the demand projections and your reasons for choosing method(s) to size the role clusters, as well as the assumptions that have been made in the modelling process. This is best done one to one, rather than in an open forum. It can also be helpful to demonstrate the depth of thinking, showing the different options and worked-through scenarios, with the pros and cons. Transparency and objectivity ought to be your top priorities throughout this process.

I'll now explain each of the six FIDRAM workforce planning methods in turn, as shown in Figure 3.2.4.

METHOD 1: FIXED ROLES

This first method is the most straightforward and should be applied to any fixed roles in the organization. As a reminder, when defining role data you would have identified which roles are fixed, and which are **variable**. There's only one position for fixed roles: in other words, the number of positions does not vary according to volumes of work, no matter what time horizon you are planning over. These are typically the roles at the top of the organization which have a strategic focus – for example, the CEO, CFO, CMO or CHRO.

METHOD 2: INCREMENTAL PERCENT

The incremental percent method is a simple way of determining how much you want to increase or decrease investment in an area over time. You would start with your baseline (your supply) and estimate an annual growth rate in headcount for an area you expect will require more investment in the future. Alternatively, you might expect to improve efficiency through process automation. This would result in a reduction in headcount over time.

METHOD 3: DRIVER ANALYSIS

Driver analysis is used for variable roles and is the main method used to model 'What-If' scenarios, alongside ratio analysis. First identify the driver influencing a change in the number and/or type of FTEs and then ask what the impact would be if that driver changed. This method is a suitable one to pick if the following factors apply:

- There is one or several variable drivers which impact on the demand for FTEs.

FIGURE 3.2.4 FIDRAM: The recommended methods to use for planning demand over time

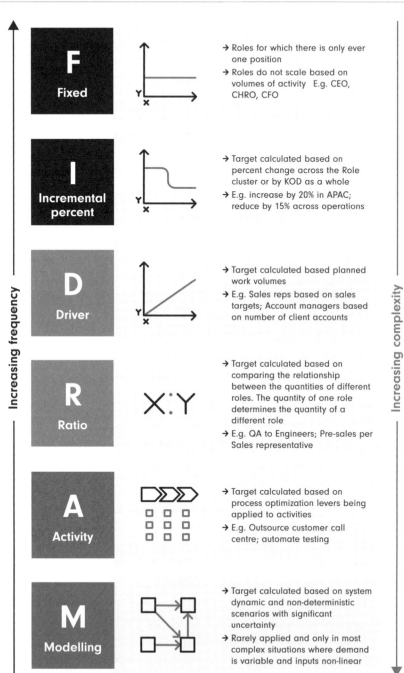

- There are significant numbers of FTEs performing the role, and therefore opportunities for benefits to be delivered.
- The driver(s) is quantifiable and measurable.

There are six steps for performing driver analysis:

1 Categorize roles into fixed or variable and focus on those that are variable.
2 Define the list of drivers that impact the demand for FTEs. These are typically a blend of context (e.g. technology use) and volume drivers.
3 Model and analyse by projecting the impact for FTEs based on 'What-If' scenarios.
4 Visualize and sense check, and remodel as necessary.
5 Estimate FTE requirements.
6 Check if the FTE requirements are affordable.

The list of drivers which can impact on the number and type of FTEs can be long. Take, for example, a call centre. The drivers determining the number of call centre agents needed to answer calls could include:

- the number of calls
- the duration of calls
- the service levels demanded by the customer
- the proportion of calls which could be dealt with by a chatbot
- the extent to which artificial intelligence is used to help agents with their responses
- the time it takes to resolve a case (which would be influenced by both the experience of the agent and the use of AI to determine responses for quick resolution)

Call centres are increasing leveraging technology such as automation to increase efficiency, reduce costs and improve the customer experience. This continues to have a significant impact on the drivers determining the number of call centre agents required. In most call centres, people are still required to answer more complex queries or be there to take over if the technology breaks down – for example if the automatic speech recognition fails or the chatbot can't resolve a query. The role of the workforce planner in this context would be to estimate how the demand for FTEs is likely to be impacted as technology continues to improve over the next five, 10 or 15 years. Will still fewer agents be needed? Will customers be satisfied with speaking to bots or will they demand more? Will there be an increased need for people elsewhere, for example an online live chat service? Will the people delivering the live chat service need a different skillset to those on the phone? What is the TTP for a live chat service role? If people are redeployed from the phones to the website, could they be up and running straight away? What about customer behaviour? As live chat becomes more prevalent, what proportion of customers is likely to use live chat instead of calling, thereby reducing the number of calls? Or, as live chat is a great way to increase leads, is that likely to increase your customer base over time, thereby creating a greater need not only for live chat agents but for call centre agents too? There is a huge array of drivers (so many, in fact, that Method 6 – mathematical modelling – may well be needed in this scenario). The point is that there are numerous What-If questions to consider when thinking driver analysis through.

In areas of an organization employing agile methodologies, a driver would be the number of epics or big programmes of work which need to be delivered. Each epic has a fixed scope of time which is ordinarily six to nine months, and will have a Mission Team assigned to it, so the number of epics dictate the number of Mission Teams. A typical Mission Team might include:

- Developers (6.0 FTE)
- Product Manager (1.0 FTE)
- QA Manager (1.0 FTE)
- Engineering Manager (0.5 FTE)

Ratio analysis can be used to work out how many Developers there should be to Product Managers or QA Managers. This is the fourth method – ratio analysis.

METHOD 4: RATIO ANALYSIS

Ratio analysis tells you how much of one thing there is relative to another thing. From a workforce planning point of view, a ratio is typically used to determine the number or cost of one role cluster, compared to another. Ratios can be used to size specific functions or role clusters, to show, for example, whether the FTEs in one role cluster make sense in the context of the number in another role cluster, or the total number of FTEs in the organization. In the agile example given above, ratios can be used to make sure Mission Teams include the right mix and number of people. For example, a team with only four Developers instead of six is likely to be suboptimal. Not only will it not get through the required work, but the Product Manager and QA Manager will not be leveraged sufficiently.

Ratios are calculated by using a numerator and denominator, for example, number of clients/business development executives. The data used should include headcount data as well as financial data and volume or output data. Combining data in this way can give an idea of whether the headcount in a certain area makes sense in the context of the revenue or profit that cluster is expected to generate over time.

Examples of finance ratios include:

- What percentage is labour of the total cost (labour costs : total costs)?

- How much of the costs of goods sold should people represent?

Examples of headcount data ratios include:

> Junior UX Designers : Senior UX Designers

> Software Developers : Quality Engineers

Volume or output data relates to the number of items produced, clients serviced, invoices processed, employees recruited, calls received, etc. Volume or output data ratios could be

> number of recruiters : employees recruited

The ratios used to size role clusters vary according to industry. Some can be interpreted as a productivity number (for example, revenue generated per consultant in a consultancy firm) while others are about balance (for example, the number of software developers per quality assurance engineer in a software development company).

There is a caveat. While ratio analysis is undoubtedly a useful way to size the workforce, be careful not to assume there's a magic number which gives 'the answer'. Such a number does not exist. A very common example of this is to use a ratio stipulating that for every 100 people in an organization there should be one HR person. But this approach is short-sighted and ignores the broader context or what each HR person does as part of their role. If you're working out ratios for Mission Teams, don't assume you need what I've suggested above. Think about what is right for your own organization. For example, how much of a QA burden is there on the team, and how much test-drive development does the Development Team do? Is testing automated? If it is, the need to do QA is reduced. Another example is span of control – the ideal is assumed to be eight, but this doesn't mean there won't be exceptions to this rule. There is always a range of questions to consider when determining which ratios to use. It's always best to use a series of ratios, rather than relying on just one.

METHOD 5: ACTIVITY ANALYSIS

Activity analysis is a fantastic way to plan future demand. I introduced Individual Activity Analysis (IAA) and the eight enhancement levers in the Reduce, Reallocate, Improve and Invest (RRII) framework in Chapter 1.2. As a reminder, the IAA documents how much time each person spends on the main activities required to perform in their role. It also asks people more qualitative questions such as: Do they enjoy the task? Could the work be improved? What level or authority do they have when performing it? How much rework is required? In short, it gives you a huge amount of information about the work currently being performed by the workforce and allows you to see the cost of every process and activity. Armed with this information, you can plan your future organization and future workforce around the highest value generating activities.

Data gathered in IAA can be analysed to get insight into how the organization is really working, answering questions such as:

- How many FTEs are involved in each process?
- What is the average cost and range of grades working on each activity?
- What percentage of time or cost is going into particular processes or types of processes?
- Are people spending their time on the right work for their role?

Based on the number of FTEs involved in each process and the amount of time they put into it, you can see your people cost rolled up in the context of your processes. From here, you can spot where efficiencies need to be made or reallocate resources across role clusters appropriately. You can see where there is a lack of investment, as well as which of the eight enhancement levers in the RRII framework need to be pulled to optimize activities over time, and what that would mean for the sizing of role clusters:

- Are there activities which should be stopped completely or reduced?

- Could any activities be consolidated by rationalizing the number of people involved? For example, if 10 employees spend 10 per cent of their time on the same activity, could this activity be reallocated to one FTE who costs less? Consolidating often results in a reduction of effort, so is linked with the 'reduce' lever.

- Should any work be reassigned to another role cluster within the same role family? This is useful if senior roles are doing work which could be carried out by a more junior, lower-cost employee.

- Could any work be reallocated to a lower-cost location?

- Could any repeatable, transactional activities such as manual data input can be automated? Could any non-critical, low value-adding work be outsourced to where it can be done more effectively: for example, a third-party provider could be employed for payroll. Remember that automating and outsourcing activities isn't just about reducing headcount. Think more in terms of freeing people up to focus on more value-adding work. If you have an oversupply of workers in an area because you are planning to automate processes, where can those workers be moved to instead to make the most of their skills?

- Does any existing activity need increased investment?

- Do you need to start any new activities to keep up with market trends? When considering the headcount implications associated with the invest lever, think whether employees no longer required on activities which are to be reduced or improved could be moved onto activities where investment is focused.

It's not just about headcount   In workforce planning, headcount and cost are often the focus. After all, that's what the executive committee is most interested in – whether the cost of the workforce can be adequately managed in line with the budget. But there is another key angle to think about when performing demand planning – that of how the competencies required to continue executing strategy might change over time, and how you can best prepare the organization for the shifting landscape.

This ties in with using activity analysis to size role clusters. As organizations adapt and evolve, some activities will no longer be necessary while new ones will come to the fore. This will inevitably mean that the demand for competencies will change. An obvious example is the impact of automation or digitization, as discussed above. When you automate a task, the competencies previously required to do that task are no longer required. At the same time, a need for other competencies might emerge elsewhere. If you can redeploy someone to another part of the business rather than letting them go, that is by far a preferable option, both legally and morally. It's crucial that workforce planners understand how to move people around the organization so that required competencies are in place when needed, both over longer time horizons and within the shorter time frames of operational workforce planning, which I return to in Chapter 3.3.

METHOD 6: MATHEMATICAL MODELLING

Mathematical modelling can be incredibly useful in scenarios where there are system dynamics impacts, such as trying to size complex pathways where the demand and productivity are variable or when the drivers are neither linear nor deterministic in nature. It provides a fantastic way of testing hypotheses and scenarios in complex situations. Increasingly, organizations are leveraging simulation technology to perform mathematical modelling, when outputs are looped back and transformed into inputs, and calculated within the model to give alternative outcomes.

The use of **feedback loops** is what sets simulation apart from other types of scenario modelling. It gives you a more realistic representation of reality, and immediate feedback on the effects of pulling levers such as increasing or decreasing headcount for role clusters, redeploying people to a different part of the organization, outsourcing work or automating processes. It allows you to see what the supply of workers would need to be if attrition was 10, 15 or 30 per cent, or if growth was x or y. The point is to plan for possible futures and understand the variability. These outcomes are not always deterministic: a change in one part of the system can have an unexpected impact on another part of the system, which makes this type of scenario modelling near impossible to perform in a linear system such as Excel.

Setting the demand plan and understanding the gap

Once you have specified a planning assumption for each role cluster according to the appropriate FIDRAM method(s) you will have your demand plan, as shown in Figure 3.2.5. Viewed by period, dimension and role family or cluster, the demand can then be directly compared to the supply to highlight gaps that need to be filled between the ideal and actual workforce, as shown in Figure 3.2.6. Visualized in this way, you can clearly see where the business requires investment.

There is almost always a gap between the demand and supply of the workforce. Demand might be greater than supply or supply greater than demand. The questions to ask are why the gap exists, and whether it matters. Is it something to be concerned about, and does action need to be taken? How urgent is it? Is it a fundamental issue which needs a root and branch investigation or just an imbalance that needs to be addressed? To answer the question about how concerning the gap is, think about the impact it will have on achieving business objectives. Which targets do you run the risk of missing if the gap is not closed? Find ways to describe the implications in these terms. You could, for example, assess the impact on EBITDA, cash burn or growth targets, or you might be able to articulate how long a product will be delayed getting to market.

Top-down projections can stipulate a permitted gap, both in terms of FTE numbers and compensation per role cluster. This can be expressed as a percentage. It's likely that for some role clusters, a certain percentage could be tolerated for the business to continue executing strategy. Could there be 5 or 10 per cent leeway either way, or should there be leeway for undersupply and not oversupply? It's useful to test high-level options for how to close the gap at this stage. This can be used to guide the bottom-up position planning (see Chapter 3.3).

The important thing is to make all this comprehensible for business leaders and instil confidence that have you have thought through the detail. Their job

FIGURE 3.2.5 The demand plan by period, dimension and role cluster

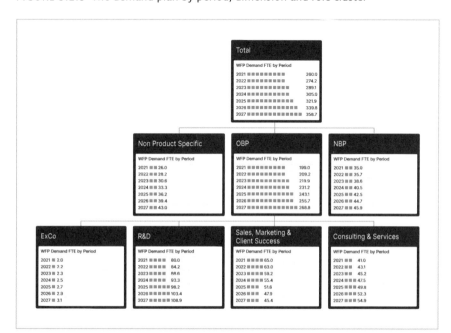

FIGURE 3.2.6 Understanding the gap between demand and supply

is to decide where to prioritize investment and/or force cost reductions. Give them the chance to kick the tyres on your thinking. Highlight areas of concern to help direct focus (as a rule of thumb, highlight between three and seven issues). If supply is greater than demand, is this a concern? Can the excess supply be reallocated elsewhere, or might natural attrition deal with the problem? If so, how many months will it take to resolve? Alternatively, can the organization absorb the extra supply provided there is a hiring freeze, or might it be necessary to put a redundancy process in place? Do the thinking for them. Keep bringing it back to strategy and the most important business objectives. Identify the biggest gaps, explain the assumptions used in the sensitivity analysis as well as which assumptions, if wrong, will result in you missing a target by the largest amount. Also highlight those assumptions which are the least certain (these are those with the greatest level of volatility – see Chapter 1.3). The more you can encourage leaders to think strategically about the gaps that exist and how to fill those that matter, the more they will anticipate risks and deal with them before they become a problem.

Final thoughts

The more thorough the top-down process, the less onerous the bottom-up one will be. Top-down planning is as much about thinking and discussion as it is about the mechanics of an analytical planning process. The efficiency of the process is important – the ease with which you can change an assumption or run a scenario will materially improve your ability to think, ask and answer scenario questions and test the plan. This, in turn, builds confidence that a variety of outcomes have been thought through. So much of successful top-down planning comes down to the questions that you ask. Asking the right questions allows you to cut to the heart of an issue so that decisions can be made. What if you won a major contract, entered a new region, or accelerated your roadmap? What gap would this create from a workforce perspective, and where would investment be needed? Identifying that demand is greater than supply is one thing, but this means little unless you also spell out whether this matters and what the impact will be. Where will it be felt and who should care? Do those who need to care know about it, and what do they think? Are they concerned, and, if so, what about?

REMEMBER THIS

1   Supply projections allow you to understand how your current headcount is likely to change over specified time periods, according to natural forces.

2   It's crucial to check that your data aligns with Finance throughout the planning process.

3   Top-down demand planning ensures that the workforce is in place to respond to the external environment to achieve long-term strategic evolutions.

4   Supply and demand are not only about headcount and cost. They should also factor in role-specific competencies that are likely to be needed over time.

5   The top-down workforce plan highlights the gap between supply and top-down demand. It is helpful to give a high-level view of how the gap can be closed.

3.3

Bottom-up position planning, finalizing the workforce plan and monitoring progress

Introduction

Bottom-up position planning takes the top-down demand plan and makes it a reality. A significant part of OP&A's role in this process revolves around negotiating trade-offs between the mathematically driven top-down plan and what the bottom-up planners feel is achievable in practice. Throughout the top-down process, the headcount requirements necessary to fulfil strategic goals will have been stipulated. This top-down plan is used to guide the bottom-up planners in terms of headcount and cost requirements. The aim is to hit organizational objectives within constraints, which can be difficult to execute. The workforce planner needs to understand where there is alignment, as well as where exceptions should be made. This can be an emotional process as it's often the case that there's more headcount than the business requires. It can also be difficult when significantly more heads are needed to execute strategy.

A significant part of OP&A's role in this process is to set up a framework for delegation. In large organizations, role clusters are assigned to designated individuals for them to model the necessary position-level changes. These individuals are tasked with adding or removing positions and specifying the scope of new positions. Bottom-up position planning is more often performed with an operational focus rather than a strategic one, so the time horizons are likely to be comparatively short – 12 to 18 months into the future rather than several years.

Bottom-up planning is not dissimilar to the process followed when building out the structure and positions in organization design (see Chapter 3.7 of

Data-Driven Organization Design). Many of the same principles apply. Positions are specified according to designed roles and within the Key Organizational Dimensions. Design principles are adhered to as closely as possible (for example, avoiding one-to-one reporting, while also checking that managers have a practical number of direct reports). Designated planners need time to reflect on their work to check that their specifications make sense and are practical. The difference is that bottom-up planning is done for a designated time period, rather than a to-be photographic snapshot. The start and end dates of positions are important, and the principles of position lifecycle management come into play.

This chapter details the second half of the six-step workforce planning process:

- Step 4: Bottom-up position planning
- Step 5: Finalize budgets and targets
- Step 6: Analyse and monitor

I give a step-by-step guide to the bottom-up position planning process, including how to specify the scope for positions and things that can go wrong. Once the bottom-up plan has been submitted for approval there is usually a negotiation before the budgets and targets are finalized – this is Step 5. Very often, agreement is reached by combining top-down and bottom-up plans, and I discuss the need for clarity about who has the final say. Once the agreed plan has been put into action, this becomes the target line, and operational workforce planning manages the ever-shifting workforce on a month-by-month basis against this target. This is Step 6, where I introduce Target, Actual and Forecast (TAF) monitoring. I discuss the need to understand the competencies possessed by people in the organization, as oversupply and undersupply of workers can sometimes be addressed by internal mobility rather than recruitment. But first, I'll begin with the need for OP&A to clarify the workflow and set up the governance process.

Defining governance and workflow

As Figure 3.3.1 shows, the executive, FP&A and OP&A Teams are responsible for developing the top-down business plan. This is then developed by the FP&A and OP&A Teams, who model scenarios and plan the number of FTEs required per role cluster. This is the process described in Chapter 3.2.

This chapter describes the responsibility of stakeholders shown on the far right of Figure 3.3.1, and the interactions between these stakeholders and the FP&A and OP&A Teams. Once the top-down plan has been finalized, each executive committee member cascades their plan down through the organization, where team managers execute the plan, performing bottom-up position planning to detail what the organization will look like over time. The bottom-up plans are then sent back up through the organization for approval. A good way to think of it is central control and local work – arming local contributors with the top-down projection and gap analysis and empowering them to plan their own teams. It can be understood through the acronym READ:

- **R**equest – The OP&A Team put in a request to the business to do bottom-up position modelling, providing them with the top-down plan and gap analysis.

- **E**dit – Individual business leaders edit the plans to close the gap between supply and demand. This is typically done with support from the HR Business Partner (HRBP – for more about this role, see Chapter 5.3). The OP&A Team, in turn, support that business partner. (This is likely to be the case in large-scale organizations. In smaller organizations without the HRBP model, this would just be done by the OP&A Team.)

- **A**pprove – The edits are agreed through an approval process, with individuals at varying levels of the organization given responsibility to approve, push back or make necessary changes (this is done at Step 5 when budgets and targets are being finalized).

- **D**istribute – The approved plan is distributed so that all those involved in the management of positions over time are in the picture, from Talent Acquisition Managers to individual Team Managers.

Distributing the input: Assigning delegated planners and local contributors

The first step is for the workforce planner in the OP&A Team to assign the delegated planners throughout the organization. The delegated planners are the business leaders with responsibility for conducting the bottom-up plans. They can be assigned according to KODs and role clusters. For example, if the KODs are function, geography and business unit, the person responsible for UX design (business unit) in Europe (geography) which sits within the

FIGURE 3.3.1 Distribution of position planning work throughout the organization

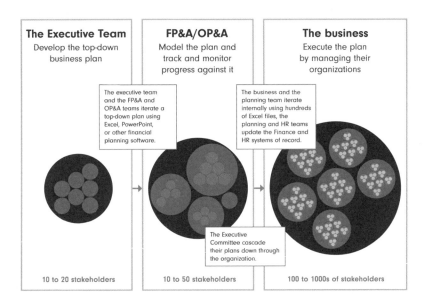

Research and Development function could be asked to plan the role clusters within UX design. These clusters could include the roles: UX Design Lead; UX Design Senior; UX Design Junior. As part of this delegation, the workforce planner should clearly communicate the following:

- the deadline for the work
- the primary objectives of the bottom-up planning process
- the degree of latitude that the delegated planners have: for example, are they expected to hit the top-down financial target and headcount exactly, or is a certain percentage of variance allowed? Figure 3.3.2 shows a permitted gap from the top-down projection, in terms of both FTE and compensation

At this stage, the OP&A workforce planner can also stipulate whether single-level or multi-level delegation is permitted, which also has implications for the approval process. Figure 3.3.2 shows that the delegated planner may be given the option to delegate the bottom-up planning further to local contributors, for each KOD and role cluster. In the scenario shown, multi-level delegation is permitted for the Product Managers and UX Designers. Rita is the delegated planner for these role clusters, but she has the option to push this down further to Paul and Arthur: Paul to plan for the Product Managers and Arthur to plan for the UX Designers. However, for lead generation, pre-sales and direct sales only one level of delegation is allowed. In cases such as this, the delegated planner ordinarily performs the bottom-up modelling.

Figure 3.3.2 also shows a Give and Get matrix for this process. As explained in Chapter 2.2, this matrix is a way of visualizing the interface design. It defines how work flows between people and stipulates the handoffs to ensure that nothing falls through the cracks. As can be seen, the delegated planner (or local contributor) 'gets' the following to complete the work:

- clarification about which role cluster(s) they have responsibility for planning
- the KODs relevant for the role cluster(s)
- the top-down demand plan for the role cluster(s) stipulating the number of FTEs required based on business assumptions and volume drivers
- the overall cost associated with the number of FTEs for each role cluster by time period
- current positions in the role cluster which can be selected to fill the gaps between the demand and the supply

Once they have completed the modelling, they 'give' the following:

- input to create, demise or repurpose positions in the time period
- submission of the bottom-up plan to the delegated planner or the OP&A workforce planner for approval

Central control: Assigning approvers

Assigning approvers is done in much the same way as delegating planners. Depending on whether there is multi- or single-level delegation, there will either be one or two levels of approval, and the person responsible for delegating work to people further down the organization is also the person responsible for approving it once it has been done. So, if the bottom-up planning is pushed down to local contributor level, the delegated planner will approve the work before submitting it to the OP&A workforce planner for final approval. If the delegated planner has done the bottom-up modelling, it gets submitted directly to the OP&A workforce planner. Whoever the plan gets submitted to, there will ordinarily be a negotiation and trade-offs will need to be made. It's therefore vital that before the bottom-up modelling begins, all parties are happy that the delegation and approval structure is in place. This involves ensuring that it is fit for purpose, and checking that things are at just the right level: there should be just enough control, just enough information and just enough people involved. It's another Goldilocks Dilemma. There should be clear boundaries but also maximum delegation to the bottom-up planners. After all, they know their area of the business the best.

FIGURE 3.3.2 Bottom-up position planning is managed by delegation and approval flow

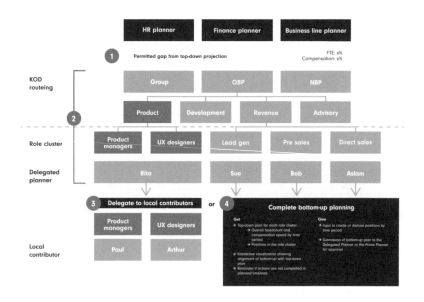

Step 4: Conduct bottom-up position planning

Armed with the top-down target figures of FTE and compensation by period, the bottom-up planner then specifies positions within their role cluster(s) for the time period being planned over. This requires deciding between the following three actions:

1 creating new positions (giving a start date for when someone needs to be in place)

2 demising positions (giving an end date for the position)

3 repurposing positions

Each position can be given a position title (for example, if a role title is Senior Sales Director, a position title could be Senior Sales Director, Financial Services), a set of reporting lines, a desired start and end date (apart from permanent positions which do not have end dates) and approval status. There are different levels of complexity when performing this work: planners might simply be required to focus on selecting simple position-level changes involved in the first two actions. Creating and demising positions is reasonably straightforward but should be performed within the context of position lifecycle management (see below). Repurposing positions is more complex. Bottom-up planners may decide to either move positions around or redesign their attributes according to the cost constraints in the top-down plan. There are times when a position might need small tweaks made to it, for example in terms of its scope and accountabilities, but it is, in essence, still the same position. There are also times when a position requires an amount of change that would effectively make it a new role, and in cases like this it is important not to just rename the position, but demise it, create a new one reflecting the changes that need to be made, and move the person from the demised position to the new one. It's very important that you don't just rename the position. Not only can this interfere with data integrity, but the person whose position has changed needs to think of it as a new role with new accountabilities.

Specifying positions according to Key Organizational Dimensions

Using the reference points from the top-down planning (for example, the top-down demand plan and the KODs relevant to the role cluster), the scope of new positions can be defined by specifying what is needed in terms of remit, location and reporting hierarchy. The bottom-up planner needs a solid understanding of how the organization is designed around the KODs, as they define how work in the organization is broken down into roles and positions and are used to determine reporting lines. Each time a new position is added, it is defined in relation to the relevant KODs. Figure 3.3.3 illustrates how the Marketing function at Hokupaa is broken down according to territory. The teams reporting into the VP of Marketing are Digital Marketing, Demand Generation, Product Marketing and Brand Communications. This part of the position hierarchy focuses on the reporting line to the Head of Demand Generation. This is a fixed role, so the number of positions doesn't vary according to the volume of work or organization dimensions. The level below the Head of Demand Generation is the Business Development Executive Coach. This role is variable, and the number of positions required is dependent on territory. There is one for each region: North America; Europe, the Middle East and Africa (EMEA); and Asia–Pacific (APAC). Say the organization strategy is to scale by entering new territories, it may follow that the top-down demand plan asks for further BDE Coaches reporting into the Head of Demand Generation. Each BDE Coach has a team of BDEs, organized by client segment within the territory served, so these positions would also need to be added, specifying the territory, client segment and the manager or managers. The bottom-up planner adds positions into the structure according to the number specified in the top-down plan. As an aside, positions can sit in multiple different reporting hierarchies in matrixed designs. So, a position might be specified according to remit of coverage (such as a BDE) or a responsibility for key clients. It could also be specified according to geographic location or the location within the organization. Aim to sort the solid lines first but document where a dotted line (for a matrix or agile work) is needed.

Taking the time to reflect

An important aspect of bottom-up position planning is taking time to reflect on the positions that have been specified in adherence with the top-down plan and ensure they make sense in the context of the role cluster(s). One aspect to think through is practicalities. It may sound obvious, but is there enough physical space to accommodate the number of positions asked for in the top-down plan? This is something that can be overlooked. In the past I worked with a client who wanted to scale from 100 to 800 people very quickly, but they hadn't thought to add up the bottom-up requests. Once we had done that, they realized that they didn't have enough space or desks to accommodate the number of people they wanted to hire, and it wasn't possible for them to scale at that speed. Their programme plan and their workforce plan were completely disconnected. It is worth mentioning here that physical

FIGURE 3.3.3 The Marketing function broken down by territory

space is less of a concern in the post-Covid world, as so many of us have become accustomed to working from home. It has become a significant lever for cost optimization as many companies are reducing office space. In this way, facility management is another stakeholder for workforce planning.

In *Data-Driven Organization Design*, I spent a lot of time discussing managerial burden and the **span of control**. The span of control is the total number of direct reports supervised by a People Manager. Small spans are indicative of excessive management overhead whereas with wide spans there is a danger of insufficient oversight. For many years, management consultants have worked out the span of control as a ratio. I don't believe it's possible to find an ideal span of control. There are many different factors which drive management complexity and the overall burden of each manager, such as the experience, performance and location of the direct reports. A **Management Complexity Index (MCI)** can be used to quantify these burdens. This aspect also needs checking by the bottom-up planner (and those with responsibility for approving the bottom-up plans) once new positions have been specified. In the example given in Figure 3.3.3, the BDE Coach of North America already has eight direct reports. The whole of the APAC region has four BDEs reporting into one BDE coach. The question is whether this should be allowed, as it falls below the ideal span of control. The answer is that it should. Only four BDEs are required, because APAC is newer, and focused on two smaller regions within that huge territory (Australia and New Zealand – ANZ; and Hong Kong and Singapore – HK–Singapore). The physical and time zone differences between APAC, EMEA and North America would make it impractical for the APAC BDEs to report into a coach in one of the latter two territories. Additionally, Hokupaa has ambitions to grow in APAC, so this structure and investment in an APAC coach makes sense and a span of control of four is therefore acceptable.

The top-down plan for the example given in Figure 3.3.3 was based on global lead generation and sales targets. The plan called for 18 BDEs and two coaches, so a ratio of nine BDEs to one coach. In the top-down plan this was seen as a perfect ratio, but it failed to recognize the need for a separate coach in APAC and Singapore because of time zone differences and physical distance. The bottom-up modelling recognized the need for a third coach and another BDE in APAC, resulting in 19 BDEs in total and three coaches, a ratio of 6.2:1 instead of 9:1. This is a perfect example of the natural conflict between the top-down and bottom-up processes. The top-down model was fine, but it wasn't done at the KOD level. The bottom-up modelling brings another level of reality.

Top-down demand planning and bottom-up position planning often involve a fine balancing act between managing business need and cost constraints. Remember that it is not just FTE numbers which are specified in the top-down plan, but the costs associated with them. After all, this is what the Executive Team and the CFO will jump to first. This is where reality starts to hit and it's very common to find that you can afford neither the ideal number nor seniority of positions that you'd hoped for. Positions that can't be afforded in the short term can be postponed until a later date. You may be able to add them once a revenue milestone has been reached or if efficiency gains are made in other areas throughout the bottom-up planning process.

Step 5: Finalize budgets and targets

As mentioned above, once the bottom-up plan for a role cluster has been approved, it goes up the approval ladder back to the workforce planner in the OP&A function and other decision makers, including in Finance. Ultimately, it goes to the business leaders. If everything aligns and the bottom-up plan has plugged the gaps between demand and supply, the bottom-up plan can be approved at this point. But, frequently, the final bottom-up plan will not align with the top-down, and trade-offs are needed. At each level of approval, discussions to determine priorities and where exceptions should be accepted need to take place. For example, the leader of several business units may have several bottom-up plans submitted to them, with many of them specifying a greater number of positions than those asked for in the top-down plan. Their job is to balance the business units to ensure a fair supply of resource before passing the bottom-up plans up for the next level of approval.

Keep an open mind throughout this process. The top-down plan isn't made in the context of putting a structure to the organization, so it's possible that the bottom-up planners may highlight investments that need to be made to realize business goals. It's important that the workforce planners in OP&A define which objectives would be missed if investments aren't made and present these to relevant business leaders.

The bottom-up plans eventually land at the top of the approval ladder where compromises need to be reached to balance the bottom-up and top-down planning across the entire group. This is where it is vital to use the budget philosophy agreed right at the beginning of the process to guide thinking. How decisions are reached varies from business to business. Ultimately, the board approves any decisions that are made, but each business will have a different decision-making process and culture. It can vary from being highly autocratic and dominated by the CEO, to highly collaborative and driven by committees. It is not the purpose of this book to articulate the pros and cons of the various approaches.

There is always a risk that the bottom-up planners ask for too many positions. The question is, how many is too many? Invest too much in an area and other areas will likely suffer, meaning that strategic priorities won't be realized, but invest too little, and the role cluster in question will struggle to fulfil its objectives. This process can get political, so turn to the budget philosophy to cut through any conflict. If imperatives, objectives and must-wins are defined up front, and those must-wins are listed in order of priority, it should be immediately apparent where investment is needed. There are three main questions to ask:

1 How much can you afford?

2 Where are the priorities?

3 What can be put off until a later date?

I'll illustrate this with an example from Hokupaa, where the strategy is to grow in North America, as well as getting a foothold in the DACH region, comprising Germany (D), Austria (A), and Switzerland (CH). The budget philosophy clearly prioritizes achieving growth in North America over any other territory. If the bottom-up position plan reveals that doing both these things would require a level of investment that goes beyond the allowance made for in the top-down plan, it's clear where the bets should be placed – North America. A decision might then be made to delay investment in the DACH region for a year.

Most often, a combination of the top-down and bottom-up plans is selected as the recommended option with which to proceed, and this becomes the workforce plan. Never underestimate the time it can take to go through the process of finalizing and agreeing on the plan. There's always a lot of discussion, disagreement, learning and plenty of iteration before you reach something that everyone is happy with. If this stage is too compressed, decisions might be made that are regretted later, so be sure to leave enough time. That said, as I discussed in Chapter 3.1, planning cycles are generally getting faster and more frequent, so if you do end up making a mistake, it shouldn't be a year before it can be rectified. This can take a lot of pressure off the finalizing process.

Once the workforce plan is signed off, it becomes the target line against which operational workforce planners perform month-by-month tracking of the ever-shifting workforce. This forms part of the final step in the process: analyse and monitor.

Step 6: Analyse and monitor

Organizations are constantly evolving. No matter how thorough the budgeting process, assumptions made in the planning process will turn out to be wrong. These assumptions could be the top-down formal assumptions, or the more implicit assumptions made in the minds of those doing the bottom-up position planning. It might be that they are out of date as the world has moved on, or they could just be plain wrong. Returning to the example in Figure 3.3.3, the lead generation capability in HK–Singapore may turn out to have been overestimated, so there may, in fact, be too many BDEs in that territory. The opposite could also happen and there may be too few.

The actual and forecasted supply of labour and the forecasted demand are monitored against the target line defined by the budgeting process.

As the world is constantly evolving, drivers are constantly changing, so demand and supply forecasts are continually reviewed and adjusted. Over time, there will inevitably be an increasing divergence between these and the target. The role of the workforce planner is to work out why this is happening and what should be done about it.

In strategic workforce planning, this target line could span multiple years, while in operational workforce planning, it represents the annual budget (see Figure 3.3.4). The role of operational workforce planning is to ensure that the required workforce is in place on a month-by-month basis to deliver the annual budget and business targets, or objectives. This is done by monitoring the progress of actual and forecast FTE and cost against the target FTE and cost. This requires understanding such things as the month-by-month change in the recruitment list, as well as the pipeline for the year ahead. On the demand side, the operational workforce planner identifies where resource has been requested but not fulfilled, or where there is a risk of redundancy. As operational workforce planning is a monthly activity, the forecast and actuals change on this cycle, from small alterations in start dates to changes in business requirements or hiring freezes.

FIGURE 3.3.4 Target, actual and forecast tracking in operational workforce planning

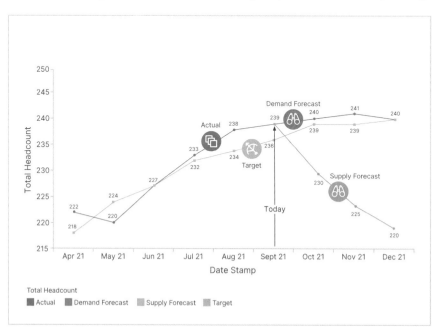

Operational workforce planning can be thought of in terms of detailed people and position planning. Figure 3.3.5 illustrates how operational workforce planning links resource supply (the current headcount in each position) with resource demand (the demand for each position). As the figure shows, there are two requested positions which need to be filled. The operational workforce planner assesses whether the demand can be met with resource currently within the organization or whether there is a need to recruit externally. In Chapter 3.2 I discussed the importance of factoring competency data into workforce planning. This is extremely important in operational workforce planning.

Using competency data to move people around the organization

When assessing gap analysis, the path ahead might, at first, seem obvious. Where there is an oversupply of labour, positions should be demised at appropriate points; where there's an undersupply, positions need to be filled by hiring new people. But it's not that simple. I'm a firm believer in internal mobility. In Part Two I discussed the need to create a talent marketplace in the organization using competency data, so that people can be moved around as necessary depending on the competencies they possess. Equipped with this data, if you can see that in six months' time there will be an oversupply of workers in a certain area, the bottom-up planner may decide to demise certain positions. But the people filling those positions shouldn't automatically be made redundant. Instead, their competencies should be checked and mapped against other areas of the organization where there might be an undersupply of workers. Not only is this the morally right thing to do, but if your strategy is only to recruit to match supply with demand, you may find yourself going to a lot of unnecessary expense. It's a lot cheaper to redeploy someone than recruit someone new. It's also likely to take less time to get the person up and running in their new role, as a current employee will have knowledge and relationships within the organization that a new recruit won't have. They will also understand the culture and how things work. The TTP for a current employee in a different role is likely to be far shorter than for a new employee in the same role. This approach not only helps to develop people's careers, but is also great for relationship building. It helps to create a more unified culture as opposed to a siloed one. In this context, workforce planning feeds into succession planning, discussed in Chapter 2.4.

The recommendations made in the bottom-up position planning for positions to be created, demised or repurposed are put into action by the operational workforce planner, alongside Operational HR. Doing this requires a firm grasp of the concept of position lifecycle management, which I will go on to look at now.

FIGURE 3.3.5 People supply and position demand in operational workforce planning

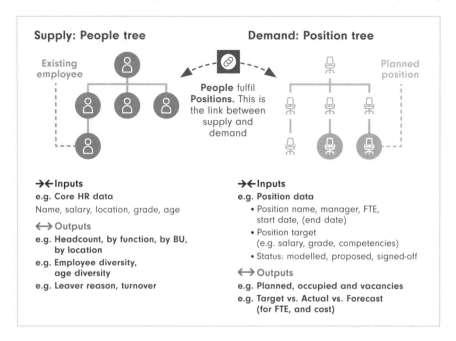

Position lifecycle management

The position lifecycle progresses through six stages, as shown in Figure 3.3.6:

1 planning

2 budgeting

3 hiring

4 filling

5 maintaining

6 closing

It is useful to understand how these steps relate to the six workforce planning steps. Following them, especially in relation to maintaining or closing a position when a position-holder leaves, gives a more accurate representation of actual FTE headcount and cost.

FIGURE 3.3.6 The six stages of the position lifecycle

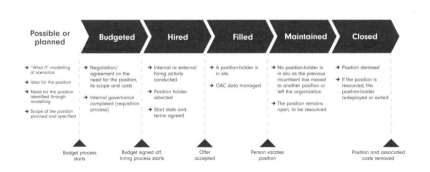

The position lifecycle is a gated process which begins with planning a position and ends with closing it. At the end of each step, the next one begins, and you can't jump into a step in the middle of the process without first completing the steps that come before it.

- Step 1 – The first step, that of planning a position, begins when the idea for a position is first suggested. It happens at Steps 3 and 4 of the workforce planning process: the need for a position is identified during both the top-down demand planning and bottom-up position planning. This is when What-If modelling and optionality take place. The scope of the position is specified during the bottom-up planning. At this stage, start and end dates for positions are set.

- Step 2 – You then move to the budgeting, when the need for the position as well as its scope and costs over time are agreed. This results in the approval of the position which signifies the end of the budgeting step and the beginning of the hiring step. (In the context of the workforce planning process, positions are approved at the end of Step 5 – this is when the budget is finalized and the target line is set for operational workforce planning to follow.)

- Step 3 – Then begins the hiring process: an internal or external position-holder is selected and start dates are agreed. The hiring step finishes once an offer has been made and accepted.

- Step 4 – Costs do not start to be incurred until the position is filled. This might sound obvious, but I have often seen planned budgets which do not take actual start dates into account when calculating compensation cost. When does the filling step end and the maintaining one begin? Once the person is onboarded, through probation and happy in their role.

- Step 5 – A position is maintained so long as there is a position-holder in place, but the real crux of understanding the position lifecycle is what do to when a position-holder moves on to a different position or leaves the organization altogether. If the plan is to backfill the position (in other words, recruit someone as quickly as possible to fill it), then it is a reasonably straightforward process: the position is maintained and continues to be budgeted for until someone is hired and it is filled once again. This is a key point: if a need for the position has been identified through the top-down and bottom-up position planning process then it should remain in the position hierarchy to give clarity on the cost and size of the workforce. Remember that people and positions are not one and the same. Just because a person goes, it doesn't mean that the position does too.

- Step 6 – If the position is not to be backfilled it should be closed, with an actual date given for when the position and the costs associated with it will be removed. This date is when the maintaining step ends and the closing one begins. If this doesn't happen, HR and Finance data become misaligned and actual costs can diverge a huge amount from the target line.

Final thoughts

The processes described in this chapter require you to think – to think through the top-down versus the bottom-up and keep a heads-up view of the world with your sights on the next quarter, year and beyond. There is also a lot of conflict resolution as trade-offs need to be made between two different sets of objectives. There are many similarities with macro operating design. Both scenarios require trade-offs, but in workforce planning your thoughts are focused more on micro detailed design objectives. Should you scale APAC or North America? Where does focus need to be directed? Making these trade-offs explicit helps to isolate the important issues and the reasons why they are important. Are you sweeping stuff under the carpet, and avoiding tough conversations? Are conversations happening with the right people, and are decisions being made for the greater good or driven by people's egos? Is the person responsible for APAC shouting for more resources for their own gain, or are they focused on the overall good? If North America is struggling and needs to be the priority for investment, are they able to see this point of view? Much of this will depend on your decision-making process and culture. My former Chairman Richard Thompson used to tell me that strategy is easy – it's timing and tactics that are hard. Aligning the top-down and bottom-up processes is all about tactics and timing. It's often not a question of if you do something, but when and how you do it.

The job of the OP&A professional is to bring the facts and implications of the options and scenarios to the table. The business leaders bring what is important and why; OP&A articulates this in the context of the options and scenarios up for debate. This is a continuous process, and to move at speed it helps to be good at it. You will need to boil down discussions to the truly meaningful conflicts. At the end of the day, this should become a strategic discussion about how best to meet your highest priority goals, while working within your financial constraints.

REMEMBER THIS

1   The aim of bottom-up position planning is to close the gaps between demand and supply highlighted in the top-down plan.

2   OP&A's role in this process is largely about identifying trade-offs and highlighting where exceptions would make sense.

3   As the world constantly evolves, workforce planning drivers continually change. The demand into the future changes as the drivers change, and the forecast constantly evolves.

4   Undersupply and oversupply of workers can sometimes be addressed by internal mobility. It's important to understand the competencies that people hold.

5   The position lifecycle consists of six steps. Maintaining or closing a position when a position-holder leaves gives a more accurate representation of actual FTE headcount and cost.

PART FOUR

OP&A analysis

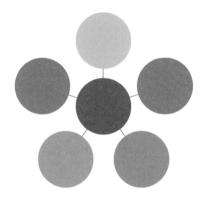

4.1

Introduction

OP&A professionals are responsible for a lot of data. They are responsible for ensuring this data is maintained appropriately and used effectively. The RPP and OAC datasets can unlock insight into many business outcomes, but to do this successfully you need the right tools and the right techniques, and you need to ask the right questions.

As these chapters will convey, effective OP&A relies on a broader range of data than just HR data. Deep, meaningful and actionable insight is reached by blending datasets together. These might be internal business datasets or data you source externally. For example, by combining competency, activity data and performance data you can start to build models and see the drivers for different outcomes. The important thing is that insight should lead to action and change. It shouldn't simply answer a question. Insight is generated from slicing and dicing data from **measures**, **properties** and **dimensions** associated with **nodes**. These are all terms that I define in Chapter 4.2.

In the next part of this book – Part Five – I describe the possible roles in the OP&A Team. One of these is a Data and Tech Leader, and another is a Data Scientist. While a Data and Tech Leader is integral to the success of the function, whether you decide to employ an in-house Data Scientist will depend on the depth of analysis you want to reach. Some analysis of data is necessary in OP&A (the clue is in the name), but there are different lengths that you can go to. Reading the chapters in Part Four before you get to Part Five will help you to decide how deep you want to go, and the roles you want to include.

My aim with these chapters is not to teach you how to be a Data Scientist, but rather to demystify terms that are so frequently discussed but rarely fully understood. When was the last time someone mentioned a **star schema** to you? How about a **graph database**? A **random forest model**? Or **neural**

network? I want to give you sufficient background so that you can converse with your Data Science Team, ask more insightful questions, and have the confidence to challenge them if necessary. Is the data they are using of sufficient quality? Have they fallen into any common statistical traps? Have they heard of the ecological fallacy, or are they aware how easy it is to confuse correlation and causation? Are they using the right tool or technique? Would an alternative one be better? Could someone else pick it up and use it? What is their dashboard design like? Is it too cluttered? Does it tell the right story?

Much of what I write about in Chapter 4.2 is very similar to Chapter 1.3 in *Data-Driven Organization Design*. The fundamentals are the same, but much larger datasets are required to plan an organization over time than to design one for a to-be moment in time. The question now is how you house these large datasets and operationalize and productionize them so that data is clean and structured on an ongoing basis.

Structure and logic for Part Four

Chapter 4.2 explains the steps necessary to ensure data integrity. A mistake people often make is to overemphasize the exciting things like machine learning while forgetting about the importance of getting the basics right. Real power comes from having solid data that you can rely on and embellish with other sources to reach richer insight. Your machine learning models are only ever going to be as good as the data they draw on. In this chapter, I explain the importance of master data management. I also address many of the challenges associated with building a strong data model as well as some of the technology and platforms you might find useful. Rather than a one-size-fits-all solution, you are more likely to need a best-of-breed technology stack tailored to your needs. The important thing is to work out what you are trying to achieve and choose the best tool or platform for the job. I conclude this chapter by looking at dashboard design and how to use dashboards effectively to tell stories with data.

I start Chapter 4.3 by outlining five of the most common statistical traps. We all have a moral duty to interpret data correctly. Far too often, people blindly follow data without questioning what they see. It's data, therefore it must be factually correct and true. Right? Wrong. There are many traps you can fall into. It might seem as though the data is telling you something, when really it's doing no such thing. The rest of the chapter is devoted to explaining various data science techniques as well as their application in an OP&A context. These techniques can be difficult to understand, but I hope I have stripped out the complexity and presented them in just enough detail to show how they can add value. The chapter concludes by looking at the role played by machine learning.

By the end of this part, I hope you will have a good sense of how to make data science work for you. This includes the tech that you need, how you need to prepare your data model, the techniques you want to pursue and whether you want to integrate machine learning capability. These decisions will have a significant impact on the roles you choose to include in your OP&A function, so you will then be ready to progress to Part Five.

4.2

Laying the foundations for effective OP&A analysis

Introduction

It's difficult to overestimate the importance of laying good data foundations for OP&A analysis, and yet in many organizations the steps described in this chapter can be completely overlooked. Many people try to jump straight into exciting statistical techniques without first making sure that the data they're using is of sufficient quality to give robust and reliable insight. They feel the pull of machine learning packages and want to start understanding their workforce on a deeper level to make predictions about the future, but these predictions will only ever be as sound as the data they are based on. Coupled with this, it is important to build a baseline understanding of an organization (or dataset) through standard operational reporting, as failure to do this can lead to people trying to predict something of little value. As my colleague Tim Archer puts it: 'being "advanced" beyond your maturity only serves to highlight the immaturity'.

I am yet to come across an organization which has its master data management practices completely nailed. Sadly, too many organizations still suffer from limited data availability with data capture happening in tools such as Excel. While organizations might hope for a unified company-wide database or warehouse, it's more likely that a range of best-of-breed systems will be needed, all capable of talking to each other and each with their own purpose. As you read this chapter and the one that follows, ask yourself where your organization is on the journey towards analytics maturity. Where you are starting from will have an impact on the kind of data science projects that you can pursue. You may have made it part-way along the journey and have disparate source systems with some data still captured in spreadsheets (although it's important to note that having a 'system' does not solve the data capture challenge. Some systems lack the ability to take daily snapshots and store them, which is critical when asking a machine to 'learn' from historical data). Your organization may have no data science capability at all. You may have a few fought-over Data Scientists, or you may have a fully fledged Data Science Team. It's important to acknowledge where you are so that you can adapt the advice given in this chapter accordingly.

This chapter addresses many of the challenges associated with building a strong data model for reliable OP&A analysis. By following the steps and advice given, you will be able to get your data managed and controlled on an ongoing basis, and make the statistical techniques I discuss in Chapter 4.3 work for you. I begin by introducing the concept of a flexible **data ware-house**, before continuing to look at different data types and how to build a data model. I end with some advice on how to design dashboards to effectively communicate the story you want to tell. Many of these concepts were explained in my book *Data-Driven Organization Design* so they may sound familiar. I am repeating and building on them here as they are fundamental not only to understanding different types of OP&A analyses, but also to any well-thought-out analytics execution, regardless of division, function or team. The kind of techniques discussed in Chapter 4.3 cannot be fully understood without first having a grasp of these basics. The main difference between the discussion in *Data-Driven Organization Design* and what follows here is that here I consider the shape of data, not just the organization as a system. As we are now concerned with analysing, designing, planning and monitoring the organization over time, the datasets necessary to do this are far bigger than those used to design the organization for a one-off photographic snapshot. So I begin here with the necessity of building a flexible and modern data warehouse that can house large datasets and be augmented as necessary with both internal and external data to reach business changing insight.

Building a flexible data warehouse

In *Data-Driven Organization Design* I talked about the datasets needed to design an organization for a to-be moment in time. Even though organization design is a mammoth undertaking, the amount of data needed for the task is relatively small compared to the amount of data that can be amassed over time in a purpose-built store for analytics, such as a data warehouse (although note that there are other ways to manage and store data for analytics which don't involve warehousing). When data is stored in a warehouse, new records are added every day, week or month to build a robust history. This data isn't just HR data, but other business data or external data that enriches understanding of people and the work that they do. This is what I mean by a flexible data warehouse: one that can accommodate a range of data points and be added to on a continual basis. These data points can be used to create insight and feed into automated and repeatable models. The datasets needed to plan and model an organization over time are therefore far larger than those needed to design a to-be organization. The role of the OP&A function is to design, build and maintain a flexible data warehouse which can house millions of fast-changing data points. Here we find ourselves entering the realm of big data.

Data warehouses are usually based on star schema relational models, otherwise known as relationship databases. I'll use the HR Information System (HRIS) to explain how relationship databases work. Every interaction a user has with the front end of an HRIS results in data being recorded and stored in database tables. These tables consist of either dimensions or facts. Dimensions and facts are connected through relationship IDs. A relationship database is often called a star schema because it is visualized as a star, with a fact table in the middle, and dimensions radiating from the central point.

In an enterprise-level HRIS, it's typical for there to be hundreds of different dimension tables, and fact tables can run into millions of transaction levels. Facts can be aggregated, such as summed or averaged, whereas a dimension is used to slice or dice an aggregation. An example of a fact is pay – tables include rows of facts showing what someone has been paid each month. An example of a dimension is gender or a function. An example of a relationship ID could be an email address or a geography. It is worth noting here that HRISs are not suitable for analytical needs, because of the way they store and manage data. In addition, the services HRISs are run on are not architected to complete resource-heavy calculations and queries.

If the relationship database is well-maintained, the vast amount of data means that you can get phenomenal insights which can be linked with other sources, especially when the data is used to feed machine learning models. The opportunities for the OP&A function are huge and I delve into many of these in Chapter 4.3. For example, machine learning models can take each change of every employee piece of data over years and use those hundreds of data points per person to understand the drivers of churn and make predictions based on the history. Similarly, data points along career paths can be used to understand the routes people take to becoming a leader in an organization, and, when overlaid with competency data, the competencies required for people to get there. Once you understand the routes people take to achieve success and the competencies that are required, you can take action to improve diversity and inclusion targets and get more female and/or Black, Asian and Minority Ethnic (BAME) employees to the top.

Connecting and blending data

One of the greatest benefits of a flexible data warehouse is being able to augment it with different data sources and combine them to reach richer insight, therefore allowing you to unlock the predictive and analytical power of data. This is where the real power of a data warehouse lies. The most interesting, challenging and sophisticated questions are those that cut across silos. OP&A professionals should continually prioritize business performance outcomes, and part of this is to assess whether there are certain competencies, activities or attributes held by people which maximize performance outcomes.

Workforce analytics is a well-established field with many different providers of standard metrics and measures related to the composition of your workforce. These include Visier, CrunchHR, orgvue, TrueCue and consulting firms such as Deloitte. Not all have the full scope: for example, orgvue uses a graphing schema and is more focused on organization design and workforce planning, while others focus on transactional data, for example churn analytics performed in TrueCue. You may want to take a best-in-breed approach. I'm not convinced that any single system will ever do it all, although some claim they can! The important thing to note is that if you want to utilize data science, you will need to go further than standard workforce analytics and blend HR data with other types of business data as well as external data. It is only in this way that you can start to answer the really interesting questions. Examples of data that can be blended to reach rich insight include people, activity, competency and sales performance data. For example, by connecting competency and sales performance data, you can see who the most successful salespeople are and work out if there is a competency profile that fits these sales people that should be emulated across your organization's sales workforce. In Chapter 2.4 I discussed Matthew Dixon and Brent Adamson's *The Challenger Sale*, which has had an enormous impact on the Sales function, just by combining competency and outcome data and applying it to the role.

Another example relates to combining competency data with client payment or churn data. Are there certain competencies or attributes that Account Managers hold that might impact these factors? Are clients more likely to pay on time for some Account Managers than others, or can the attributes of Account Managers account for deals falling through or clients churning?

External data can also be brought in to augment the data warehouse, but the data that you choose will depend on your industry. For example, when doing location strategy work, you could pull in data around the supply of labour, salaries, unemployment levels, or even LinkedIn data (spikes in activity on LinkedIn can be a sign that someone is a flight risk and thinking of moving on from their organization). Another example relates to tactical workforce planning such as scheduling. Although this type of workforce planning is outside the scope of this book, it's an interesting example to consider here. Imagine a weather-dependent industry such as a recreation park, farming, construction or road clearance. In these types of industries, long-term weather forecasts can be considered to determine how the weather might have an impact on scheduling, and predictive models can be created to work out staffing levels.

Other types of databases

There are two other types of database it might be helpful to be aware of, other than a relationship database: **transactional** and **graph**.

Transactional database

As its name suggests, this database records transactions. Think of transactions like events, for example when someone joins or leaves an organization, or moves to a different position. It might also record a salary move, or someone's date of birth. Transactional databases are therefore often used to record workflows.

Graph database

Think of a graph database like a network containing nodes and links between those nodes. In data science, these links are referred to as 'edges', but for me, calling them 'links' makes the graph database easier to visualize and understand. The nodes contain data, as do the links between them. For example, a person would be a node, containing data such as gender and date of birth. An activity, for example 'conduct role design', could also be a node. The link between those nodes could contain data such as the amount of time the person spends doing the activity, how often they do it, and whether they enjoy it. We all use technology based on graph databases every day. Facebook is one example. Another is the mapping technology used by Uber.

Understanding the different types of data

Nodes

A node is the smallest 'thing' you have information about. In a relationship database, nodes can be thought of as the 'records'. A node could be an individual employee in a people dataset, a specific position within a positions dataset or a specific task within an activity (processes) dataset. These are just some examples. Returning to the organization system framework, each component is a dataset, and connecting the system with data enables efficient organization design, planning and monitoring.

Properties, dimensions and measures

Properties are the information held about nodes, which, in a relationship database, can be thought of as fields. For example, in a people dataset where each node is an employee, you will typically find information such as position title, location, start date, salary, age, gender and so on. These are just a few examples of the 50 to 100 properties typically found in people datasets.

Properties are used to describe, categorize and aggregate nodes; to create sub-groups according to defined characteristics using the information you have. A simple example could be to use the property 'gender' to split the workforce into male, female and non-binary sub-groups. This property is being used to describe the nodes (the gender of each node) and create sub-groups.

Properties can be calculated. For example, the age of an employee is dynamic and changes daily, so this is calculated from their date of birth. Similarly, the tenure is calculated from their start date. Due to the temporal nature of data, these calculated properties constantly change: every day employees get a day older, and the length of time they have been at an organization increases.

In some graph databases (orgvue is one example), dimensions are found within properties: they are categories each property has. More broadly, dimensions are attributes and are defined through master data management. A dimension is the thing you want to see the data by, for example by region or by year. The job of a dimension is typically to filter, group or label. In the previous paragraph the property 'gender' was used to create sub-groups. These sub-groups are defined according to the dimensions which are specified. In this example, the property 'gender' had three dimensions: 'female', 'male' and 'non-binary'.

Let's think about the differences between two of the properties we've used in our examples above. These examples illustrate two main types of data:

- Properties with 'continuous' data have values which could be any number on a (theoretically endless) scale. In the examples above, age and tenure contain continuous data. Salary, span of control or the number of organizational layers are other examples.

- Properties with 'discrete' data are those which have defined dimensions. The example of 'gender' used above is an example of a property with discrete data; other examples include 'function', 'grade' and 'location'. Dimensions also have hierarchies, as do dates. In fact, a date hierarchy is one of the best understood hierarchies there is, with year at the top, progressing down through quarter, month, day, hour, minute and, finally, second. Measures (or facts) can be aggregated up and down the hierarchy. Dates can be both continuous and discrete, as can some other properties such as 'grade' or 'age'.

There are further definitions of data types – for example, within continuous data there is ratio and interval data and within categorical data there is ordinal and nominal – but for our purposes the distinction between continuous and categorical is sufficient. Categorical data can be created from continuous data, for example categorizing ages into bands: younger than 18; 18–24; 35–44, etc.

Measures are defined to generate insight on the organization and workforce. The old cliché 'if you can measure it, you can manage it' rings very true: measures are created by applying simple statistical techniques to properties, and are usually represented as a sum, an average, a percentage or a ratio.

Measures provide insight to show how effectively the organization is performing.

Measures are generated to analyse specific questions. For example, a company wanting to understand gender diversity may use measures such as the percentage of female employees at the top three layers of the organization or the percentage salary difference between different male, female and non-binary employees.

Good practice is for measures to be defined and calculated as simply as possible. The insight generated through measures needs to be communicated and understood so excessive complexity and sophistication should be avoided.

Measures can act as dimensions if you put them into categories, often referred to as 'bins'. They are most seen when drawing histograms with continuous data. Take income. You could group income into less than £20,000, £20–30,000, £40–50,000 and so on in increments of £10,000. Note that, in this example, you wouldn't necessarily want all groupings to be equal. The higher the income, the fewer people will be earning at that level, so rather than continuing in increments of £10,000 you might then go to £100–150,000, £150–200,000 and £200,000+. When you're categorizing measures to make them dimensions, think carefully about the cut-off points.

RATIOS AND PERCENTAGES

Ratios and percentages are special types of measures that can help to add context to most situations and allow for good comparisons between different categories. They are noteworthy as they are calculated on the fly. They cannot be hard coded. They are calculated as different aggregations take place – if this didn't happen you would end up summing or averaging a ratio which might not make any sense. Ratios are used in workforce planning – two examples are the ratio of one function to another or of sales reps to business development executives. Percentages are frequently used to benchmark. For example, in FP&A, you might want to look at the percentage of spend that is Selling, General and Administrative (SG&A).

Using properties, dimensions and measures to generate insight

Figure 4.2.1 shows how properties, measures and dimensions can be used together to generate actionable insight. In this example, insight is being sought into whether the workforce is diverse and inclusive. The question under investigation is whether the organization is at risk of losing part of its workforce because of retirement. The properties to answer this question are

FIGURE 4.2.1 Properties are used to calculate measures which are analysed by dimensions to generate insight for action

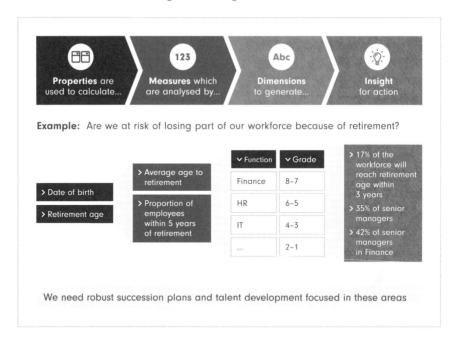

'date of birth' and 'retirement age'. The next step is to drill into the measures related to those properties which are going to help you best understand the situation. Initial questions always lead to further questions, which guide you in slicing and dicing and drilling into the data to reach the insight you need. In this example, the first question is whether or not there is risk because of retirement, and the next is where that risk is, which is answered by drilling into the dimensions. When measures are analysed by dimension, you can start to see where in the business action needs to be taken. In this case, insight reveals that succession and talent development plans are needed in the Finance function because 42 per cent of senior managers will be reaching retirement age within the next three years.

Building a data model

This section repeats the nine-step iterative process necessary for laying data foundations which I outlined in my book *Data-Driven Organization*

Design. If you are already familiar with this then feel free to skip to page 246, where I outline some thoughts on dashboard design. The steps take you through building a data model, and then using it to analyse the data and act on it, as well as two principles you should aim to adhere to throughout those nine steps: making the process valuable for all and visualizing and telling stories with data to inspire action. The steps and principles are shown in Figure 4.2.2. It starts with building a baseline of existing data, without which you can't monitor progress or understand trends. This baseline should be built from the data that you already have in your organization. The data model is created in steps two and three of the process. These two steps can be performed rapidly, and get you to a place where you can begin to use your data to answer questions, form actionable insight, make predictions and, most importantly, act on the insight your questions have given you. As you progress through these steps you can begin to lay sustainable data foundations for the future and implement master data management. In Step 8 you can start to automate the process and make it continuous. Your ultimate goal is to be able to maintain high-quality datasets which everyone in the organization recognizes as the 'one version of truth' and which can be continuously monitored to assess progress. This allows for the continuous creation of actionable insight so that, where necessary, change can be implemented quickly and confidently. I'll now walk through the different steps of Figure 4.2.2, starting with the two key principles.

FIGURE 4.2.2 Building and automating a data model

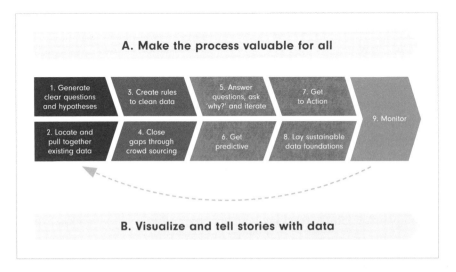

Key principle A: Make the process valuable for all

As a rule, people don't like to provide data. It costs them time and effort; it can cause embarrassment and show their shortcomings. Some people aren't influenced by authority, and those providing data can be highly creative in their delay tactics, or worse, creative in the data that they produce (building untrustworthy data into the process). So the process must be made worthwhile. At a high level, make sure you can answer the key questions of why you are collecting the data, how they are going to help, what the consequence of not getting the data will be, and what is in it for them. In Chapter 2.3 I introduced WIFM analysis: 'What's In it For Me?' Articulating how it's going to benefit people in the long run is vital for getting buy-in.

At the lower data processing levels, the concerns of those performing the day-to-day tasks associated with processing and managing data will need to be addressed. You'll again need to think from a WIFM perspective – if they are going to process data, how can you demonstrate the benefits to them? There are six key points to note here:

1 Check to see if the data already exists, and if it does, use that as the starting point. No one likes duplication of effort, and it is usually much easier to correct something than create it from scratch. Asking someone to start something anew, to later discover that they didn't need to, is a sure way to set off on the wrong foot.

2 Ensure the data owner can see the value they are contributing or getting back. For example, an Individual Activity Analysis (IAA) survey can include meaningful qualitative questions like: Do they enjoy it? How could the work be improved? Are the accountabilities clear? What is their authority? How much rework is required? In answering these questions, respondents can see how they are likely to benefit from the process. Data playback is another great way to do this. If you can automatically summarize someone's data and give it back to them, preferably with some insight on what they provided, it not only gives them a record of the data they have processed but also helps them to see the holistic benefits the data will lead to.

3 Gamify the process. Set targets turn it into a contest, to appeal to people's competitive nature. Tracking people's progress against one another tends to work a treat and can make it much more fun.

4 It's imperative that something positive comes from the work, or people will be reluctant to help you again. It is essential that you use the insights to improve (see Step 7 in the data model, 'Get to action').

5 Make your request with conviction and confidence. Too often, initiatives are either short-lived or change shortly after they start. This leads people to question the value of running the process.

6 Attempt to automate output directly from the input. For example, timesheet entries are chased weekly, when the data is sitting in a database waiting to be used. Emails can be automatically sent to all employees who haven't completed 40 hours, saving the delivery time. If they are not completed to 40 hours within a set time, the email can be resent and copied to their line manager.

Creativity is essential to get the most out of your data, both in how you analyse it, and in how you get it in the first place. After all, data sits with people, so it's important to find ways to make it worthwhile for them. The last thing you want is someone huffing at you and informing you that they have a 'day job'. Everyone must be able to understand the value and see that it's worth their effort and time. It's important to note here that while automation is a great way to collect data, it still requires a level of input.

Key principle B: Visualize and tell stories

Visualizing data is a key part of the data and analytics process. Try to stay away from Excel, which can turn people off before they even get going. Where possible, it's best to use specifically designed software that helps bring all your data together in an interactive and visual way using dashboards. If you have the technology available to you, this is undoubtedly the best way to go. Dedicated software allows the creator to build something interactive and beautiful that the consumer can instantly engage with. Later in the chapter I delve into some dos and don'ts around good dashboard design.

Realistically, though, many people do not have the tech (or the capability or skills to operate the tech) to create dashboards and will use PowerPoint for presenting and telling stories with data. PowerPoint can be an extremely effective medium for storytelling, so long as you follow the key tips I give below. Whatever software you use, visualizing the data as early as possible in the process will bring it to life and achieve buy-in from people working with it and affected by it. It may also start uncovering some basic insights to help reaffirm the hypotheses you generate in Step 1 and ensure you are going in the right direction.

There is a key distinction to be made between using visualizations to hypothesize and using them to tell stories. As I explain in Step 1, with hypothesizing you are exploring and finding insight by slicing, dicing and drilling into the data. When you visualize with the purpose of telling stories, you need to build a narrative around that insight to inspire action and change. In Step 1 I explain how to create a hypothesis tree: this can be used to structure your narrative.

We've all heard the well-known advice for giving successful presentations:

1 Tell your audience what you're going to tell them.

2 Tell them.

3 Then tell them what you've told them.

As I'll demonstrate below, when storytelling with data, this translates broadly into:

1 Give your audience a call to action.

2 Tell them why you believe this to be true, supported by data and insights.

3 Give your audience an action plan, tied back to your call to action at the start.

The whole point of storytelling with data is to communicate key messages in a way that is going to inspire people to act. I always advocate following the *Pyramid Principle* developed by Barbara Minto in 1987.[1] The Pyramid Principle asserts that when structuring your ideas, you should do it in the shape of a pyramid, starting with your 'big idea' – or call to action – at the top, followed by answering why you believe this to be true, followed by a more detailed breakdown of supporting data to back up those 'why' statements. To ensure that your audience is left in no doubt of what you want the key takeaway to be, it's best to lead with your big idea rather than revealing it at the end. It also helps to focus your audience's attention from the start, so that they hear everything you say in the context of your call to action. At every stage of the pyramid, tie the discussion back to the strategic goals of your organization, which will give clarity as to why your audience needs to care about what you're saying. Answers to the 'so what' question should be obvious with every point you make.

After conveying your call to action, the next stage is to isolate the main reasons why you believe this call to action to be necessary. This is where you explain the insight which has led you there. Think of your 'whys' as buckets containing supporting data which you will articulate at the next stage of your story. At this stage you should include any exceptions or unusual insight, and anything that gave you an 'a-ha' moment. The trick is to focus on the primary message you want each 'why' statement to give, and to make it as lively, interesting and relatable as you can. Adding humour at opportune moments can keep people engaged so highlight what you found surprising, and anything that made you chuckle.

The next step is to dig into your 'why' buckets and explain each one in the context of your supporting data. The point here is to tell your audience how you got to the 'what' (the 'what' being the insight communicated through the 'why' statements). Below are my top tips for providing a compelling narrative at this point:

1 When talking about your supporting data, be sure to give context and explain the process you went through. For example, you should explain:

   o how you collected the data and what you did

   o the scope of the population (for example, size)

   o the shape, functions and geographies

   o any issues or notable points around data integrity

   o the number of measures and properties

   o the timeframe – when you started, and when you stopped.

2 Give examples of depth and breadth, with well-chosen and representative deep-dives and make it relatable to your audience.

3 Compare the extremes and get any notable issues out into the open. In my experience, it always works best to highlight potential concerns before anyone else does! By highlighting them yourself you will prevent them from becoming a distraction. Some issues may deserve further discussion, but be the one to decide which issues these should be, not the audience.

Conclude the narrative with an action plan giving calls to action with distinct and quick wins. Relate the action plan back to the 'why' given at the start, and articulate how you're going to measure the impact of the actions you are proposing.

One final thing: don't be tempted to jump straight into the detail before getting the red line of your story sorted first. An excellent way to do this is to create a storyboard based on your hypothesis tree (see Step 1). Storyboarding helps to get your thinking straight and can be used to ensure that the message you are crafting makes sense. It's a way of creating an outline for what you want to present, checking that the structure works and that the key messages (and story) are crystal clear for the audience. There are various ways to put a storyboard together, but I like to create a Message House, which I introduced in Chapter 2.3.

From this point onwards the process of visualizing data to tell stories will add value throughout each stage of your data model. Visualizing data integrity alone helps identify where the gaps are in your data and where there may be inaccuracies. When crowdsourcing data, handing visuals back to data owners helps them identify outliers and inaccuracies in seconds (Step 4). And as mentioned above, visualizing data and storytelling with that data can be an incredibly powerful way to inspire action (Step 7) and monitor change (Step 9).

EMERGENT STORIES

Some stories take shape through discussion. While you could argue that this is done through the Message House (away from software), software can play a role too. A well-designed analytical tool will enable people to learn, discover and create their own stories along the way. Confidence intervals exist for a reason. Machine learning algorithms include forecast accuracy as a key measure. Why? Because not everything can be stated with absolute certainty. Often, you may not have enough data points, or you may have had limited time. But that doesn't mean the insight you get is of no value. The data may be revealing things through weak signals but it's important not to dismiss these signals just because of an element of doubt. Learn from them, build on them, and allow a story to emerge.

Another point to note is that things change. At Hokupaa, we were working to certain predictions based on machine learning algorithms which became obsolete once Covid-19 hit. From that moment on, life changed and things that were true before the pandemic were suddenly no longer true.

Things can also change through the Hawthorne effect, which states that by observing something you change it. While you might have observed that fewer women choose to go into commercial roles, and that being in a commercial role is a significant predictor for getting to the top, once the observation has been made and more women start going into commercial roles, over time this will cease to be the reason why fewer females reach senior positions, if this indeed remains the case.

These emergent stories work at an operational level as they don't require as much strategic thinking and can be completed at the speed of thought. But they do rely on well-built, carefully thought-through dashboard creation, which I address below.

Step 1: Generate clear questions and hypotheses

In data science projects, it's very tempting to start playing with data immediately, but that way danger lies. For decades, strategy consultants have used a hypothesis-led approach to focus investigations – and it works. The most common method is to use a hypothesis tree. Hypothesis trees allow you to focus and build up a complete argument by breaking down a problem into a set of Mutually Exclusive and Collectively Exhaustible (MECE) hypotheses that may explain that problem. By segregating problems in a MECE manner, you ensure that things are clear with no overlap (ME) and that nothing has been left out (CE). Hypothesis trees are excellent for narrowing down an investigation to the essentials. They focus on the 'so what' of any data presented, hence they are a good starting point to any data analysis. Figure 4.2.3 provides a set of hypotheses to investigate the high-level problem: 'Why are there fewer women in leadership positions than men?' It first breaks this question down into three areas of exploration which could be used to answer this question:

1 More men than women are recruited to junior levels.
2 We fail to retain talented female employees.
3 Leadership development and selection processes favour male candidates.

These hypotheses can be broken down into further hypotheses which can then be tested to find out whether they are true.

Developing a hypothesis-led mindset is crucial when performing any of the statistical techniques presented in Chapter 4.3. That chapter begins with some common statistical traps that people fall into when finding patterns and relationships in data, many of which could be avoided through cultivating a habit of asking 'why?' This is the key to the quality of the output of any statistical investigation. One exception to this is naïve analysis, which I also look at in Chapter 4.3. This statistical technique allows patterns and

FIGURE 4.2.3 Building a hypothesis tree provides a complete picture which can be tested for validity

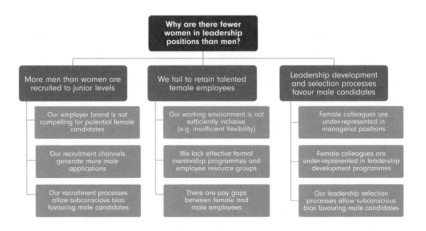

insight to 'emerge' from the data and generates insight which is not guided by any kind of hypothesis. Arguably, however, this element of discovery should always be combined with a hypothesis-led approach to establish the reason why the data is giving the insight that it is giving.

As an aside, it's worth mentioning that you can draw trees to answer business questions which don't always take a hypothesis-led approach. A good example is a people analytics tree. There are over 200 standard questions which are frequently asked which can be classified into chapters and sub-chapters, forming a tree.

Step 2: Locate and pull together existing data

It amazes me how often organizations jump straight to implementing new data collation and creation, overlooking their existing data. Very often, much of the data needed to analyse the organization is already in place; it just needs bringing together. Using your existing data to create insight early in the process has several benefits:

- Those working hard to provide the data can see that they are being used and how you are using them.
- You can start to answer some of your hypotheses and make sure you are collecting the right data for your needs.
- You can gain a much better understanding of the data-cleaning and further collection processes ahead in Step 8.

The starting point is to be extremely clear about the data you need to collect. There is not the room to talk about the types of baseline properties you might focus on here to support planning and monitoring the organization. For that, please refer to *Data-Driven Organization Design*. Once you know what data you need, the next step is to determine where to source it. In doing this, understand:

- What systems are used in the organization and where are they being used? For example, often different geographical locations or business units may use different systems, especially if there has been a history of mergers and acquisitions.

- How do the required properties map to the various source systems and which properties currently don't exist in any system?

- Do you have the ability to bring data together? This is often done through **Application Programming Interfaces (APIs)** and connectors. I won't go into detail about how APIs work but imagine them like middlemen between systems, pulling data and following set rules to allow systems to talk to each other. As well as having APIs in place, it's important to also have consistent primary keys across systems. An example of a key could be an employee number (in some work situations, not all employees have email addresses, so this cannot always be relied upon as a key for employees).

- Who owns which system and what is the process for getting the data extracted?

If you need to repeat the extraction process, ensure you document and test the process. Good sources to begin collecting data from include:

- HRIS – This is the best place to start, although position data is typically a shambles as strict data controls aren't usually defined or adhered to.

- Payroll – You would be surprised how often payroll doesn't match other source systems. For example, comparing performance management systems with payroll is a great way of testing the integrity of your people data. If they are the same, then great, but if they are different you need to look at your data integrity.

- Enterprise Resource Planning (ERP) systems.

- Financial systems for customer revenue and margins, and P&L cost information.

- Purchasing systems for suppliers, contractors and temporary labour – Be sure not to exclude this type of labour. You want to understand the entire workforce, not just permanent employees. How often does an organization complete a Reduction In Force (RIF) only to hire the same people back on day rates?

- Applicant tracking systems.
- Learning management systems.
- Excel spreadsheets – I have not seen an organization yet that does not have multiple Excel islands, with pockets of information siloed away. It is a constant problem. Bringing all this data together is a good chance to collect all that 'lost' data.
- Customer Relationship Management (CRM) for sales and marketing performance metrics.
- External economic and workforce data (especially for multinationals as it is important for storytelling).

Step 3: Create rules to clean data

Inevitably when you bring data together and start visualizing it, you will find data integrity issues. According to the European Spreadsheet Risks Interest Group, 94 per cent of spreadsheets contain hidden errors.[2] Remember that your goal is to end up with a single version of the truth with a level of data integrity which everyone in the organization accepts.

So how do you get to having one version of the truth? First, you need to establish whether your data is clean and quantify its quality. Second, you must create clear rules to clean it. These two steps form the beginning of laying your data foundation, covered in Step 8.

The quality of your data can be quantified by visualizing it so that you can easily see gaps, inconsistencies and errors. This is an important point: as I have said, data integrity is often used as an excuse for not generating information. In my experience, however, if data is being used and presented in an understandable way, it will drive behaviour which will naturally improve its integrity.

Cleaning data is not a one-off exercise. Given that people are collecting and cleaning data in different offices or even different countries, once your data is clean you need to make rules about data collection and storage. This is master data management, and is covered in Step 8. It provides a framework for all employees to follow when managing data so that there is consistency around what things are called and what things are. It is often centred around how the data is categorized or '**dimensionalized**'. A common and easy property to grasp is location. In the same dataset, I have seen the property 'location' with multiple dimensions intending to signify different regions and countries: for example, a region might be defined as both North America, US or USA. Consistency is key. Be clear about what locations are called, and then break those locations into regions and countries. Is it New York or NY? UK or UK&I? This is essential for accuracy in reporting data by location.

Organization design is typically done under significant time pressure. If the data isn't right, you probably won't have time to fix the fundamentals at source. Don't worry for now. At this stage in the process your focus is to clean it sufficiently to meet your immediate needs. Step 8 shows you how to keep it clean and ensure you build data integrity for the future.

Step 4: Close gaps through crowdsourcing

The data you need to further improve integrity or for new properties will sit in different places across the organization. Technology now exists to make it easy for people to provide and alter data at speed, for example through surveying capability, which automatically updates a person's records once completed. For many organizations the data around who reports to whom is incomplete. In these cases, a two-question survey can be sent to all employees asking 'Who do you report to?' and 'Who reports to you?' Collate the data, generate an organization chart and very quickly you will expose any confusion or inaccuracies.

Below are three tips to help you when crowdsourcing data:

1 Make data easy to upload. If the upload process is complex people will become disengaged and turn to other work instead. For example, sending out a webform that takes two minutes to complete will give you instant updates on your data.

2 Report data back to owners. Those who know the data should be the ones who interact with it. They will get new insights from the process. They are the ones who will identify outliers and be best placed to uncover data quality issues.

3 Make the process mobile. Often, the best time to spend a couple of minutes uploading or analysing data is when you are in transit or a little bored. If the data is available at all times and on all devices such as smartphones and tablets, it makes it easy to review charts and add insight.

To begin with, collecting data from different areas of the organization will come down to you and your team. However, the sign that you are getting this right is when the data is seen as a business issue and function leaders come to you to drive new insights and get further data.

Step 5: Answer questions, ask 'why?' and iterate

As the HR Information Systems Manager at one retail client once said: 'One of the most exciting things about bringing all types of organizational data together and visualizing is that you can start to answer questions that people didn't realize they needed the answer to.' Having consolidated your data, just enjoy yourself. Start exploring, slicing and dicing the data and asking why things are the way that they appear.

Bring together your people data with data from across the organization and see what you can find. To make sense of it all, break down areas of insight into topics by organization or theme. For example, functional areas: HR, Finance, Procurement, Manufacturing; or organizational areas: People, Process, Systems; or strategic: Operational, Transactional. Using these categories, you can start performing advanced analytics and asking 'why' questions to get to root causes. For instance, can you see whether sales performance links to education or recruitment channels? Do those who attend training have lower attrition? Which actions post an employee engagement review had meaningful impacts? What human factors drive profit, productivity or retention? The answers to your questions will inevitably lead you to new ones. Getting to the root cause is always an iterative process of asking 'why?'

Step 6: Get predictive

As well as using your data to answer questions and ask why, consolidating your data allows you to make predictions and lessen the chance of you being taken unawares by events. The whole point of building a baseline of data is so that you can both measure progress against it and combine historical and current data to detect trends and make predictions about the future. This is the subject of much of the content in Chapter 4.3. Much of the predictive analytics done by the OP&A Team relates to two factors:

1 Churn and flight risk. There are many drivers for churn, some of which are obvious, such as reward, or the amount of time since someone received

a promotion. Other drivers are less obvious, including managers being located at different sites to those who they manage, or the time of year that someone joins an organization, and the amount of time between them joining and having a performance review discussion.

2 The impact of competencies on outcomes. Your data can tell you which competencies have the greatest 'predictive' impact on what matters most. One of the problems with competency management is the amount of conjecture that can surround their assessment. Some competencies, such as generalized behaviour competencies, are also harder to measure than generic business skills or specialized functional skills (see Chapter 1.2).

Step 7: Get to action

It's not what you know, it's what you do with what you know that counts. Throughout this chapter I've talked about the need to create actionable insight. Not insight for insight's sake, but insight which can be used to bring about change and improvement in the performance of your organization. All too often, I see people with analysis paralysis. They are drowning in data and insight, but with no clear path showing how it can bring about change.

To understand this, think back to the question posed in Figure 4.2.1: Are we at risk of losing part of our workforce because of retirement? This figure shows how measures, properties and dimensions are used to generate insight, but that question alone didn't go far enough. To get to the action, the next stage would be to drill further into the data and establish where the risk was, and what needed to be done about it. From the insight obtained, a plan would need to be formed, and people given accountabilities and objectives to deliver that plan. As noted above, one of the best ways to communicate these actions is through creating compelling narratives around visualizations.

Step 8: Lay sustainable data foundations in phases to allow data to be productionized

As I mentioned in Step 3, when you're consolidating your data at speed to reach a point where you can start to answer your questions, get the insight and act, you typically won't have time to think beyond the immediate exercise. It is one thing getting data clean, but it's another keeping it that way. Once you have done most of the leg work to clean up your data, it's vital that you start laying a sustainable data foundation which will enable you to consistently have clean and high integrity data at your fingertips.

This is master data management. Once introduced, it gives you a framework to continually clean your data against, as well as clear rules around how to structure and store it so that it can remain clean and structured on an ongoing basis. These rules should be automated, repeatable and scalable. A huge part of master data management is the **productionization of data** and the **operationalization of analytics**. Productionizing data smooths data processes so that data is continually updated and insight can be continually obtained. This, in turn, allows you to operationalize analytics. The techniques I discuss in Chapter 4.3, such as survival curves should not be built as one-offs but as a continuous model. This is all about moving analysis on from being a one-off intervention to making it repeatable over time. The idea is to ensure that the right people have the right data at the right time on a continual basis. One of the biggest problems many organizations must overcome is the way that data is pulled and analysed to reach one-off instances of insight. The insight gives a snapshot of a moment in time, and action might be taken on the back of it, but what next? How do you know that your action has had the desired effect, and what's to stop the problem you were trying to address recurring? Too often, management follow 'hot topics', for example employee attrition, and focus all their attention on it until it has been 'solved' in the short term. They then move on to the next thing, and the next, and then three years down the line realize that attrition is high again. To have sustained impact, KPIs must be operationalized and tracked on an ongoing basis. You may be doing deep, sophisticated analytics, but is it sustainable? Is it going to show your progression (or otherwise) over time? Relevant questions should be asked on repeat so that decisions can be made to keep the organization on track. Part of laying sustainable data foundations is to put thresholds into place against your KPIs and set up an alert if these thresholds are broken. This can then trigger a questioning process to establish what has gone wrong.

This leads me on to another large part of laying the data foundations: getting definitions straight. For example, say you want to calculate attrition, are you doing this on an annualized basis or every six months? Are you excluding temporary labour? When setting the threshold for attrition, what are you assuming to be a healthy level? Have you checked this against benchmarks for your industry?

Organizations evolve over time and definitions evolve with them. Two functions might merge and be renamed, but when doing analysis, you need to be able to look back and understand the data that related to these functions before they merged. When new products are introduced, someone needs to decide what to call them. Similarly, new geographies and regions need to be given a specific name for everyone in the organization to follow. Being clear about what you're calling things and why you're calling them that puts you in control. Without this governance, inconsistencies abound, and categorization and analysis become impossible.

Once you have the definitions of things agreed, the OP&A Team can put a data management process into place to ensure inconsistencies don't creep in again. Governance is critical, so that data associated with any changes, such as the introduction of a new product, a merger or entering a new region, is clearly defined and named.

An important consideration when structuring your data is to decide how colour should be used. Colour coding is important to describe the type of data. In addition, each dimension should be consistently represented in the same colour – using countries as an example, the USA could always be red, New Zealand black and Australia gold. This saves on cognitive load – by being consistent, you don't need to keep referring to the key to see what each colour means.

Another key part of master data management is to introduce **data controls**. Data controls are calculations which show where there are inconsistencies. An example of a data control could be flagging where a span of control is greater than an expected maximum, or limiting the number of competencies specified for each employee.

Step 9: Monitor

The last step in the process is to monitor progress, a continuous exercise and key theme in this book which links back to the point made above about asking questions on a continual basis. Using insight to get to an action is all well and good, but the action itself doesn't mean anything unless you have a way of monitoring its impact. Monitoring is crucial. It tells you one of two things: either that the action has had the impact you were hoping for, or that the action has failed, and was therefore wrong, or insufficient. Monitoring forms part of a continuous feedback loop: if your actions don't fully deliver, you need to return to the data and continue hypothesizing and exploring to reach fresh insight. If your actions succeed, however, it doesn't mean the monitoring process should stop there: you need to keep monitoring to ensure that you see continuous improvement as well as identify potential risk or variation from the plan.

Creating dashboards

I'll end this chapter with advice on how to use your data to create dashboards. Dashboards are collections of visualizations which are shown in a single view to communicate related information clearly and effectively. They can be used to monitor and report on a wide range of HR metrics such as headcount, diversity and inclusion, talent acquisition or Learning and Development. Many platforms incorporate pre-packaged dashboards as well as an automated end-to-end process to refresh dashboards on a regular cadence so they can be used for regular monitoring of key metrics.

Dashboards are storytelling devices. The starting point is deciding what story to tell, and this should guide every decision you make when creating your dashboard. There's always a trade-off when deciding how to tell your story between flicking through multiple different dashboards and having everything in one place. The former approach runs the risk of the viewer losing track of the story as you flick from one sheet to another, but on the flip side, having too much information in one place can be overwhelming and too much for the brain to process all in one go. Like with any good design, clutter is a no-no. Ensure enough white space so that the viewer doesn't get overloaded and it's clear where the eye needs to go.

Revisit the advice on storytelling I gave earlier in the chapter, as much of this is applicable to dashboards. Stories begin with the question you want to be answered. Different sheets can be combined to build up a more detailed view of your business. With modern technology there is a range of different options that can be used to create different views and pull them together.

Figure 4.2.4 shows an example of a dashboard related to flight risk. The following aspects make it exemplary:

- The questions ('Which current employees are at risk of leaving? Which features contribute most to leaving or staying?') are at the top of the dashboard.
- The questions are clearly answered by the graphs and graphics which have been chosen. The most important information – who is likely to leave and which features contribute to someone's decision to leave or stay – are given centre stage. Those who are a flight risk are shown in the middle at the top of the dashboard, and the reasons why are middle bottom.

FIGURE 4.2.4 An example of good dashboard design

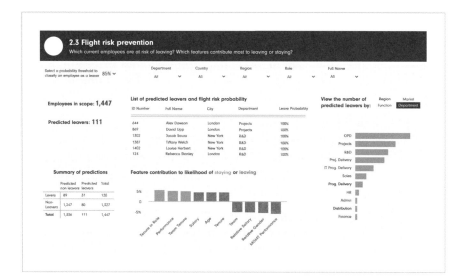

- These two graphics are sufficient to answer the main questions, but supplementary information is given at the sides of the dashboard to augment the story.

- On the right-hand side you can view the number of predicted leavers by region, market, function and department. Filters are used to allow you to decide on the information you want to present, depending on the story you want to tell.

- Key metrics are shown on the left and are sized in a way that draws the eye. The viewer can quickly see the headline that 111 people out of a scope of 1,447 are a flight risk.

- White space between objects on the dashboard is important so that the viewer isn't overloaded with information.

- Colour is used to aid fast understanding. Features which contribute to staying are in blue while features contributing to leaving are in red.

Final thoughts

The overriding message throughout this chapter is that of discipline. Laying sustainable data foundations requires rules and routines to be followed by all stakeholders on a consistent basis. Failing to get this message across in your organization will hamper your efforts from the start. Emphasize the importance of master data management with everyone involved in the process, and ensure that everyone is clear why building strong data foundations is key to sustained business performance over time.

Once you have your data in place, there are hundreds of questions you could ask to understand your organization in more depth. Where do you begin? Go back to your business goals to ascertain which questions are the most critical, and start there. Once you've started answering some of these questions, build momentum and answer more. Identify further sources of data, both internal and external, to add to your data warehouse so you can reach increasingly rich insight. This will maximize the potential of machine learning models, which I cover in Chapter 4.3. There is no point in insight for insight's sake, so once you have it, think carefully about how to present it to instigate change. The necessary change might seem obvious to you, but it may not to those who are further away from the data. Use the advice given in this chapter around storytelling and dashboard design to inspire that change.

It's unlikely that just one system will meet all your needs. You're far more likely to need a best-of-breed technology stack. New tech emerges all the time. It's critical to stay in a heads-up mindset and keep abreast of what's on the horizon. See what's coming and consider how it could help you reach deeper insight and more meaningful action. The tech you invest in will have an enormous impact on the data science projects you can pursue. I'll consider some of these in the next chapter.

REMEMBER THIS

1   It's not what you know, it's what you do with what you know that counts.

2   Build a flexible data warehouse which can accommodate a range of fast-changing data points from internal and external sources – by combining and blending data you will reach richer insight.

3   Data models need to be automated and repeatable.

4   There is unlikely to be one tool for the job. Use a range of best-of-breed technology to meet your needs.

5   Security is key so think about who has permission to see what, and when. HR data is very sensitive, which is another reason to stay away from Excel.

6   Think about the dashboards you create and tell good stories. Getting people to act takes more than just analysis.

Notes

1 Minto, B (2021) *The Pyramid Principle: Logic in writing and thinking*, FT Publishing International.

2 Pollack, L (2015) A testing time for spreadsheets, *Financial Times*, 21 July. www.ft.com/content/0fdc6e62-2f23-11e5-91ac-a5e17d9b4cff (archived at https://perma.cc/8ZBY-8QKA)

4.3

Ignoring statistical traps and leveraging data science

Introduction

Having lived through the Covid-19 pandemic, we have become accustomed to hearing about the need to 'follow the evidence', 'be led by the data' and 'listen to the science'. If only it was that simple. Even with the noblest of intentions, conclusions can be drawn from data that are completely wrong, which can lead to harmful action. There are also many moments when the intent is less than noble. If someone has a conviction that something should be done, they might use the authority of erroneously presented data to get their way. In situations like this, it's not that the data is wrong (a 'you have your facts and I have mine' situation), it's that data can easily, with or without intent, be prepared to show something that isn't necessarily true. In this chapter, I show that I can present compelling evidence that rich people are more likely to vote Democrat or sharks love to eat people who have just consumed an ice cream.

Science is a process. Defined by the Science Council as the 'pursuit and application of knowledge and understanding of the natural and social world following a systematic methodology based on evidence',[1] it requires, among many things, critical analysis, evidence, measurement, testing hypotheses, inductive reasoning and repetition. In other words, data is a necessary but insufficient criterion for scientific endeavour. There are many traps when working with data, some more obvious than others, that are all too easy to fall into.

I also believe that those of us who work with data and use it to make decisions have a moral duty to educate ourselves to prevent unintentional harm with the veneer of data-driven, evidence-based and rigorous work. In other words, it's possible to use data to create significant authority, but still be wrong. The scientific approach helps us to reach the truth, while recognizing that we might struggle to know something with absolute certainty. 'Absolute certainty' isn't part of a scientist's vernacular. It is more about putting forward our best guess based on the evidence, and thinking analytically to test against our intuition, which can often be faulty.

Is it simple? No. I wish I could say it was, but the world is full of colour, it's not black and white. Remember the phrase 'All models are wrong, but some are useful'?[2] The tools that we use to measure have their imperfections and there will always be gaps in our knowledge. The purpose of this chapter is to plug some of those dangerous gaps and make you more aware of the art of the possible. Many of the modelling techniques discussed can be used to understand your workforce on a deeper level, as well as make predictions and plan scenarios. My aim isn't to teach you how to build these models, but more to show you the kinds of questions you can answer by using them and then identify helpful actions to continuously improve. I begin with some common statistical traps and how to avoid them.

Common statistical traps

Data can often be misrepresentative and insights are only as good as those who draw them. I'm starting this chapter with a look at the kinds of statistical traps that people fall into time and again, which results in erroneous conclusions being drawn from data. The world is full of wrong and dangerous analysis and statistics. Linear correlations are calculated with high correlation coefficients (R) at the wrong level and bad science is peddled as robust analysis. There are many PhD dissertations that can be written on bad analysis. Given the scope of this book, I am going to focus on the six statistical flaws that I see most frequently. This doesn't mean you should stop the learning here. More, I hope, that you gain an interest to want to learn more and avoid making recommendations that give the illusion of being robust but are not. Whatever the exploration you are making with data, you should always maintain a questioning mindset to ensure that the conclusions you are drawing are valid and correct. The six traps I am going to cover are:

1   the ecological fallacy
2   taking correlation for causation

3 ignoring statistical significance

4 averages versus medians

5 the McNamara Fallacy

6 ignoring data, biases or bad data

The ecological fallacy

In the 2004 US election George W Bush won the 15 poorest states and John Kerry won nine of the 11 wealthiest. The conclusion: wealthy people vote Democrat and poor people vote Republican. And yet 62 per cent of voters with annual incomes over \$200,000 voted for Bush, while only 36 per cent of voters with annual incomes of \$15,000 or less voted for him.[3] So that conclusion is completely inaccurate.

This is a great example of the ecological fallacy. 'An ecology fallacy is a logical fallacy in the interpretation of statistical data where inferences about the nature of individuals are deduced from inference for the group to which those individuals belong.'[4]

In the context of HR, an example of the ecological fallacy in practice is the likely hypothesis of a correlation between performance and absenteeism as measured through the Bradford Index. The Bradford Index weights the number of absence instances higher than the total duration of absence. The theory is that short, frequent and unplanned absences are more disruptive than longer absences. The formula is $B = S^2 \times D$ where S is the number of spells (instances) and D is the duration. For example, if someone were sick once for 10 days, their Bradford score would be $1^2 \times 10 = 10$. But if they were sick 10 times a day at a time, giving the same total of 10 days, their score would be $10^2 \times 10 = 1,000$. For a given group of employees, the histogram (in Figure 4.3.1) clearly shows that those with a Bradford score below 100 have an average performance of 5.6 out of 10, while those between 600 and 700 have an average of only 3.

This is proven even more emphatically through the 'scientific-looking' correlation in Figure 4.3.1. The figure on the left shows the average performance for each Bradford Index group while that on the right takes each of those six groups and draws a correlation between each group's performance and their average Bradford score. The same groups of employees (those with Bradford factors less than 100, between 100 and 200, and so on) are correlated with their performance ratings. Unsurprisingly, the correlation (r) is –0.97 or almost perfect (a score of r = 1 or –1 is perfectly correlated while

FIGURE 4.3.1 Histogram and aggregate scatter with linear regressions of average performance rankings by average Bradford Index category

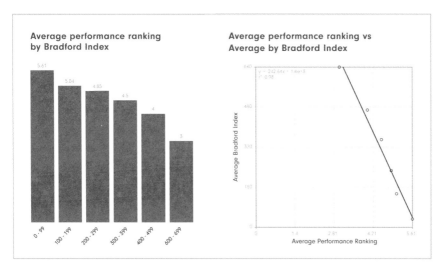

a score of r = 0 means there is zero correlation). Wow, think the people reviewing these numbers. Conclusions are drawn: 'We need to sort out the poor-performing employees.' 'It's so logical that it's these people who aren't performing!' The analyst gets a pat on the back and now the management team thinks it has the proof and burning platform to take action against these low performers.

However, in this instance, they are all wrong. In fact, they are terribly wrong. They have just fallen for the ecological fallacy. In the above example, if you dig just a fraction deeper, the distribution of the 46 employees included within the analysis is shown in Figure 4.3.2.

You can see, straight away, that there are very few (three) data points of those with a Bradford score above 300. You can also see a large range of performance rankings of those with a Bradford score below 100. In fact, if you draw the scatter chart at the individual rather than group level, you can instantly see there is, in fact, no correlation (it is just 0.023). There are only two employees with high Bradford scores and poor performance scores.

This is a good example of what is officially called 'outlier analysis'. No drastic or group action is necessary on the basis of this data. Instead, a quick investigation into their historical performance to find out if they have always been poor performers would be advisable (if possible). Then a conversation can happen either to find out if something or someone is affecting their performance, or how the manager can help bring them back on track. This is

FIGURE 4.3.2 Departmental and individual scatter plots of performance rankings by Bradford Index category

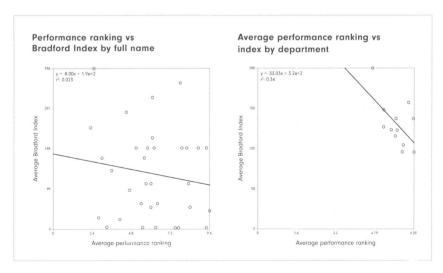

obviously a tailored example, but it is an excellent reminder of the value of digging into statistics, questioning what you see and avoiding sweeping conclusions which are wrong and could have a negative impact.

Correlation versus causation

Did you know that it is dangerous to eat ice cream and then go swimming? Sharks love ice cream. They have a craving for it, almost equal to any toddler. How do I know this? Through a highly comprehensive study covered over decades, there is almost a perfect correlation between ice cream consumption and the likelihood of shark attacks. R, the correlation coefficient, is almost one. It's almost perfect. Sharks like people who have just eaten ice cream, right? Clearly, no. So how can they be correlated? The real correlation is that the hotter it is, the more ice creams people eat, the more they swim and the more likely it is that they are going to be attacked by sharks. This may be obvious, but every day people jump to overly simplistic and inaccurate conclusions, confusing correlation with causation.

A correlation is just a number. It happens to calculate the strength of a linear relationship between variables, but it does not carry any information about causation. Why? Because causation is far more complicated than the idea of how nicely it can fit a line to data. In general, it is very difficult to show causation because we need to rule out all other factors that could influence the relationship.

In a business context, we can show correlations are high and use these effectively for prediction. But it is important to ask why this correlation is occurring to examine causation. For instance, suppose that performance ratings were inversely correlated to number of absences. However, the driver of the relationship is unclear. That is, we cannot determine whether performance ratings were assigned as a penalty for absences or whether missed days contributed to lower performance. The causation is unclear, but the correlation is still useful to drive a conversation, investigate the potential drivers before acting (for example, by using the Five Whys technique to find the root cause, which I covered in *Data-Driven Organization Design*) and run relevant analysis for future conclusions to be drawn. Asking why and trying to understand underlying reasons is fundamental to scientific method. One of my economics professors always used to ask us to articulate the intuition behind our findings.

Ignoring statistical significance

If we are going to draw conclusions about a set of data, then we should have some understanding of how strongly we can draw those conclusions. I am going to use a simplified example to demonstrate my point. The example below shows that, for a set of employees, men are higher performers than women. So does that mean that we should only hire men? The problem here is that the statistics can get quite complex, so here are a couple of simple tools and thoughts. The first is to look at the variation within the dataset. The greater the standard deviation, the less likely you can draw the conclusion. Why? Standard deviation measures the average of how spread out the data is. You can think about it this way: if female employees all have similar performance measures, then it is possible to make better generalizations about that group. More similarity means a small standard deviation. If, instead, some are performing well, some are performing poorly and some are doing okay, it is harder to tell a story about what is happening to the whole group. This is a situation with a large standard deviation – lots of differences, a more spread-out group.

A good way to visualize this is through the box plot diagram, which is described in Figure 4.3.3. The box plot shows the distribution of the data. For the median, there is a thick line and a box is drawn to show the majority of the data points. This could be the upper and lower deciles (the latter is where 90 per cent of the points are above it and 10 per cent of the points below) or quartiles (the same, but 25 per cent and 75 per cent). A further set of lines

FIGURE 4.3.3 Box plot explanation

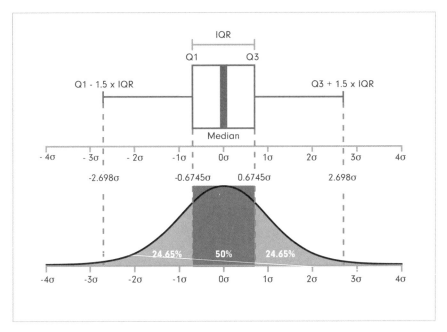

shows the upper and lower limits of the data. This could be the max and min, or the 99 per cent and 1 per cent points (the percentiles). The box plot gives you a visual sense of distribution, which helps to indicate where there is more than just a simple story in the data.

The risk of using bar charts and the power of the box plot is highlighted in Figure 4.3.4. The left-hand bar chart shows the performance scores of males and females. At face value it appears males are performing far better, with an average of 6.4 out of 10 compared with the female average of 5.9. But when the same data is plotted using the box plot, another picture emerges. The median performance for females is actually 7.5. There is far more variability within the female population, with the lowest scores of 0 being 'achieved' and therefore taking the average down.

The next thing to look at when thinking about statistical significance is the sample size. The smaller the sample size, the greater the danger. This also makes sense. If you want to make a claim about the performance of women and you only measure the performance of 10 women, how confident are you that they reflect all women the company would ever be interested in hiring? If you get performance measures from more women, you have a clearer idea of what is happening on average. How can we make a statistical decision

FIGURE 4.3.4 Average and box plot of gender performance levels

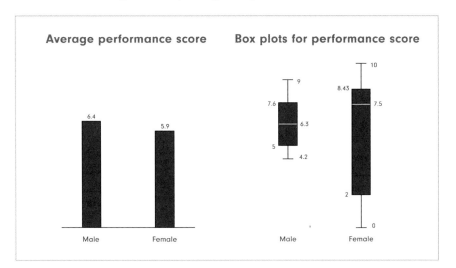

about whether men perform better on average? We turn to the most common statistical significance test, which is called the t-test. We can plug all of these numbers into the formula for a t-test comparing two averages. The result from such a test is a single percentage called a p-value. (It is not in this book's scope to outline the t-test. For further reading on this please see the suggestions at the end of the chapter.) In our scenario, this value is 15 per cent. Great – so how do I get any information about my employees' performance based on this number? In this scenario, the p-value measures the likelihood that these differences in employee performance arise completely by chance rather than due to any real average performance differences. It is standard practice to conclude that a p-value of less than 5 per cent indicates a 'significant' difference. Here, with our value of 15 per cent, we cannot make this claim. Are men performing better than women on average? Yes. But are they performing significantly better on average? No. So should we hire only men to boost performance scores? Not according to the data.

If you are told that a value is 'statistically significant', you should ask: 'Statistically significant compared with what?' and 'According to which statistical test?' Statistical significance is used within a section of statistical analysis called hypothesis testing (see below) and is used to infer how likely it is that we observe data by chance. Instead of using the phrase 'statistical significance', you will save a lot of energy and confusion by just explaining in words the conclusion your data leads you to. For example, it isn't (statistically) possible to conclude that men are performing better than women. It is also good practice to include details about the statistical test used to reach your conclusion and the number of data points included in the calculation.

Averages versus medians

The danger of averages can be appreciated through a simple thought experiment. Imagine you are in a bar of 100 environmental change leaders, and someone told you their average wealth was $1,850.5 million. Wow, you might think, I'm not paying a penny for my drink given that these are all billionaires! But then, someone tells you that Elon Musk is in the room. This means that the average of the remaining 99 is $500,000, as Elon Musk, at the time of writing, is worth £185 billion. Given what you've just found out, a more accurate way to describe this group would be 'Hey, did you know the median income in this bar is $250,000, with the top percentile being worth $185 billion? And by the way, who managed to get Elon Musk here, and is he buying? However, sadly, just over a quarter of this group has zero effective wealth'. It doesn't always pay to be an environmental change agent, but at least the beer might be free.

The McNamara Fallacy

The McNamara Fallacy is named after the former US Secretary of Defense, Robert McNamara. Known for being data-driven and scientifically minded, McNamara made a vital mistake during the Vietnam War. He used one quantitative metric – body count – to make decisions. Body count data was easy to get, and he used that and that alone to gain insight into how the war was progressing.

Statistical blindness such as this is an easy trap to fall into. It's akin to putting your head in the sand. The result is a disregard for things that cannot be measured (or are comparatively difficult to measure) and an assumption (whether implicit or explicit) that those things are therefore unimportant or don't even exist. If we manage what we measure, we also don't manage what we don't measure. By becoming fixated on one single thing, we risk overlooking things of statistical importance. Avoid the trap of measuring what is easy rather than thinking about what really matters.

Ignoring data, biases or bad data

We all have biases which can lead us to be selective in the data that we use. There is a strong human tendency to ignore data that doesn't conform to our views and emphasize that that does. This tendency is easy to spot and call out. But what if the data that you are using is just wrong, or bad data?

The danger of using bad data is illustrated brilliantly in the discovery of planets. Certain planets are bright enough to be seen by the naked eye, and so have been known about since the beginning of time. The ancients knew that Mercury, Venus, Mars, Jupiter and Saturn existed as they could be observed from Earth. It took until 1781, with the aid of a telescope, for the astronomer William Herschel to discover the next one, which was to become known as Uranus. But when he first observed it through his telescope, he was confused. No one had ever discovered a planet before, so it didn't cross his mind that that's what this might be. Instead, he wrote of a comet in the night sky, or a star. Seeing something for the first time can be confusing.

The other confusing thing was its path and 'wobble'. Amazingly, using the data they had at the time and what they knew about Newton's Laws of Gravity, they were able to make mathematical predictions, and figure out that there had to be another major planet tugging on Uranus and making it wobble. This became known as Planet X. It wasn't until 1846 that this prediction was proved to be correct. The Berlin Observatory got the location right and found Neptune. Bang. Success to science.

After more observations, it seemed that Neptune was being impacted in the same way that Uranus had been, which led scientists to believe that there had to be yet another planet somewhere. After much searching, Pluto was found in 1930. Pluto was too small and in the wrong place to have the observed impact on Neptune, but never mind, we'd found our Planet X. Except we hadn't, and hadn't even needed to. Further investigation found that Neptune wasn't acting with the same 'wobble' that Uranus had been; it was simply that the data collected by the Washington Observatory had been wrong. Once this 10-year span of data was excluded from the sample of observations, everything made sense. Neptune was moving as you would expect it to move, and there was no other Planet X tugging on it.

Predicting and finding Neptune was a triumph to science, so falling into the trap of having the data predict another planet comes into the realm of confirmation bias. We look for data that conforms to and confirms what we expect to be true. This story also highlights, as Neil deGrasse Tyson explains so well, that science is *hard*.[5] This is why medical researchers do double-blind sampling, debate evidence and prove conclusions wrong. It is why things are so hard to prove right. In science you need to be able to replicate results. But move forward we must. We need to test our findings and be open to our conclusions being wrong. As the evidence changes, so too should our views. Is it perfect? No, and it never will be, but just wishing or expecting something to be true is a greater evil. I personally love the idea that I'm on a constant journey of discovery. Yes, it can really hurt to have a belief or conclusion proved wrong. We find ourselves attached to things we believe to be true, especially if we discovered them. But it's a fact of life I try to accept.

As I hope this section has shown, the key to avoid falling into these six traps is to perform statistical analysis in a questioning mindset. Always ask why the data is showing what it is showing and question it. It is true? Could it be misleading? This mindset is necessary when applying any statistical technique. I'll now take you through some common ones used by OP&A.

Statistical techniques

Technique: Survival analysis

Survival analysis was first developed for use in the medical field to predict the efficacy of drugs and how they might prolong the life of patients who take them. Survival rates typically form a curve over time. For example, there might be a 100 per cent survival rate in the first year, dropping to 70 per cent in the second, 50 per cent in the third and so on. From this, predictions can be made about the probability of a patient being alive at a point in time along the curve if they take medication. This well-established technique is often adapted to understand churn, both of customers and clients but also, from an OP&A perspective, of employees. The aim is not only to predict when someone might leave, but also to understand the drivers behind that decision.

APPLICATION

When using this technique to understand churn, you first need to know the history of who stayed and who churned over time, and then manipulate and reshape the data so that everyone starts at time point 0. From this, you can then build the survival curve. Once you can see the curve, you can overlay such things as workforce segmentation and dimensions such as the manager, location and the time zone of the manager versus the employee. This overlaying of data helps to answer the following sorts of questions:

- Which groups are likely to leave and why?
- Are lots of people leaving in the first six months?
- Does the location of the manager have an impact on how quickly people churn?
- Does the start date have an impact? Are people who join in one month more likely to stick around than those who join in another?
- Do pay reviews have an impact? Is the timing of these reviews significant, and the amount of increase agreed?
- Do performance reviews have an impact? How had those employees who churned been performing?

As mentioned in Chapter 4.2, answering these questions is not simply about gaining insight but also about identifying the actions that could be taken from that insight. The more data you have, the greater the level of insight you can reach, and the more specific the action. If, for example, you can see from the curve that lots of people are leaving in the first six months of their employment, that could suggest a process failure – could you be hiring the wrong people or are people joining the company with the wrong expectations? Are roles being oversold in the talent acquisition process, or does your onboarding process need to be looked at? If the curve shows high churn after a longer period, it could be worth looking at management. Are you giving the right kind of management training and the right level of support to People Managers?

At Hokupaa, survival curve analysis was used to gain insight into the relationship between higher churn levels and the time of year that people joined the company. It revealed that churn could be dependent on whether people joined close to an annual or biannual performance review as this had an impact on the clarity of their objectives. The longer the time before the review, the higher the level of churn. This insight led to specific action to improve the chances that people would stay longer at the company.

Technique: Regression

Regression analysis is a common statistical method used in decision-making to understand the relationship between two or more variables. Correlation is a type of regression. Regression is usually presented in graph form, with an x and y axis. We often think of linear regression as being represented by a fixed line – this is simple linear regression with one x and one y variable. Not everything in the world is linear, so multiple linear regression is also needed to understand the relationship between one y and two or more x variables.

Linear regression can be used to understand such things as:

- How is the data distributed? Is it normally distributed?
- What is the average, standard deviation, minimum and maximum?
- Are there any significant outliers?
- Can some modes or clusters be identified?

APPLICATION

Regression can be used as a first port of call to see if there's anything in the data worth investigating further. For example, you might want to see if there's any correlation between experience and pay. It's easy to fall into traps when performing regression. For example, you might be able to draw a line of best fit, but the correlation is so low and there's so much variability that it doesn't really mean anything.

Technique: Classification

Classification identifies categories, or classes, that observations belong to. It helps you to answer the following sorts of questions:

- Is the dataset balanced?
- How many observations are there by class?
- Do the different classes share any apparent similarities?

APPLICATION

Classification is a helpful technique to use to identify causes of churn. If you're looking at employee churn by country and grade, you may find that North America has thousands of data points over a five- or 10-year period, while Chile, where fewer people are employed, has less than 50. With fewer observations, drawing conclusions is a lot more difficult.

Technique: Association analysis

Association analysis uncovers hidden patterns to find interesting relationships in large datasets. It works by trying to find rules in the data which can be used to make predictions.

APPLICATION

Association analysis can be used to look for patterns to predict churn. It may be that attrition is particularly high for people who have managers in different locations or for those who didn't go through the onboarding process properly. To use this technique in the context of onboarding, you first need data about who followed all the right onboarding processes; you can then overlay this data with those who are churning. You'll then be able to assess whether onboarding could be a factor. You might also be able to overlay performance data to assess whether high or low performance has an impact on churn, or competency data to see if certain competencies, or lack of them, can be an accurate predictor.

Technique: Clustering

Clustering is a statistical process used for discovering inherent groupings in data. It groups sets of objects or observations in such a way that objects in one group are more similar to each other than to objects in the other groups. There are many practical applications of clustering, including:

- Customer segmentation – Brands with thousands of customers can leverage clustering to classify their customer base, and generate more targeted products and advertisements.
- Topic modelling – Clustering can be used to organize large bodies of texts into similar topics.
- Outlier detection – Clustering and similarity measures can be used to spot abnormal observations in a dataset.

APPLICATION

It can be useful to group together those with similar competencies, or who are doing similar work (this can be identified through an Individual Activity Analysis (IAA)). Clustering is also an excellent way to create a role grid. Once you've done your IAA and used clustering to find the people who are doing the same work, you can assume that they are probably the same role, which can then become the basis of your role grid (see Chapter 1.2).

Technique: Hierarchical clustering

Hierarchical clustering doesn't result in a single set of clusters, nor a static mapping of observations to a cluster. Instead, the algorithms generate a hierarchy of clusters.

Hierarchical clustering can be used in competency assessment to determine:

- which people have similar competencies
- how they form into sub-groups
- which elements best predict success, i.e. define output measures that are inherently good or bad and assess whether competencies have any impact on these outputs

Hierarchical clustering can also be used to sort roles into sub-role families and role families or to understand reasons for leaving. Reasons can be clustered into groups to gain insight into key problem areas.

Technique: Naïve analysis

Sometimes, the most interesting insight is that which you would never have thought to look for. This is the premise of naïve analysis, a statistical technique which, unlike every other technique described in this chapter, does not start with a hypothesis. Naïve analysis spills out insight related to an outcome (for example, churn) using any data, for example join date, manager name, the location of the manager and the number of levels between the employee and manager. The data it chooses to use might also be seemingly unrelated to the outcome, such as the first letter of a surname or employee height. Due to the random nature of the data it selects, the understanding gained can either be amazingly insightful or completely useless. It might tell you that your male employees are taller than your female employees. Is this useful to know? No. The insight derived from naïve analysis still needs to be questioned. First, ask whether it's interesting and relevant, and second, if it is, apply a questioning mindset and ask if it is valid. It might tell you that sharks like ice cream! Make sure that you're not falling into any of the statistical traps outlined above, such as correlation versus causation.

At Hokupaa, naïve analysis was used to discover that if certain types of people managed certain other types of people, it led to higher churn of the people being managed. This insight was neither looked for nor expected. It simply emerged through the data.

Technique: Organization Network Analysis

Organization Network Analysis (ONA) is a method for studying communication and relationships within organizations. It has the potential to transform understanding of the organization by looking at how people connect, how knowledge and information flows, and how and where people collaborate to get things done, thereby helping organizations to harness the potential their people provide. Influencers can be identified to help accelerate change and innovation. New recruits can be onboarded faster by connecting them to knowledge hubs. Your talent retention strategy can be focused on areas of highest risk, and you can analyse and understand the behaviours of your highest performing people and teams.

For ONA to be successful, it's vital to first identify the problem that needs to be solved. You can then pinpoint the type of social interactions that might help. Then you need to work out how best to quantify relationships within the organization that relate to the identified problem. One way is to look at email traffic – who emails each other a lot and how quickly does it take people to respond? What about other systems, such as Teams or Slack? You can also send a quick questionnaire to people, asking them who they trust in the organization and the kind of relationships they have.

APPLICATION

An excellent use of ONA is to gain insight on the people in your organization who are thought of as being highly proficient in a particular skill. This can be done via a competency survey where people are asked to name those they go to for advice in particular competencies. Performing this exercise at Hokupaa led to some fascinating insight. When performing self-assessment, people were asked to rate their proficiency level on a scale of one to five in a specialized functional skill in data science. Many of the British and American 'guys' rated themselves as a 4, and rightly so. They were all highly proficient and had trained hard in the skill and practised it for many years. However, an equally highly trained woman in the team who was Chinese in origin rated herself as a 3. Yet when we asked 'the guys' in the same survey who they went to for advice in this skill, they all pointed to the same person, to the woman who had rated herself as a 3. At the time, she was one of 17 people in the world with her level of accreditation in this skill, and the first woman to achieve it, but she still rated herself lower than 'the guys'. Without this type of ONA, highly talented and modest people who are reticent to put themselves forward may forever be hidden stars in an organization.

Overlaying ONA with competency data can be incredibly powerful, and allows you to answer the following types of questions:

- How long does it take for someone to be a trusted part of the network after they join?
- Who are the highly proficient and trusted people in the organization?
- Who are the connectors across geographical silos? Can we move those people around to help strengthen relationships?
- If it takes too long to get connected in a certain part of the organization, does that lead to churn six months down the line?

Technique: Career path mapping

I wrote about the application of career path mapping in Chapter 2.4. It's a kind of temporal analysis that tracks how careers evolve over time.

APPLICATION

By tracking people's career paths, you can make predictions about who future leaders might be and understand the paths that are most likely to mean that people reach the top. This insight can then be used to help certain groups make career choices to help them get there. For example, if in your data you can see that fewer women reach leadership positions in your organization than men, you can analyse the paths that male and female leaders have taken and assess any similarities and differences. When this was done for a consumer goods client, it was discovered that women who had commercial experience in their background were far more likely to reach leadership positions. Targeted talent development strategies were then employed to give potential female leaders the experience that they needed.

The opportunities for career path mapping are huge. Split by function, gender and ethnicity, it can feed into diversity and inclusion analysis, and modelling can be done to assess whether five-year diversity and inclusion targets are achievable. Problem areas that need immediate attention can also be identified, such as any areas of concern which might be a result of unconscious bias.

Machine learning

Machine learning is a branch of data science which uses the kind of statistical techniques described in this chapter to train algorithms. Data is fed to the algorithms on a cadence, perhaps every day, week or month, and the algorithm gradually learns over time so that it can make better and more accurate predictions. This section is not intended to make you an expert on machine learning – there are plenty of books and resources out there that can do that. More, it's to give you an overview of how a machine learning project is set up and the kind of things that need to be thought about. My intention is to arm you with sufficient knowledge to work with the Data Scientists on your team and ensure that the right models are being built to answer the right questions.

As you progress through a machine learning project, you are likely to encounter the terms 'supervised' and 'unsupervised' learning. These refer to how algorithms learn. Most machine learning projects use supervised learning, whereby inputs are mapped to outputs. In other words, the datasets 'supervise' the algorithm's learning. **Supervised learning** is generally used for classification and regression problems. The main supervised learning algorithms used to solve these problems are:

- linear models
- support vector machines
- decision trees (random forest is a supervised machine learning algorithm which is based on decision tree algorithms)
- similarity-based algorithms
- ensemble learning
- neural networks – models which mimic the functioning of biological neurons to generate predictions. They connect many artificial neurons – simple processing elements – together, thus allowing the model to account for complex and non-linear relationships. Neural networking can be applied to the talent selection process. Using competency data, neural network models can help to find hidden gems and must-keep talent. They can be used to predict outcomes like higher retention, team retention and sales performance

With **unsupervised learning**, there is no output variable, so the algorithm is not 'learning' how to reach an output. It is left unsupervised to uncover interesting patterns and relationships in the data. Whereas supervised learning is often used for classification and regression problems, unsupervised learning is often used for clustering and association analysis problems.

Machine learning projects are generally divided into distinct phases which are completed one after another. The purposes of these phases broadly span experimentation and productionization. The experimentation phase ensures the right model is chosen to fit the right business questions. Productionization ensures that insight is not only generated on a one-off basis but continuously over time. As the amount of data increases, the ability to predict gets stronger, which is why the productionizing phase is so critical.

The experimentation and productionization phases can in turn be split into four stages, the first two relating to experimentation and the latter two to productionization:

1 Discover

2 Alpha

3 Beta

4 Live

The focus of the Discover phase is to define the business questions which need to be answered by the machine learning project. This is best done through engaging stakeholders to establish their requirements and dig into the problems they are facing. Business questions permeate all aspects of a machine learning project's architecture (inputs, algorithm design and outputs) so they need to be clearly defined and signed off before exiting the experimentation phase. To help define these questions, ask yourself the following:

- What is the task at hand (is a supervised or unsupervised learning algorithm needed)?
- What is the business use case? How will the model be used?
- How interpretable should the model be?
- Is predictive accuracy the main target?
- Should the model also generate recommendations for actions?

Once you know the problem, you'll have a good idea of the data you need to solve it, so the next step is to perform a thorough assessment of the nature of the data and availability. This is the Alpha stage. You can also process and consolidate any existing datasets so that they can feed into the machine learning model. Much of this goes back to building the data model, discussed in Chapter 4.2. Assessing the nature of the data can be done by answering a few important questions:

- What is the quality of the data?
- Is any data missing? Why is it missing, and what can be done about it?
- What is the distribution of the dependent variable (see regression and classification, above)?
- What are the distributions of the input variables?
  - How are the numeric columns distributed?
  - What are the correlations between the different inputs with the outputs?
  - Are there any categorical columns?
  - Are there any free text columns? Can these fields be used?
  - Are there any date columns? What is the minimum and maximum date?
  - Are there any missing features? Are there features that need to be engineered?

Once you know the purpose of the model, your team can then develop a general model architecture, using one of the many available technologies, for example Python, R, Alteryx, AML designer or Auto-ML. The goal is to build a functional end-to-end pipeline, from data processing to prediction output. The model can then be optimized by fine tuning the algorithm to improve its accuracy. This is effectively your dry run, so at this point the results of the model are played back to check whether it is doing what it is intended to do. Check that it meets the business case outlined at the end of the Discover stage.

Next is the Beta phase, the purpose of which is to fully understand the model to be productionized. A key aspect of this is to set up the necessary accesses to data and the cloud machine learning environments. Another task during the Beta phase is to design the end-to-end solution architecture, from data ingestion all the way to writing and visualizing predictions.

Another aspect of this phase is automating the machine learning model. Schedules are implemented to both retrain the models and generate predictions. By the end of the Beta phase, the model needs to run on a 'business as usual' basis. As the data being fed into the model evolves, the performance of the model should be tracked, and models will need to be retrained regularly. During the Beta and Live phases, ask the following questions:

- On which platform is the model going to be productionized?
- What security measures should be implemented?

- What performance monitoring systems should be used?
- How frequently should the model be retrained?
- How frequently are new predictions going to be generated?

Once you've answered these questions, you should have a fully production-ized machine learning pipeline, from data processing to prediction generation. Most platforms also provide dashboards connected to the predictions.

How the technical architecture is documented is extremely important. The models will be handed over to and used by people who are not Data Scientists, so there needs to be a detailed description of the different stages of the data management process which can be followed. The same goes for documenting the code. Sophisticated models should be developed and documented in 'blocks' and 'modules' so that the process is clear.

Final thoughts

I hope this chapter has armed you with just enough detail to understand the potential of data science for OP&A. Many of the techniques discussed can be used to understand the workforce, make predictions, and plan scenarios related to the future workforce. By blending HR data with other types of internal and external data, you can reach insights that you hadn't even thought to look for. Importantly, employing the techniques in this chapter can help you to understand the composition of your workforce and take action to hit DEI targets. It's all about identifying necessary actions. If survival curve analysis shows that too many people are leaving in the first six months, what does that mean? Could there be a process failure? Are you hiring the wrong people? Are jobs being under- or over-sold in the recruitment process? Data science is a way of researching and implementing ways to derive more information from data. It's creative, exploratory and uses established models, as opposed to statistical models, which tend to be bespoke. But remember, it isn't guaranteed to turn up something interesting – it's science!

My intention has not been to make you an expert. I don't expect you to be able to build a survival curve or a random forest model based on this chapter. I hope I have improved your awareness of the possibilities and perhaps made you feel that having a Data Scientist in your OP&A Team would be a worthwhile investment. I also hope that you now might feel confident challenging data and insight and know that you are making recommendations based on robust findings. I have only just skimmed the surface. If you would like to know more, I've made some recommendations for further reading at the end of the chapter.

Data analysis often isn't as much of a magic wand as many people think. Just because insight is based on data, it doesn't mean it's sound. Too often, people work hard to build a data model and leave the 'insight phase' of the work to the last minute. They jump to erroneous conclusions because they don't think deeply enough and make too many predictable mistakes. Unfortunately, from what I have observed from countless business presentations, much of the business world is full of terrible statistics. The bar chart is probably the most common stats tool used, yet, as this chapter has shown, it hides a whole range of flaws. Every one of us has a moral obligation to ensure that we interpret data correctly. This is true not only for the Data Team in the OP&A function but for the OP&A Leader, Organization Design Leader and Workforce Planning Leader. It's true for every single one of us.

REMEMBER THIS

1 All models are wrong, but some are useful.

2 This is a science. Be responsible and draw the right conclusions. Use analysis as guidance for further questions and be mindful of the many hidden statistical traps.

3 Blend HR data with other sources of internal and external data to reach richer insight.

4 Machine learning projects are divided into distinct phases.

5 And finally... sharks prefer to munch on people who have just eaten an ice cream!

Notes

1 Science Council (2022) Our definition of science. https://sciencecouncil.org/about-science/our-definition-of-science (archived at https://perma.cc/X8LU-8UEK)

2 Thought to have been first said by the British statistician George Box.

3 Gelman, A (2008) *Red State, Blue State, Rich State, Poor State*, Princeton University Press.

4 Robinson, W (1950) Ecological correlations and the behavior of individuals, *American Sociological Review*, 15 (3), 351–57.

5 deGrasse Tyson, N (2020) Neil deGrasse Tyson explains why science is hard, StarTalk, 29 September. www.youtube.com/watch?v=w8PoG3mvqk8 (archived at https://perma.cc/7HUN-J7PF)

Further reading

Frankfort-Nachmias, C, Leon-Guerrero, A and Davis, G (2020) *Social Statistics for a Diverse Society*, 9th edition, SAGE Publications.

Salkind, N and Frey, B (2019) *Statistics for People Who (Think They) Hate Statistics*, 7th edition, SAGE Publications.

PART FIVE

The OP&A function

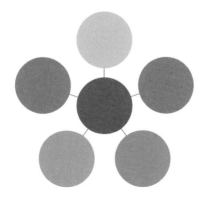

5.1

Introduction

One of the greatest truisms in management is the statement 'People are our greatest asset'. It is repeated time and again. Almost as common a cry is a plea for 'a seat at the table'. No other function wants a seat at the table more than the People function – the function responsible for organizations' greatest asset. It's been spoken and written about almost endlessly, but alongside the articulation of the desire, a concern is often expressed – if the People function were to get a seat, what would it do with it? How would it make the most of it and use it to secure relevance within the organization? Businesses are just as frustrated with their People functions as the People functions are with not having that seat. The seat needs to benefit not only the function but the entire business too. While commentators have had difficulty reaching a consensus on this point, I hope this book has demonstrated that a big part of the answer lies with OP&A. Not only does it have the potential to make the People function far more relevant, but it is vital to the success of organizations over time.

You have now reached the final part of the book. The preceding parts have laid out the work of the OP&A function, in both transformation and 'business as usual' contexts alongside the numerous benefits of having one in your organization. As demonstrated, OP&A enables organizations to stay focused on the future and make appropriate adaptations to continually perform. It can make Operational HR sub-functions like Learning and Development, Compensation and Benefits, and Talent Acquisition far more effective, enabling businesses to make the most of their people. People are organizations' greatest asset, but without active planning of the organization system within which people perform, this asset can become an expensive liability. Having the right people, with the right skills, doing the right work, in the right numbers with real alignment to achieve strategic objectives makes the workforce more engaged and productive. Waste is minimized and political game playing is diluted.

Introducing OP&A capability is a big step for any organization, and, while the benefits are clear, cannot be entered into lightly or without sufficient preparation and planning. Remember that statistic quoted in Chapter 1.1 – that 98–100 per cent of time in most People functions is currently dedicated to transactional tasks. Rebalancing this to bring the function more in line with how the Finance function splits its time between transactional tasks and FP&A often requires dramatic change and a significant shift in mindset. Very few organizations will have the bandwidth, capability and, sometimes, the executive support to achieve it in one go. The path to a full OP&A function is most often a journey where capability is added incrementally, and value is proved along the way. But how do you determine the path that is right for you? How should you go about it, and what should you prioritize? How do you ensure that the introduction of OP&A is supported through all levels of the organization? These are all questions that the chapters in this final part help you to answer.

What does successful OP&A look like?

OP&A capability can take a variety of different forms and success looks different depending on your goals and aspirations. Do you want to create first-class capability and use it as a driver of change? Do you want to test the water with minimal capability to see how it goes? What level of support and service do you want from OP&A? Do you foresee needing it only in certain circumstances, or do you want OP&A to be a constant presence and fundamental to the decision-making process?

Chapter 5.2 lays out different design options for OP&A capability. They include outsourcing OP&A to a third party, installing a Centre of Excellence or shared service, having a virtual organization and, finally, implementing a full OP&A function. My view is that if you want to achieve all that I discuss in *Data-Driven Organization Design* and this book, and you genuinely want the People function to have a seat at the table with FP&A, then OP&A needs to be a distinct function within the overall People function, with accountability and ownership. The other three options are simply not enough. This, I believe, is what truly successful OP&A looks like – a function which works in service to the business and asks strategic and operational questions to define what the organization should look like over time. A function which has equal footing with FP&A and defines how the requirements laid out by FP&A should be delivered by the organization. Implementing a full function gives organizations the best chance of leaving the boom-and-bust restructuring cycle behind, thereby avoiding situations which give rise to the kind of horror stories described in Chapter 2.3.

OP&A is rooted in the belief that organization design and workforce planning are processes that should be owned by a single function. All the pieces of data discussed in *Data-Driven Organization Design* (for example, the role grid and the Objectives, Activities, and Competencies taxonomies) are owned by OP&A. So too is the analytics of that data – it is vital for this to sit with OP&A so it can drive performance (in many organizations, this would historically have been owned by the People Analytics function).

The full remit of an OP&A function includes a high level of business influence and spans both organization design and workforce planning processes, as shown in Figure 5.1.1. This translates into a mandate consisting of eight key aspects:

1 Optimize the performance of the organization through organization design to deliver the company strategy effectively and efficiently, ensuring the right people, with the right skills, are doing the right work, in the right numbers with real alignment.

2 Monitor the organization on an ongoing basis and adjust the micro detailed design to maintain organizational health.

3 Plan future adaptations of the organization and workforce through modelling potential scenarios based on potential and anticipated market developments.

4 Advance the impact delivered by the People function through the application of data-driven methods. Gain insights through data to improve performance.

5 Provide executive, business line and functional leaders with integrated financial and workforce planning, forecasting, analysis and reporting for company and business line steering (coupled with FP&A).

6 Design and maintain motivating roles for the organization so that every employee understands their contribution to overall company and business line goals.

7 Provide analysis and insight to inform talent acquisition and management decisions. Understand who to recruit and when, and track and manage career paths to enable optimal internal moves.

8 Provide analysis and insight to understand the required competencies needed in the workforce now and in the future and fill existing or anticipated gaps. Understand training requirements now and in the future to feed into Learning and Development decisions.

I will return to this mandate throughout this part as it is used to inform many of the decisions that need to be made.

FIGURE 5.1.1 The scope of OP&A spans both Data-Driven Organization Design and workforce planning processes

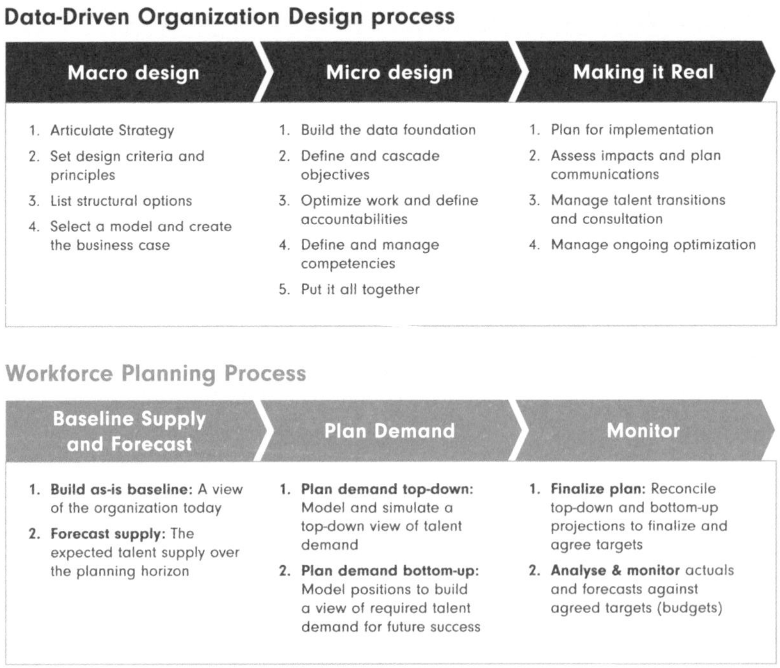

Data-Driven Organization Design process

Macro design	Micro design	Making it Real
1. Articulate Strategy 2. Set design criteria and principles 3. List structural options 4. Select a model and create the business case	1. Build the data foundation 2. Define and cascade objectives 3. Optimize work and define accountabilities 4. Define and manage competencies 5. Put it all together	1. Plan for implementation 2. Assess impacts and plan communications 3. Manage talent transitions and consultation 4. Manage ongoing optimization

Workforce Planning Process

Baseline Supply and Forecast	Plan Demand	Monitor
1. **Build as-is baseline:** A view of the organization today 2. **Forecast supply:** The expected talent supply over the planning horizon	1. **Plan demand top-down:** Model and simulate a top-down view of talent demand 2. **Plan demand bottom-up:** Model positions to build a view of required talent demand for future success	1. **Finalize plan:** Reconcile top-down and bottom-up projections to finalize and agree targets 2. **Analyse & monitor** actuals and forecasts against agreed targets (budgets)

Structure and logic for Part Five

Before you begin, I'd strongly recommend revisiting Chapter 1.2 to refresh your memory of the steps involved in macro operating and micro detailed design. It is also essential to have read Part Two: Making it Real. The chapters in Part Five serve as a mini case study for how to step through the macro operating and micro detailed design phases as well as Making it Real:

- Stage 1: Scoping the macro operating design and writing the business case (Chapter 5.2)
- Stage 2: Detailing the OP&A function (Chapter 5.3)
- Stage 3: Making the OP&A function real (Chapter 5.4)

These stages are illustrated in Figure 5.1.2.

FIGURE 5.1.2   Implementing an OP&A function follows three stages: macro operating design, micro detailed design and Making it Real

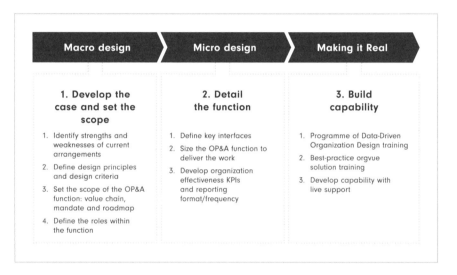

Chapter 5.2 begins by looking at the big picture: mapping out your vision for OP&A and your strategy for how to achieve it. It gives a high-level view of the OP&A value chain and processes, so that you can articulate the value delivered through each step of the chain. It also contains a helpful diagnostic tool to help you assess where you are on the OP&A maturity curve. This, in turn, helps you to define your case for change and priorities for implementation, which are laid out in the business case. A large part of macro operating design involves setting out design principles and criteria and prioritizing these so that they can inform your design options. Chapter 5.2 defines four potential options and sets the scene for the remaining chapters in the part, which assume that the chosen operating model design is that of a separate OP&A function. Figuring out where to begin

with implementing an OP&A function can feel overwhelming, and a roadmap is useful to define the major milestones along the way to full functionality. This chapter helps you to identify an 'on-ramp' to that roadmap that will work for you – this is largely defined by your current strengths and weaknesses and business need. Should you prioritize competency design, activity design or workforce planning? Are you even ready to start thinking about these or do you need to focus on getting your data straight first? These are all considerations that need to be mapped out at this stage before being picked up on in Chapter 5.4, which looks at how to make the function a reality. Throughout this chapter, sample text is given which could be used as a blueprint when writing your business case for OP&A.

Chapter 5.3 takes the high-level vision for OP&A mapped out in Chapter 5.2 and explains how to use it to detail what the function should look like. This is the equivalent to the micro detailed design. It shows how roles can be defined and designed in the context of OAC data, the ways that the key interfaces can be detailed and how to rightsize the function to deliver the work.

The last chapter in this part, Chapter 5.4 is concerned with making OP&A real – this is where you prepare for building the capability to ensure every aspect has been thought through. Where do you start? You have your roadmap for implementation, but how do you make this a reality and roll out an initial programme of work? What HOWWIP questions need to be addressed? What do you need to think about when interviewing to fill OP&A roles? These are the sorts of questions this chapter helps to address.

By the end of this part, my hope is that you will have a clear process to follow to implement OP&A in your own organization. Following the three-stage gated process outlined in Figure 5.1.2 breaks down what might at first feel overwhelming into achievable steps. I hope that you find it a constructive way to finish this book, and that it helps you to take meaningful and practical action, as well as provide you with the motivation, energy and drive to sustain that action.

5.2

Stage 1: Scoping the macro operating design and writing the business case

Introduction

This chapter is all about big-picture thinking. It's about figuring out how and where OP&A capability could sit in your organization and agreeing on a vision and strategy for its implementation. In other words, it helps you to think through the macro operating design for OP&A. My intention is to provide a blueprint for the decisions that need to be made so that you end up with a capability that fulfils your needs in the short term, and a roadmap for where you want to get to in the longer term. In 1965, American psychologist and computer scientist, JCR Licklider wrote that 'People tend to overestimate what can be done in one year and to underestimate what can be done in five or ten years'.[1] This thinking later became known as Amara's Law, when American scientist and futurist Roy Amara applied it to our tendency to overestimate the effect of technology (such as the internet) in the short run, and underestimate the effect in the long run. Bear this wisdom in mind when scoping the high-level design for OP&A. There is a huge amount of detail to think through and it's important that you are realistic about what can be achieved in the short term, while articulating how revolutionary it could be in the longer term. Once you have a fully operational OP&A function, it can completely transform your organization's performance. In the initial phases, many people underestimate just how impactful the long-term outlook can be. And many (or most) corporate managers focus on optimizing the short term.

Every organization is different, and how you integrate OP&A capability will depend on numerous factors, such as your starting point, budget, size of your organization and the amount of support for OP&A at an executive level. My fundamental belief is that OP&A capability should be housed within its own function, but, realistically, not all organizations will have the budget and support to implement this. I have seen it executed in different ways, three of which are briefly outlined in this chapter as alternative design options. Is it better to go with one of these rather than no capability at all? Undoubtedly. But realize that to get the kind of results outlined in this book and in *Data-Driven Organization Design*, an OP&A function with true accountability and ownership is needed.

Before reading this chapter, remind yourself of the full OP&A mandate outlined in Chapter 5.1, bearing in mind that this mandate will vary depending on the design option that you choose. This chapter takes you step by step through the macro operating design for OP&A. Working through it will enable you to:

- map out your vision and strategy
- map out the high-level OP&A value stream and processes
- perform a maturity curve assessment to understand your current must-keep strengths alongside weaknesses, which form the backbone of your case for change in your business case
- consider possible design criteria and design principles for OP&A
- think through different design options
- devise an implementation plan, including a roadmap for your OP&A journey

By the time you've worked through this chapter you will have much of the material necessary for writing your business case. To give you a head start, I have included boxes throughout containing sample business case text which can be adapted for your own circumstances.

Vision and strategy

Your vision conveys your overall aim. It should be a simple, succinct statement which communicates how you envisage integrating OP&A capability in the long term, tying together both value and purpose. As you might remember from *Data-Driven Organization Design*, your vision informs your strategy, which in turn informs your goals (the results you want to achieve). This is where you nail down why you want to do this. Think through the following questions:

- Do you want to invest in OP&A capability or rely on third-party providers?

- Do you have existing capability in OP&A (for example, in People Analytics, Workforce Planning or Transformation Teams)? What percentage of HR investment does this make up?

- Do you want to provide support as and when it's needed?

- Do you want to dip your toe in the water and provide minimal capability – perhaps in the form of a pilot or Agile Team to focus on a specific part of the business?

- Do you want to achieve everything in *Data-Driven Organization Design* and this book, create a world-class function and use it as a driver of change?

Your answers to these questions will inform your design criteria, which in turn inform the design option you choose (see later in the chapter). You may or may not be constrained by a budget at this point (this is often assigned only once the business case has been signed off), and so you might be limited in what you can do from the off. It will take time to come up with your vision, as it not only involves a lot of thought about what is right for your organization, but distilling this into a single statement can take a lot of iteration and discussion! A sample vision statement could be:

> *To optimize organizational performance over time by having the right people, with the right skills, doing the right work, in the right numbers with real alignment.*

This statement would feed into your strategy, which defines how you are going to achieve the vision and gets translated into strategic goals. The mandate outlined in Chapter 5.1 is a useful starting point for devising your strategic vision. Example strategic goals are shown in the next box.

OUTLINING STRATEGIC GOALS FOR OP&A CAPABILITY

The strategy goals support the defined vision. Five goals have been identified:

1   Implement agile ways of working to accelerate strategy execution.

2   Define clear roles with meaningful accountabilities to reduce churn and establish clear career paths.

3   Create a more skilled workforce focused on higher impact work, with lower-level tasks automated.

4   Optimize the workforce cost base through forward-looking positions management.

5   Ensure effective succession development to mitigate talent risks.

OP&A value chain and processes

It also helps to map out the value chain and high-level processes at this point. As a reminder, a value chain shows how the 'raw materials' (whether that's ideas or parts) needed for a business to operate can be broken down or transformed into value – be that a final product or a service. In other words, it summarizes the key steps necessary for the OP&A function to deliver value to the business. The seven steps in the OP&A value chain are shown in Figure 5.2.1 alongside a short description of the step and the value proposition implicit within each.

FIGURE 5.2.1 The seven steps of the OP&A value chain

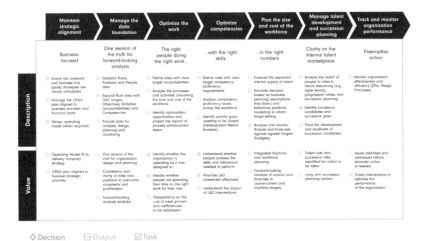

◇ Decision   ⊟ Output   ☑ Task

It's important to spell out the short- and longer-term impact that OP&A can deliver so that the more immediate value can be understood alongside a vision for the future. For example:

1   Maintaining strategic alignment ensures that the operating model is fit to execute strategy. When the OP&A plan is aligned to business strategic priorities, organizational strategy runs through the entire organization and all employees are clear about business priorities. In the shorter term, it prevents wasted effort. In the longer term, it prevents a business from falling apart.

2   Maintaining the data foundation gives one version of the truth for organization design and planning. This in turn allows analysis and insight to be reached at speed, and buys time to think, make decisions and act. In the short term, it makes everyone's lives easier. People can feel confident that they have access to correct and current information. The longer-term business benefits from accurate scenario planning.

3   Optimizing the work identifies whether people are spending their time on the right work for their role and gives transparency on the cost of each process. It improves efficiency and motivation within the workforce and results in more time being spent on the highest impact work. This allows for a more streamlined organization in the short and longer term.

4   Optimizing competencies allows you to understand the current skills and behaviours in the organization as well as those needed to maximize business performance in the future. It allows for competencies to be tracked over time and for the creation of an internal talent marketplace to analyse current role fit. This in turn means that L&D investment can be prioritized, and the impact of interventions understood. It makes for a happier workforce in the short term and ensures that the longer-term needs of the organization can be met.

5   Planning the size and cost of the workforce allows for integrated financial and workforce planning and forward-looking analysis of actuals and forecasts. This, in turn, results in less waste and a more streamlined workforce over time, equipped to maintain pace with disruption.

6   Managing talent development and succession planning improves careers and leads to less undesirable churn. It makes for a happier and more motivated workforce and also identifies risk over a long-term planning horizon.

7 Tracking and monitoring organization performance removes organizations from the boom-and-bust restructuring cycle, allowing issues to be identified and addressed before drastic action is needed. It also sheds light on connections that wouldn't otherwise be seen.

Building the case for change

Your case for change identifies issues and problems which are having a negative impact on performance, and which could be solved by the implementation of OP&A capability. It should focus on business need and be clearly tied to your strategy. Much of this comes down to identifying your strengths and weaknesses, which I like to do through an exercise called **'Imagine you are moving house'**. Moving house can be a painful but liberating experience. It often involves sifting through everything you own and deciding what to throw or give away and what to take with you, as well as identifying the things that you will need in your new place that you don't currently have. Thinking through your strengths and weaknesses when it comes to OP&A capability is very similar. Three questions should be asked:

1 What are you currently doing, perhaps in small pockets in the organization, that you want to continue as you build OP&A capability? These are your strengths.

2 Are you currently doing anything that is destroying value and should be stopped? These are your weaknesses.

3 What are you not doing, but should be doing to increase value? When should you start doing it?

To help answer these questions, I've provided a list of further questions below, arranged to help you map out your strengths and weaknesses against the steps in the OP&A value chain. These questions have been designed for 'yes' or 'no' answers to allow you to ascertain your organization's current level of OP&A maturity, using a classic maturity curve framework. Engage a range of stakeholders and ask what you are and aren't doing so that you can arrive at an answer for each question. I recommend that you get input from the OP&A sponsor or lead, if they are already in place, as well as HR Leadership Team members and representative Business Line Leaders. Keep track of your scores listed on the left-hand side as the summation of these will indicate your current level of maturity. There are four categories:

1 foundational

2 developing

3 maturing

4 advanced

Very few organizations will come out of this exercise with scores of 4 across the piece (if you do, please call me), and a huge number won't even be at the foundational level, so don't worry if that's you. See this assessment as a valuable input into prioritizing the order with which you introduce new capability. I discuss this more later in the chapter with reference to the OP&A roadmap and on-ramp.

OP&A maturity curve assessment: A diagnostic tool

STEP 1: MAINTAIN STRATEGIC ALIGNMENT

1 Do you have clearly articulated company and business line strategies in place? Is the strategy broken down into goals and a set of actions so everyone in the organization is clear about how you will win in your marketplace?

1 Is your operating model clearly defined?

1 Is macro operating design work needed to support the articulation of the strategy?

2 Do you know where you need to invest and the action you need to take to execute the strategy? Do you know where you need additional resource, and what activities you need to invest in?

2 Does the Executive Team ask 'What-If' questions and have an eye on the horizon?

2 Do discussions centre around the continual performance of the organization rather than stalling at where people are positioned on the organization chart?

STEP 2: MANAGE THE DATA FOUNDATION

1 Do you have a role grid in place, with each of the components of the organization system clearly defined in terms of the flow of data, and an infrastructure to link Roles, Positions and People data?

1   Do you have clear definitions of concepts in place to allow for a shared understanding across all stakeholders (particularly OP&A and Finance)? For example, do all parts of the organization define the 'number of employees' in the same way, or is this understood in different ways, with some assuming it's FTE and some assuming it's overall headcount?

1   Is your position data separate from people data rather than people and positions being thought of as one and the same?

2   Does position data include start and end dates and position costs?

2   Is efficient and effective master data management in place in the organization?

STEP 3: OPTIMIZE THE WORK

2   Are defined value chains and process taxonomies in place?

2   Is there an infrastructure to link target accountabilities to roles?

3   Is there an infrastructure to measure the actual work conducted by the workforce over time and calculate cost?

3   Are you doing some work in an agile way, e.g. do you have people in multiple positions, with multiple reporting lines?

5   Do you know the cost and level of fragmentation of the work?

4   Are you pulling the RRII levers to optimize the work now and into the future?

STEP 4: OPTIMIZE COMPETENCIES

2   Is there a defined competency taxonomy in place and a proficiency level framework?

3   Is there an infrastructure to link target competencies to roles and feed into talent acquisition?

3   Is there an infrastructure to measure the actual competencies possessed by the workforce, including self-assessment, management assessment, 360 review and third-party assessment?

3   Is this measured on an ad hoc basis?

3   Are the gaps identified?

4   Are your Learning and Development programmes designed around closing the gaps?

4   Is this measured on a continual basis?

STEP 5: PLAN THE SIZE AND COST OF THE WORKFORCE

2 Do you have an infrastructure to forecast internal talent supply?

2 Is a talent marketplace established?

1 Do you have defined business financial targets and underlying assumptions in place?

3 Do you use driver and ratio analysis to model demand?

3 Is sensitivity analysis done on key assumptions?

3 Are you predicting churn, do you know its root causes and are you systematically reducing it?

4 Is sensitivity analysis automated?

STEP 6: MANAGE TALENT DEVELOPMENT AND SUCCESSION PLANNING

2 Are role families and levels sufficiently defined within the role grid to allow for clear progression routes and career paths?

3 Are there defined role-level competency targets?

3 Do you have clearly defined individual-level competency data?

4 Have you identified the career paths that are most likely to lead to leadership positions?

4 Are you using this insight to address DEI imbalances?

STEP 7: TRACK AND MONITOR ORGANIZATION PERFORMANCE

1 Can you answer basic people questions like headcount, FTE, spans and layers? Can you do this by Key Organizational Dimension?

1 Is your pay, promotion and hiring fair and reflective of the community you are part of, from a DEI perspective?

3 Are organization effectiveness KPIs in place, including design principles?

3 Does your FP&A function perform top-down financial planning?

3 Do you use a rolling budget which is consistent with FP&A?

3 Does your FP&A function use a system with modelling capability?

3 Is there capability within your organization to perform analysis and pull levers?

4 Do you apply data science to understand the root cause of key outcomes, e.g. churn, flight risk or promotion?

4 Do you combine HR data and business data to reach richer insight, e.g. use competency data to predict business outcomes?

Once you have completed this exercise, add up your scores for an overall maturity assessment and make two lists – one of your current strengths (those questions you answered 'yes' to) and another of your current weaknesses (those questions you answered 'no' to). Reframe these lists in terms of the three 'moving house' questions asked above, so that you end up with:

- a list of strengths you want to keep
- a list of things hindering strategy execution that you want to stop doing (these problems may relate to both how things get done from a practical point of view and prevailing mindsets within the organization, and may need additional input from stakeholders)
- a list of activities you want to start doing through implementing OP&A capability

You may also want to refine these lists in terms of Now, Next, Later (see Chapter 2.3). Which gaps do you want to close immediately? Which should follow swiftly afterwards? Which ones should be closed once that's done? These lists form the backbone of your case for change, and may look something like the example text given in the next box.

THE CASE FOR CHANGE
(Example business case text)

We currently lack the ability to track organizational performance on a consistent basis. We have no way of managing the organization system to deliver the company strategy effectively and efficiently. We lack planning capability and we do not plan over long enough time horizons. This means that our organization is not responding quickly enough to change, and we are losing out to key competitors (recent examples include...). We don't have the necessary competencies within the organization to allow for future mobility, and our Learning and Development programmes are wasted because we cannot identify training needs with enough precision.

We also need the work that we do to be more fun, with less of an emphasis on political game playing and more on problem solving.

We do have some key strengths that we need to retain:

- Agile Teams with an internal marketplace
- organizational chart modelling capability

We want to stop doing the following with immediate effect (i.e. *now*):

- finance forecasting the labour cost separately from the workforce plan
- creating a workforce plan once a year and doing it for a whole year
- hiring based on inconsistent role definitions
- developing Learning and Development plans for individuals which are not sufficiently informed by the company's requirements

We want to start doing the following:

- develop a competency taxonomy to be consistently applied across the organization to define role targets, analyse the skills of the workforce, career paths, training needs analysis, talent management, succession development – *now*
- measure actual competency proficiency levels to understand gaps to inform Learning and Development investment priorities – *now*
- implement a continuous planning process, enabling us to react faster to opportunities and threats alike – *next*
- understand root causes of churn to mitigate those and reduce churn from 20 per cent to 10 per cent – *next*
- optimize the work through process enhancements – *later*

To start these things, the business needs a new core OP&A capability to optimize the performance of the organization and deliver the company strategy effectively and efficiently.

Design criteria and principles

In Chapter 1.2 I briefly explained design principles and criteria in relation to macro operating design. These concepts need to be understood before considering design options for OP&A, so recap Chapter 1.2 or refer to my book *Data-Driven Organization Design* if you are in any doubt as to what they mean. As a brief reminder, design principles are key measurable objectives that are translated into design rules which must hold true irrespective of the design option under consideration. The following are all examples of design principles which you may decide to use for OP&A:

- All data aligns with FP&A. The same measures are used by both functions and the reporting cadence is the same.

- OP&A uses the same exchange rate as Finance.

- Organization units for reported key organization measures match the units used for financial and business performance reporting, for example cost centres.

- The function is sized for 'business as usual' demand and augmented with specialists (e.g. management consultants) at times of peak demand.

- An OP&A Lead and a Data and Tech Leader are in substantive permanent positions with key accountability.

- The OP&A time horizon is strategic and operational, not tactical.

- Data is not siloed – data is to be entered only once within the data flow and is secure with clear and enforced permissions as to who can see and change what.

- The master data is owned by the OP&A Lead.

- Shared definitions and assumptions are in place across functions. There is a clear, accessible glossary of terms in place, which is understood and used as part of standard operating procedure.

Design criteria are critical business goals used in the design process to evaluate options and decide which one should be chosen. The design criteria are informed by your maturity assessment and list of identified weaknesses and clearly state what you are trying to do. To form them, you need to have a firm grasp of your current situation, what the challenges are and the ideal that you want to get to. The following could all be examples of design criteria related to OP&A:

- Provide OP&A support on an ad hoc basis to the Leadership Team.

- Provide accessible and individual thought partners to the Leadership Team and CEO.

- Keep the business lean.

- Maximize time to impact.

- Make the People function more aligned to business strategy.

- Maximize organizational performance as measured by productivity.

- Improve planning capability to anticipate the future.
- React to disruptive change more quickly.
- Design more motivating roles.
- Understand workforce demand.
- Introduce agile ways of working.
- Minimize cost in the organization.
- Drive efficiencies in the organization.
- Ensure FP&A is joined at the hip with OP&A.
- Ensure Finance and the People function are aligned and consistent.

Prioritizing design criteria

Once you have your criteria, list them in order of priority, with an emphasis on determining the single most important one you want to achieve. This top criterion must be significantly more important than the second, which, in turn, must be significantly more important than the third. This prioritization is vital to allow trade-off decisions to be made. I won't go into detail about how to make prioritization decisions here (for that, refer to *Data-Driven Organization Design*). Involve the group of key stakeholders who had input into the strengths and weaknesses. Once you have your list, sign it off to ensure that everyone is agreed on the direction of travel before mapping out design options.

Thinking through design options

A design option is a conceptual model, consisting of frames and features, which describes how a function or organization could work (refer to *Data-Driven Organization Design* for a detailed guide for how to create a design option). Your aim is to end up with a design option that optimizes the design criteria that matter most to you. There are four potential frames you could consider for OP&A capability:

1 outsource to a third party
2 a shared service or Centre of Excellence (CoE)
3 a virtual organization
4 a distinct OP&A function

As I've explained, I believe that to get the most out of OP&A, a distinct function should be created, but before delving into this in more detail I'll briefly consider the other three options listed above, and when you might decide to opt for one of them.

If your most important criterion is 'Make the People function more aligned to business strategy' with 'Provide accessible and individual thought partners to the Leadership Team and CEO' somewhere towards the bottom of your list, you might decide to outsource OP&A work to a third party, at least in the short term. This would help to demonstrate the potential of OP&A to the business and show what it could look like if you brought the capability in-house at some point in the future.

If your most important criterion is 'keep the business lean' – say you're a small business and reluctant to make significant investment – a shared service or CoE could be the way to go. Think of this option like an internal customer service business which charges business units for providing a service. The service has the necessary capability and is engaged to perform OP&A work as and when required.

Say your most important criterion is 'Provide OP&A support on an ad hoc basis to the Leadership Team', with 'Make the People function more aligned to business strategy' fairly near the top of the list, you might think about Option 3, creating a virtual organization. With virtual teams, people from FP&A, HR Business Partners and perhaps also external consultants meet virtually to perform the work of OP&A. They have the capability, but it's done on periodic basis rather than a continual one. Rather than an ongoing soap opera, OP&A is seen as more of a movie with a beginning and an end.

Obviously, if your most important criterion is 'Provide accessible and individual thought partners to the Leadership Team and CEO', with 'Make the People function more aligned to business strategy' near the top along with the final seven criteria in the list above, a function is the only way to go. This is what I believe provides the most significant ongoing value in organizations. If this is the option you choose, the rest of this chapter and the two that follow provide a framework for putting it into action.

When writing your business case, show that you have considered the strengths and weaknesses of all the options by demonstrating how each optimizes certain design criteria. HOWWIP questioning is extremely important when performing this exercise – show that you have thought through the HOWWIP with each option and provide some examples in your business case. An example of how to do this is given in the next box.

DESIGN CRITERIA
(Example business case text)

Our design criteria are listed below, in order of priority:

1 React to disruptive change more quickly.

2 Provide accessible and individual thought partners to the Leadership Team and CEO.

3 Design more motivating roles.

4 Improve planning capability to anticipate the future.

5 Maximize organizational performance as measured by productivity.

6 Introduce agile ways of working.

7 Understand workforce demand.

8 Ensure FP&A is joined at the hip with OP&A.

9 Ensure Finance and the People function are aligned and consistent.

These design criteria were assessed against a range of options:

- Option 1 would be to outsource the work to external consulting partners. While they could help us to *design more motivating roles* or *introduce agile ways of working*, it would not allow us to achieve many more of the design criteria, specifically *react to disruptive change more quickly* or *provide accessible and individual thought partners to the Leadership Team and CEO*, which are the top two criteria on our list. We see OP&A as a core organizational capability needed for ongoing monitoring of performance. The expense of hiring consultants on an ongoing basis should also be considered as a downside of Option 1.

- Option 2 would be to create a shared service or Centre of Excellence. Again, this fails to optimize our top two criteria, particularly *provide accessible and individual thought partners to the Leadership Team and CEO*, as it would be in a different location. We see OP&A as a function with decision-making authority and accountability, rather than an advisory centre. It may also be harder to attract and retain the best talent to a shared service as opposed to a distinct function.

- Option 3 would be to create a virtual organization. This would lean heavily on FP&A and the HR Business Partners, who already have a full workload cutting across Operational HR activities such as dispute resolution and talent acquisition, and are likely to struggle to fit this work in. It is therefore unlikely to mean that we can *react to disruptive change more quickly*. As the team would meet only occasionally, it would also fail to *provide accessible and individual thought partners to the Leadership Team and CEO*. It would also not allow for institutional knowledge or team resilience to be built.

- Option 4 is to create an OP&A function and optimizes our top two criteria alongside many others. In the initial stages, the function would focus on organization design and basic analysis and data management. Building this strategic capability will enable us to monitor performance on an ongoing basis and make data-driven structural changes when necessary to *maximize organizational performance as measured by productivity*. It will also provide a foundation from which we can add further steps in the OP&A value chain, particularly 'Plan the size and cost of the workforce', thereby fulfilling the criterion *understand workforce demand*.

Option 4 has been selected as the one that optimizes the greatest number of our design criteria, specifically the critically important objective of providing the Leadership Team and the CEO with an accessible thought partner, which none of the other options achieve.

The Give and Get matrix

Part of mapping out design options is showing that you have thought about how they will work in practice, which can be done by thinking through key interfaces. If you are undecided about which option to choose, it can help to perform this exercise for all your listed alternatives to understand how work will get done in each of the scenarios. It's all about bringing each option to life by defining who gives what to who – I call this the Give and Get matrix (see Chapter 2.2). If you are proceeding with Option 4 – that of a function – it's important to think through how that function will interface with the rest of the business. In a typical organization, there are likely to be at least seven interfaces, which I list below. Note that this list is not exhaustive. For example, you may also need to specify how HR operations/technology is likely to be impacted. The seven primary interfaces are as follows:

1 Executive and Business Line Leaders

2 FP&A

3 HR Business Partners

4 talent acquisition

5 Learning and Development

6 talent management

7 reward

I detail these interfaces in Chapter 5.3, but at the macro stage aim to think through the basics at a business unit level rather than role level.

The starting point is to outline the mandate of each of the organization units, as shown in Figure 5.2.2, and from this summarize the interfaces:

- The Executive Leadership Team gives OP&A the company strategic plan, and OP&A articulates this to provide the basis operating model design. OP&A performs the operating model design when required.

- Business Line Leaders give OP&A the business line strategic plan, and OP&A articulates this to provide the operating model design. OP&A performs the operating model design which Business Line Leaders approve and sign off.

- OP&A provides analysis and insight on competency gaps and training needs. Learning and Development devise a plan to address these gaps.

- OP&A provides talent management and succession planning analysis including role fit and talent risk classification. Talent Management devises strategies for retention, motivation and engagement of workforce segments based on this analysis.

FIGURE 5.2.2 Detailing interfaces starts with the mandate of each of the related organization units

Choosing an option and devising a roadmap

At this stage, it might be obvious which option to choose, in which case go for it and move straight on to how you could implement the option and develop your business case. Often, the decision is not an obvious one and the benefits and drawbacks of each option will need to be assessed. In my book *Data-Driven Organization Design*, I detail how you can assess this against the design criteria through first performing a SWOT analysis and, if that doesn't lead you to an obvious answer, moving on to a weightings analysis, which ordinarily yields results.

Once you have your option, think through the basics of how it should be implemented. As mentioned, if you're implementing a full OP&A function, this often requires significant change and can't be achieved in one go. For this reason, it's useful to devise a roadmap, which acts as a communication tool to explain the strategy behind the implementation and sets out a staged plan for how the end goal will be reached. But where do you begin? Your starting point should be informed by an assessment of your current maturity and business priorities (defined in your design criteria). This is how you pick your on-ramp onto the road to begin your journey. The roadmap then defines the phases in which elements of the value chain will be addressed by the OP&A function.

The roadmap can also set out the resources that will be required at each stage, and therefore the cost. These are important factors to include in the business case. To do this, you need an understanding of the different roles in the OP&A function, which I cover in Chapter 5.3 – you may find it helpful to refer forward to these descriptions when working through this section.

The first thing to do is return to your maturity curve assessment. Most organizations will complete this exercise and find that they have some Level 1 gaps to fill before they can move on to Level 2. It's very important to complete the foundational level before moving on to more advanced capability. Similarly, if you've answered 'yes' to all the questions at Level 1, but 'no' to some of those at Level 2, priority should be given to filling in the Level 2 gaps before attempting to tackle anything at Level 3. Don't try to run before you can walk.

Two foundational questions are particularly important to address before you do anything else – these are the first two listed under Step 2: Manage the data foundation:

- Do you have a role grid in place, with each of the components of the organization system clearly defined in terms of the flow of data, and an infrastructure to link Roles, Positions and People data?

- Do you have clear definitions of concepts in place to allow for a shared understanding across all stakeholders (particularly OP&A and Finance)? For example, do all parts of the organization define the 'number of employees' in the same way, or is this understood in different ways, with some assuming it's FTE and some assuming it's overall headcount?

I'll start with the first. My mother's maiden name is Hammerstein, and I grew up believing that I am a distant relation to Oscar Hammerstein II. Whether this is true or not, I don't know (my mother swears it is) but, regardless, I've always felt a special connection to the film *The Sound of Music*. As Julie Andrews famously tells us in the film, starting at the beginning is always a good idea. When you read you begin with A-B-C, when you sing you begin with do-re-mi and – I'd like to add – when setting up an OP&A function, it's RPP. Role, Position and People data is the foundation from which everything else follows. Remember Otto Pretorius's quote (see Chapter 1.2): 'Role and role grid design means to human capital what the general ledger design means to Finance. Although few see it, it's omnipresent. It anchors design, integrates process and provides context for meaningful analytics.' It's vital that you begin here.

Until you have a role grid, you can't set target objectives, competencies and accountabilities, and nor can you formulate the role clusters necessary for performing top-down workforce planning. It provides a consistent basis for Organizational Planning and Analysis by mitigating the proliferation of multiple job titles and is the foundation for many things: career paths, rightsizing and reward structures, to name but three. Once in place, it can be enriched and enhanced over time with additional properties, for example activities and accountabilities as well as competency proficiency targets and role criticality.

If you don't have your RPP data secure, refer to Chapter 1.2 or to my book *Data-Driven Organization Design*, and remember that part of getting this data right is implementing strong position management (see Chapter 3.3). This is worth reiterating because, in many organizations, it requires a mindset shift. People and positions should never be seen as one and the same thing. This on-ramp also includes providing a standardized approach to monitoring organization design across the business.

The second fundamental aspect to get right is ensuring that there is a shared understanding of concepts across the organization. Time and again organizations trip themselves up because concept definitions and assumptions are inconsistently applied across functions, so things can mean one thing in one function, and quite another somewhere else. As OP&A is so closely coupled with Finance, it is particularly important that these two functions agree about what certain things mean. HR reporting structures must be aligned with Finance reporting units so that data can be sliced and diced for comparative analysis. Below is a list of concepts and questions to ask in relation to each one:

- Should the number of employees be defined as FTE or headcount? Should contractors be included or excluded?
- Should the size of the workforce include in situ employees only, or in situ employees plus all open positions?
- Should the cost of the workforce include salaries only, or also include projected bonuses, and the cost of benefits, or the fully loaded cost taking account of employer taxation?
- How should you accommodate the cost of vacant positions?
- When supply planning, should the employee turnover rate be calculated as voluntary turnover and/or involuntary turnover?
- When supply planning, should a company-wide measure be applied or should it be done by role cluster?
- What age is applied to calculate retirement?

If you don't have these two fundamental design aspects secure, then this is where you begin. For this, you would only need a minimal function, covering four steps in the value chain:

- Maintain strategic alignment.
- Establish and maintain the data foundation.
- Manage organization and workforce data and systems.
- Track and monitor performance.

This could be managed with two or possibly three roles – an OP&A Lead, a Design and Tech Lead and, if the scale and complexity of your organization is sufficient and your budget allows it, an Organization Design Lead. It's worth mentioning here that it is possible to outsource data management to sit within a shared service, depending on the scale of your organization. For larger organizations employing more than 10,000 people, I would always recommend that this role is kept in-house. This would also be the better option for medium-sized organizations of between 1,000 and 10,000 employees. But if your organization is smaller, perhaps employing under 500–1,000 people, you may well be able to outsource this resource.

Picking your on-ramp

Once these two fundamental phases are complete, you're ready to pick your on-ramp and get on the road. But what are the on-ramps? How should you choose between them? How do you set the path ahead once you're on the road? The three on-ramps to choose between are listed below. Each of these aligns with a step in the OP&A value chain, and each is a significant undertaking. They can't all be done all at once, so choose which to do first, second and third. Each time you implement another phase you will be adding another step to your OP&A value chain and be closer to your vision for full capability. Be led by your prioritized design criteria and case for change. For example, if 'Introduce agile ways of working' is close to the top of your list, you may decide to prioritize competency design and the talent marketplace. If 'Drive efficiencies in the organization' is closer to the top, you may decide to prioritize activity design. There are also other factors to consider. Which of these three things will take the longest time to implement? Which will require the most significant change in the organization? If the design criteria point towards activity design, this doesn't necessarily mean it's the right on-ramp for you. As I explain below, the cultural implications of implementing this step are an important consideration.

THE THREE ON-RAMPS

1 Activity design (Optimize the work)
   I explained activity design in Chapter 1.2. Activity analysis is used to answer business questions such as:

   - Is our organization operating in the way that it was designed to?
   - Are people spending their time on the right work for their role?
   - What is the cost of each process and activity?
   - Are there pressing process inefficiencies which need to be addressed?

   Pulling the levers to optimize activities is likely to result in decisions to automate, move, redesign, consolidate or outsource work. This can cause disruption and anxiety within the organization and requires change management to reassure people and bring them along on the journey. Remember that the work doesn't change by itself – there is a lot of work involved in changing the work! There will be business cases to write and conversations must take place with finance, particularly if investment in automation or outsourcing is required. If you decide to outsource a chunk of work this will involve working with procurement too. Due to all these different factors, you might decide that this step is best saved for when the OP&A function is established and trusted. Or you might feel that the value gained through starting with this step is the best way for OP&A to gain trust. This is a decision to take based on your own context and set of circumstances.

2   Competency design (Optimize competencies across the workforce and manage talent and succession planning)

If you feel you're being held back because your talent is out of whack, then you may decide to prioritize competency design. Refer to Chapter 1.2 for the questions competency design can help you to answer. Remember when pursuing this route that it's very easy to get competency design and management wrong, and that often bad competency design is worse than no competency design at all. It's likely that you'll need to make some fundamental changes to how your organization approaches this vital dataset. Refer to my book *Data-Driven Organization Design* to ensure you are getting those fundamentals right.

3   Workforce planning (Plan the cost and size of the workforce)

Once you have your role grid and RPP data secure, it is possible to progress straight to workforce planning. While I would ordinarily advise getting your competency and activity datasets sorted first, you may want to begin with the workforce planning piece if you foresee a lot of change on the horizon, for example if your organization is rapidly growing or declining and you feel there is a lack of top-down control to guide the bottom-up planning processes.

To get an idea of cost, you'll need to think through the roles you would need for each of these on-ramps. For example, if you choose activities or competencies, you will need an Organization Design Lead and/or more junior staff to support the roles already in place. (As an aside, this can be a fantastic job for bright graduates – they can do much of the heavy lifting, particularly taking charge of the huge amount of documentation that is needed to implement these steps.) If you choose workforce planning as your on-ramp you are likely to need a Workforce Planning Lead straight away, unless your scale and complexity are such that an Organization Design Lead who is already in place to set up the RPP data can absorb this into their workload. Organization design and workforce planning can be combined into one role in the initial stages, especially if this role is supported by junior staff, but you do need to think through whether this would be too much for one person to take on.

Another question to ask yourself when making this decision is the importance of team resilience. If you have one Method Lead overseeing organization design and workforce planning, what happens when they go on holiday, or are off sick? The next box gives some sample text for laying out the implementation plan in your business case. Remember to refer to Chapter 5.3 for clarification of the OP&A roles which are mentioned in the text.

IMPLEMENTATION PLAN AND COSTS
(*Example business case text*)

Implementing a full-scope OP&A function is a hugely ambitious goal, so we propose breaking the work into four distinct phases:

- Phase 1 – The first step is to implement a role grid to ensure that we have the basic Roles, Positions and People data in place to structure the workforce. Without this, we cannot begin to augment with other data such as competency and activity data. This phase will focus on getting our organization design right.

- Phase 2 – Our planning assumption is that we will then be able to progress to understanding the skills of the workforce. We have identified this as our priority after the role grid as we are struggling with talent and do not see enough internal mobility. Our L&D budget is wasted, and we know that we're missing out on upskilling our current workforce because we do not understand competency gaps. This phase will therefore focus on optimizing competencies across the workforce.

- Phase 3 – This phase will see us implement workforce planning capability. The business has seen rapid growth over recent years and because of that the demand and supply of the workforce are out of alignment.

- Phase 4 – In this phase we'll introduce the activities piece. Here we will implement capability to optimize processes and understand the work that gets done and the accountabilities across the workforce. This is the phase that will have the greatest impact on our organization and requires the biggest change. Understanding activities and accountabilities gets to the heart of how we do what we do, who does what and where it gets done. We are leaving this phase until last because we want to prove the worth of the OP&A function in the earlier phases and earn the right to do this work. It will be vital to have earned the trust of the organization before implementing this phase. We also want to get the foundations in place first.

Although these phases reflect our current planning assumptions, we do not need to remain committed to these decisions. If, for example, at the end of Phase 1, we feel it makes more sense to pursue workforce planning before competency design then the phases can be switched around. It would be preferable to leave activities analysis and design until last.

We envisage the following approximate timelines:

- Phase 1 – four months
- Phase 2 – between six and nine months
- Phase 3 – between three and five months
- Phase 4 – between four and six months

We expect to have a fully operational OP&A function within two years.

Top-down budgeting assumptions

The number of FTEs required in each phase is shown in Figure 5.2.3.

FIGURE 5.2.3 The phases of OP&A implementation by FTEs, duration and cost

Phase	FTE	Months		Cost (FTE Months)	
		Min	Max	Min	Max
1	3	4	4	12	12
2	4	6	9	24	36
3	4	3	5	12	20
4	6	4	6	24	36
Total		17	24	72	104
Years		1.4	2.0	6.0	8.7

We intend to size for a base, 'business as usual' demand and augment with consulting firms in times of peak demand. We have identified three consulting firms with the expertise that we need, and we will hire them as necessary depending on the function and geography.

In Phase 1 we will need a team of three people:

1 an OP&A Lead who will work directly with the Head of FP&A and ensure alignment across the Executive Team

2 a Data and Tech Leader who will ensure that all our data is clean and refreshed daily, and that the flow of data works throughout the organization.

This role will also prepare monthly reports for the business and ensure the data can be used by HR Business Partners as they make ad hoc requests

3 an Organization Design Lead who can define and maintain the role grid and structure

In Phase 2 we will augment this core team with a Skills Analyst who can support the Organization Design Lead with the implementation of the competencies piece.

In Phase 3 we will recruit a Workforce Planning Lead. We considered whether the Organization Design Lead could also head up the implementation of this phase but decided it would be too much for them, especially given the amount of work involved in Phase 4.

To complete the work in Phase 4, we suggest recruiting one or two junior members of staff to support the Organization Design Lead, especially in the running and documenting of workshops.

We have thought about how OP&A will work to support each part of the business, and, in particular, the close working relationships with FP&A, HR Business Partners, the Executive Leadership Team and Operational HR. There are numerous critical interfaces which are documented alongside critical execution questions in the appendix.

The expected business outcomes are as follows:

1 Halt the confusion between Finance and the People function and reduce wasted time.

2 Enable the ability to accelerate planned growth.

3 Support the corporate objective to be more agile and get new products to market faster.

4 Drive the increase in revenue per employee by 10 per cent by focusing on the most important work.

Final thoughts

When writing your business case, bear in mind that it has a dual purpose: first to inform and then to persuade. It should demonstrate to decision makers that you have thought about a range of options and considered the pros and cons of each. Get your thinking as watertight as possible as this builds confidence, both with yourself and with the decision makers. Aim to build a compelling story to get your design for the function approved. You want to achieve *real* buy-in and sign-off. OP&A is exciting – make sure this comes across! Why are you excited? Why do you think they will be too?

The business case also serves as a reference guide for detailing the function (the subject of Chapter 5.3) and when you come to implement the function in practice (Making it Real – the subject of Chapter 5.4). It should therefore be written so that someone not involved in this macro stage of the design can pick it up and understand it. There may be times in Stages 2 or 3 when it makes more sense *not* to follow the recommendations laid out in the business case. This is another reason why the original thinking and reasoning needs to be crystal clear so someone can feel confident making a decision which deviates from the plan.

Most importantly, the business plan needs to resonate with your leadership. In fact, my hope is that you are a leader or someone who can take action to lead – to champion the function and steer your organization through the next two stages: the micro detailed design and, finally, Making it Real.

REMEMBER THIS

1 People overestimate what can be done in the short term and underestimate what can be done in the long term. Don't just focus on optimizing the short term.

2 The full OP&A value chain consists of seven key steps.

3 Devise your case for change using the 'Imagine you are moving house' exercise and prioritize into Now, Next and Later.

4 OP&A capability is best housed within its own function but there are three other design options you could consider.

5 Address the two fundamentals before picking your on-ramp to your roadmap.

Note

1 Quote Investigator (2019) People tend to overestimate what can be done in one year and to underestimate what can be done in five or ten years. https://quoteinvestigator.com/2019/01/03/estimate/ (archived at https://perma.cc/5SNK-C65H)

5.3

Stage 2: Detailing the OP&A function

Introduction

This chapter is inherently 'meta' since it can be thought of as a worked example of much of the micro detailed design described in Part Three of *Data-Driven Organization Design*. This is where you take the high-level scope set out in Stage 1 and get into the nitty-gritty of what your function is going to look like.

Stepping through this chapter will help you to answer the following questions:

- What roles are needed?
- What will those roles be responsible for?
- Will you need to source outside help?
- Where does accountability for key elements of the value chain sit?
- Who will be responsible for data flow?
- Who will manage senior stakeholders?
- How will OP&A interact with other areas of the business?
- How will the function provide value to other areas of the business?

The answer to many of these questions is: it depends. It depends on the size of your organization, the number of business units, and the number of different geographies in which you operate. It also depends on the number of projects, and the context of the work that the team will be doing. My hope is that this chapter helps you design a function that will work for you.

As you enter Stage 2, you are likely to know the allocated budget for the function. This may or may not have been the case during Stage 1, so alterations to the high-level design may be needed with budgeting constraints in mind. Remember that the business case put forward in Stage 1 was a recommendation.

It set out an achievable pathway for establishing an OP&A function, but it needn't be followed to the letter. You may find that you need a broader or narrower range of roles than you anticipated, or more external help than you thought. For this reason, it's vitally important to keep a HOWWIP questioning mindset and continually ask yourself how things are going to work in practice. This is the key to ensuring that things go smoothly when it comes to making the function a reality in Stage 3.

I begin with an explanation of the roles you could have in the OP&A function and the various permutations you might choose to meet your needs. I focus on four of these, OP&A Leader, Organization Design Leader, Workforce Planning Leader and Data and Tech Leader, and explain how to design them in the context of the objectives to be achieved, the processes and work activities to be conducted and the competencies necessary to succeed. Next, I look at the key interfaces between these roles and the rest of the business before explaining how to rightsize the function to deliver the work.

Define the roles within the function

One of the first questions often put to me is what an OP&A function would need to look like in terms of the roles and positions. Figure 5.3.1 shows the range of possible roles. I want to be clear that this is an *example*, showing how a function might evolve over time from an initial scope of four roles to a full scope of eight. It is not intended to be prescriptive and there are several different permutations you could have as you progress along your phased roadmap. This book has been written for organizations of more than around 500 people, or high-growth businesses of around 300 people which are expected to scale quickly. For full disclosure, most of my past clients have had well over 2,000 employees, and the vast majority over 20,000, but I have led as a CEO at a smaller scale. It has been assumed therefore that your organization has sufficient scale and complexity to need a full-scope OP&A function at some point, but how you reach that full scope and how you choose to structure your function throughout the implementation journey are questions to now ask yourself. Much of this is budget-dependent, and you may be limited in the number of roles you can afford, at least in the initial stages. At every stage of the OP&A journey, the function should have an OP&A Lead and a Data and Tech Leader (assuming data management sits within the organization rather than being outsourced). This could be 50 per cent of an FTE for smaller-scale organizations of under 500 employees. If your initial function can include only two roles, this would be a great place to start.

Consider the following scenario: you have decided to implement a very basic function while fundamentals such as RPP data and a role grid are put into place. For this to happen, you would not necessarily need the four roles shown in the initial scope in Figure 5.3.1. Two would suffice:

1 an OP&A Leader responsible for organization design and workforce planning

2 a Data and Tech Leader responsible for data flow, master data management and slide and insight production

As you scale, two more roles could be added: an Organization Design Leader and Workforce Planning Leader, both of which would report into the OP&A Leader. As you scale further, more roles can be added until you are operating at full scope, including all the roles shown in Figure 5.3.1.

In this chapter, the focus is on describing the roles and their respective responsibilities. In Chapter 5.4 I'll discuss aspects to consider when recruiting for these roles, including many of the skills and attributes needed by people to do the job well.

FIGURE 5.3.1 An example of how an OP&A function might evolve over time

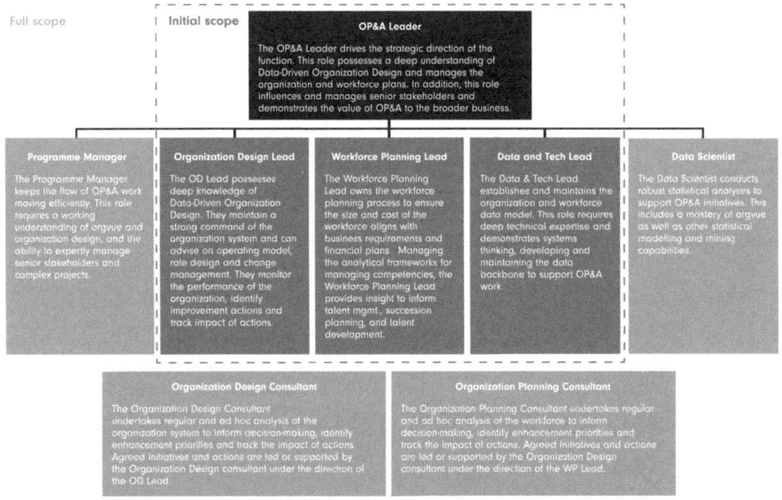

OP&A Leader

While not responsible for setting the strategic direction for the business (this is done by the CEO, Board, and Leadership Team), they must fully internalize the strategy and have it at their fingertips – the priorities and the why, what and how. The OP&A Leader is key to executing the strategy and is one of the guardians of it. Whatever the strategic direction (be that growing in a certain market, launching a new product, focusing more locally, or doubling down on customer service) there will be implications for the workforce. In just the same way the CFO is responsible for translating the strategy into a financial plan, the OP&A Leader is responsible for presenting a people plan which both complies with the financial plan and fits the overall strategic direction of the business. They monitor the organization against the design criteria on an ongoing basis, approving exceptions and ensuring that those exceptions make sense. In a 'business as usual' context, their role is one of keeping on top of the Analyse–Design–Plan–Monitor cycle. A core part of their role is to take information from all levels of the business and use it to influence and manage senior stakeholders and demonstrate the value of OP&A to the organization.

In my view, the Leader of the OP&A function should report directly to the CHRO, being one of their more important lieutenants. They also work with the CFO and in tandem with the FP&A Leader to present the financial and workforce plans. Think of them as one team, sitting across the People and Finance function silos, and breaking those silos down. The OP&A Leader should have a deep understanding of both D-DOD and workforce planning and strong coaching skills so that their knowledge and skill can be disseminated to their team members. The OP&A Leader could be responsible for people strategy or there may be a separate Head of People Strategy. The high-level role responsibilities for the OP&A Leader revolve around strategic alignment and operating model design:

- Ensure the company and business line goals/strategies are clearly articulated.
- Engage with EXCO, business leaders and functional leaders to identify OP&A priorities.
- Set the direction and develop the plan for OP&A aligned to the overall business strategy.
- Ensure the company and business line operating models are fit for purpose through regular tracking of compliance through design criteria and principles.

- Operating model design (when required, for executive or business leader approval).
- Build and run the infrastructure and process for integrated financial and workforce planning in alignment with FP&A.
- Track, monitor and report the contribution of OP&A to the business and the value delivered.
- Manage the OP&A budget.

Organization Design Leader

The Organization Design Leader is responsible for the work outlined in Chapter 1.2 and in my book *Data-Driven Organization Design*. Their job is to know the business inside and out and be responsible for a host of master data management. The Organization Design Leader is the custodian of organization design methodology and developing the right tools and frameworks. They are also responsible for educating the rest of the People function and business on its adoption. They also advise on any necessary changes to the operating model and are the go-to person for advice on role design and the role grid. They should have a thorough understanding of the work and who is doing that work. The high-level responsibilities of the Organization Design Leader are as follows:

- Establish and maintain the data foundation:
  - Develop and maintain a role grid.
  - Maintain enterprise/functional value chains and process taxonomies.
  - Maintain the taxonomy of competencies.
  - Define, document and maintain the hierarchy of objectives.
  - Maintain consistent role descriptions specifying target objectives, accountabilities (activities) and competencies.
- Track and monitor organization performance:
  - Develop, maintain and enhance the KPIs for monitoring organization performance in line with design principles.
  - Analyse and report organization performance.
  - Identify potential improvement actions.
  - Gain stakeholder alignment on insights and buy-in to process optimization actions.

- o Track and monitor the impact of process optimization programmes, initiatives and actions.
- • Optimize work:
  - o Maintain process optimization frameworks.
  - o Analyse and report on process efficiency.
  - o Identify potential process optimization initiatives.
  - o Gain stakeholder alignment on insights and buy-in to process optimization actions.
  - o Track and monitor the impact of process optimization programmes, initiatives and actions.

Workforce Planning Leader

The Workforce Planning Leader is responsible for budgeting and detailing what the organization should look like over time to meet the financial plan. They are responsible for the top-down workforce plan discussed in Chapter 3.2 as well as supporting the bottom-up planners and HR Business Partners throughout the bottom-up modelling process discussed in Chapter 3.3. Much of their role involves monitoring the performance of the organization system and tracking the delivery and impact of agreed plans. The high-level responsibilities of the Workforce Planning Leader are as follows:

- • Plan the size and cost of the workforce:
  - o Maintain the workforce planning process.
  - o Forecast the expected internal supply of talent.
  - o Model and simulate top-down talent demand.
  - o Model positions to build a view of required talent demand.
  - o Reconcile top-down and bottom-up projections to finalize and agree workforce plans.
  - o Develop plans to match supply and demand projections.
  - o Gain stakeholder alignment on workforce plans.
  - o Analyse and monitor actuals and forecasts against the agreed targets.

- Optimize competencies across the workforce:
  - Maintain frameworks for analysing competency proficiency levels.
  - Analyse and report on competency proficiency levels.
  - Identify priorities for competency gap closure/training needs analysis.
  - Track the effect and impact of Learning and Development projects/programmes.
- Manage talent and succession planning:
  - Maintain frameworks for managing the organization's internal talent marketplace.
  - Identify succession candidates, readiness and risks.
  - Track the development of succession candidates.

Data and Tech Leader

The main job of the Data and Tech Leader is to ensure that data is set up right and flowing throughout the organization. It needs to be secure with clear and enforced permissions. This is the person with the deep technical expertise who the Organization Design Leader and Workforce Planning Leader turn to for help with statistics and analysis. There's a lot of master data management involved in the role, as well as building dashboards and packs and ensuring everyone has the right information. The Data and Tech Leader is not responsible for some of the more advanced analytics discussed in Chapter 4.3 such as building random forest models and machine learning. For this, a Data Scientist is likely to be needed (see below). The high-level responsibilities of the Data and Tech Leader are as follows:

- Manage organization and workforce data and systems:
  - Maintain master data: one version of the truth for organization design and planning.
  - Maintain data management systems.
  - Provide data to meet analysis requirements.
  - Undertake analysis to support the insight requirements of the OP&A Team members.
  - Maintain data security and protect data sensitivity through access rights, controls and permissions.

- o Ensure data is secure.
- o Ensure permissions are clear, reflect the agreed access rights and are flawlessly implemented.

Organization Design Consultant

The Organization Design Consultant undertakes regular and ad hoc analysis of the organization system to inform decision-making, identify enhancement priorities and track the impact of actions. Agreed initiatives and actions are led or supported by the Organization Design Consultant under the direction of the Organization Design Leader. This is to support specific projects and areas of your business.

Workforce Planning Consultant

The Workforce Planning Consultant undertakes regular and ad hoc analysis of the workforce to inform decision-making, identify enhancement priorities and track the impact of actions. Agreed initiatives and actions are led or supported by the Workforce Planning Consultant under the direction of the Workforce Planning Lead. Like the Organization Design Consultant, they will support specific projects.

Programme Manager

As organizations grow, there is likely to be a range of design projects and workforce planning programmes happening at any one time. Your business is therefore likely to reach a point where a Programme Manager is needed to keep the flow of OP&A work moving. They will also support the process of bringing in outside help as and when needed, and helping to manage that help. This role is unlikely to be needed until you have reached the full scope of your OP&A function and are working in a very large enterprise with significant change.

Data Scientist

The Data Scientist conducts the kind of robust statistical analyses outlined in Chapter 4.3 that are needed to support OP&A initiatives. They need a mastery of a variety of statistical modelling and mining capabilities. Their job is to provide predictive insight, so you can move faster and sooner. They pull levers you wouldn't even think about.

Design the roles

As laid out in Chapter 1.2, full role design takes account of numerous pieces of data such as role family and sub-role family, level and grade and pay benchmarking codes. What follows here are not detailed explanations of how to assign all this data to each of the roles in the OP&A function as this is sufficiently covered in the advice given in *Data-Driven Organization Design*. Instead, I focus on how to design the roles in terms of the objectives to be achieved, the work to be carried out and the competencies which need to be held by the people performing the roles. As highlighted in Chapter 1.2, the starting point for each of these aspects is to determine OAC taxonomies for the OP&A function. Each of the sections below includes an example taxonomy. When building these, refer to the 'seven rules of taxonomy building' in my book *Data-Driven Organization Design*. This process should have input from the OP&A Leader, HR Leadership Team members and representative Business Line Leaders.

Objectives design

The people in the OP&A function are business enablers. They help the business to get things done so that company-wide and business line strategies can be put into practice. As such, the objectives assigned to those in the OP&A Team are often driven by context. They centre around defining what company-wide and business-line objectives and goals mean in terms of ongoing organization design and workforce strategies.

Start by identifying the goals and list potential objectives for the roles needed along your roadmap. As I explain in *Data-Driven Organization Design*, these objectives should be checked against frameworks such as SMART (Specific, Measurable, Attainable, Relevant and Time-Bound) and/or FAST (Frequently Discussed, Ambitious, Specific and Transparent). This is important to allow for effective measuring and the management and tracking of the objectives over time. At this stage, objectives can only be determined top-down from management. Once people are in positions, they can act as a 'starter for 10' to firm up individual objectives.

Objectives can then be inserted into a taxonomy and cascaded and connected to Roles, Positions and People in the function. When assigning objectives to each role, use the high-level processes outlined in Stage 1 as a guide. Take each process and determine SMART or FAST objectives which will enable that process to happen. For example, Figure 5.3.2 shows an example of an objectives taxonomy for Hokupaa. One of its goals is to 'be more customer-centric'. A way to do this is to develop standard libraries to accelerate client speed to value. All learning from clients alongside additional research can be available 'out of the box'. Content – such as stories and workflows – is loaded into the platform, alongside accessible digital training to add value for clients. Each objective gets broken down into milestone objectives (e.g. to deliver standard libraries with workflow for client adaptation by Q1) and measure objectives (e.g. achieve a promotion score of Y per cent for each standard library).

FIGURE 5.3.2   Objectives tree for the goal 'be more customer-centric'

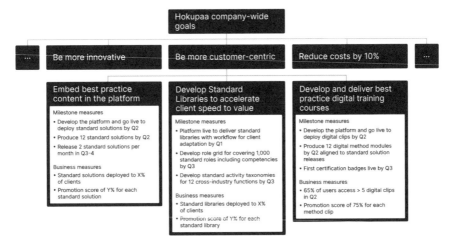

For the OP&A Leader, an important objective involves identifying conflicts between company-wide objectives and ensuring that all decision makers understand the trade-offs that need to be made. Take the three goals shown in Figure 5.3.2:

- Be more innovative.
- Be more customer-centric.
- Reduce costs by 10 per cent.

There is a conflict between these goals. Any organization would struggle to be more customer-centric and innovative at the same time as reducing cost, so a job for the OP&A Leader is to articulate this conflict and work with senior leadership to define the priorities. In my experience, reducing cost is frequently cited as a goal, but it isn't always legitimate and often shouldn't take priority over other strategic goals. To help business leaders to make these trade-off decisions, an objective for the OP&A Leader could be to quantify the impact of company goals: for example, stipulating the roles, capabilities and competencies that would be needed to achieve a goal and showing the gap between the current situation and what would be needed.

Many of the objectives for the OP&A Leader, Organization Design Leader and Workforce Planning Leader are very similar. An example is to articulate and quantify exceptions and explain the logic behind them. For example, there may be times when it makes sense not to follow a design principle, such as the common one of ensuring a span of control of eight. A client had this problem with their Auditing function. In some smaller regions, the Data Science Team had two or three accountants reporting to them. To follow the design principle of always having a span of control of eight, my client had two options: remove Data Science Teams from these smaller markets so that the accountants reported to a Data Science Team in a different location, or hire more accountants in these regions to make it up to the ideal span of control. Neither of these options made sense. Removing the Data Science Team would be too risky (because of differences between markets and the need for specialized knowledge) while hiring more accountants for the sake of it would be inefficient.

A further objective common to these three roles is to build confidence and become trusted by senior decision makers. An exception such as the one described above shouldn't require a long discussion (I'd say 15 seconds at most – 10 for OP&A to present the facts and a further five for the decision maker to get it, approve it and be ready to move on to the next on the list). But for it to be this fast, there needs to be trust. There will be other exceptions that require deeper thought and discussion time should be saved for those. There are only so many senior leaders, so there's a scarce resource of cognitive processing power. OP&A needs to get this cognitive processing focused on the right topics.

Another objective which spans the OP&A Leader, Organization Design Leader and Workforce Planning Leader is to ensure that organizational costs fall within financial constraints. This involves understanding the financial constraint, articulating it, and then helping to optimize within it. There may be times when a strategic objective cannot be achieved within these constraints, which should be brought to the table by OP&A. For example, if there's a financial constraint that Sales and Marketing shouldn't be more than 30 per cent of revenue, but to achieve your growth ambition there's a belief that it must be 35 per cent, a trade-off needs to be made.

The objectives of the Data and Tech Leader are somewhat different. They centre around implementing the data model described in Chapter 4.2. It's their job to ensure that data is secure, high quality, well-structured and productionized so that the right people have access to the right data at the right time. Objectives for the Data and Tech Leader include:

- Work with those in information security to ensure that data is secure with the right permissions defined and implemented.
- Ensure that data is structured in the right way for rapid design and planning work.
- Ensure the **golden thread of data** is defined and followed, that data is only entered once into their 'master system' and leveraged by other systems.
- Ensure data is shaped so that analysis can easily be performed.
- Ensure that definitions of data (e.g. dimensions, measure, fact tables, node properties) are clear, consistent and up-to-date, with appropriate controls implemented to maintain changes.

Activity design

When designing activities for the roles in the OP&A function the starting point is to create a taxonomy using the high-level processes outlined in Chapter 5.2. An example activity taxonomy for the OP&A function is shown in Figure 5.2.1.

It is important to understand how these activities fit together in the context of the function. A great way to do this is by creating Match Attax-inspired process cards as described in Chapter 2.2. As a reminder, each card could have:

- the value chain component and the process and sub-process
- what the activity is and whether it is a Decision, Output or Task (DOT)
- how it fits within the taxonomy (i.e. what the parent processes and value streams are)
- colour coding and icons for the key dimensions, such as daily, weekly, monthly or annually)

- if it has been defined, clarity of who is responsible
- a succinct description on the back of the card

Once you have the cards, lay them all out on a table and divide them into the roles you have defined along your roadmap. You will quickly be able to see if the activities make sense in the context of the roles and identify any that are missing. This will also help you to clarify whether the roles you thought would be needed along the roadmap (see Chapter 5.2) will work in practice, given the activities involved.

While doing this work, identify an appropriate enhancement lever for each of the activities from the eight enhancement levers in the RRII (Reduce, Reallocate, Improve and Invest) framework. Many of the activities you define won't currently be done within the organization, or may be done very minimally, so they will come under the 'invest' lever.

Competency design

Competencies assigned to roles in the OP&A function can be defined at either the activity level or the role level:

1 At the activity level, each element of the process map is defined in terms of the competencies needed for the process to happen effectively.

2 At the role level, you make a leap and assume what competencies are needed for each of the activities for which that role is responsible. The competencies each role needs will vary depending on how your OP&A function is structured, both in the initial phases and as you progress along your roadmap. For example, if, in the initial phases, there is one person doing the work of the Organization Design Leader and the Workforce Planning Leader, that person will need a range of competencies, to match a wide scope of processes they are responsible for.

As a reminder, roles are linked to target proficiency levels and people are linked through actual proficiency levels. See *Data-Driven Organization Design* for how target proficiency data is set and actual proficiency data is collected.

Remember that there are four types of competencies:

1 behavioural

2 cognitive (thinking and problem solving)

3 generic business skills

4 specialized functional skills

Figure 5.3.3 shows a competency taxonomy for the OP&A function, which includes the behavioural, cognitive and specialized functional skills components. The first layer below the root shows the competency type (whether it is behavioural or cognitive competency or a specialized functional skill) and the second layer is the competency dimension. The third layer is a group of 'sub-competencies', and it is these that are assigned to roles and/or activities. For example, influencing people and selling ideas are key parts of OP&A – this is a behavioural sub-competency which comes under the dimension of 'focus on self'.

FIGURE 5.3.3   An example competency taxonomy for OP&A

The next step is to define the proficiency level of each competency (for a detailed explanation of how to do this, see *Data-Driven Organization Design*). These proficiency levels then need to be linked to roles and/or activities. In Figure 5.3.4 they have been linked to the four OP&A roles. Two of the four types of competencies are listed – behavioural and specialized functional – with the target proficiency levels. For example, 'management of conflict' is a key behaviour the OP&A Leader should have mastered, with proficiency Level 4. The same is true for 'business acumen' and 'building relationships'. The Organization Design and Workforce Planning Leaders need higher levels of proficiency in being 'action and results-driven'. There is a large set of specialized functional skills the Data and Tech Leader needs, e.g. 'people data analysis and insights' and 'data modelling', that the other three don't.

In Chapter 5.4 I translate this grid into a list of attributes to look for when hiring for these roles. As Figure 5.3.4 brings into focus, if you plan for the Organization Design Lead and Workforce Planning Lead to be a combined role in the initial stages of the function, it may prove challenging to find someone to tick all the boxes, in terms of both competency and proficiency level.

FIGURE 5.3.4 Linking competency proficiency levels to roles for the OP&A function

Behavioural	OP&A Leader	Organization Design Lead	Workforce Planning Lead	Data and Tech Lead		Specialized functional
Influencing – selling ideas	4	4	3	4	5 6	2	Data-Driven Organization Design methods
Management of conflict	4	4	3	4		2	Organization design
Business acumen	4	4	3	2	5 4		Strategic workforce planning
Building relationships	4	4	3	2	5 4		Operational workforce planning
Action and results driven	4	2	4		4	5 4	Human capital technologies
Planning and coordination	4	5	3		4 4		Competency architecture and modelling
Strategy implementation	4	5		4	4		Job architecture
Systems thinking	4	4	4	4	5 4	5	Data story telling and visualization
Teamwork	4		5	5 4	5		Workplace optimization
Problem-solving and reasoning	4	4	3		5 4		Business planning
Agile work methods & planning		2	4	2			Business process architecture
Abstract resoning	4		5	4 5	4		Business re-engineering
Numerical reasoning	4	5	2	5	4 4		Human capital data-models and mgmt
Business communication	4		5	5		4	People data analysis and insights
					5	Data architecture
					5	Data engineering
					5	Data security architecture
			4		4	Data modelling
	4	4	2			Writing and editing skills

Detail the key interfaces

In Chapter 5.2, I explained how to define the high-level interfaces between OP&A and the rest of the business. Now it's time to detail these at the role level using the Give and Get matrix (rather than the business unit level, which was done in Chapter 5.2). Interfaces will change as you progress along your roadmap and as additional responsibilities are added or split between more roles. Defining appropriate interfaces for your organization is dependent on four factors:

1 the size of the company
2 the HR operating model
3 the data maturity and analytical capability across the People function
4 the agreed scope and value chain for OP&A

As no two organizations are the same, my intention is not to be prescriptive but to get you asking the right questions applicable to your own set of circumstances. Remember that in a typical organization the most common interfaces to define are the following seven:

1   Executive and Business Line Leaders

2   FP&A

3   HR Business Partners

4   talent acquisition

5   Learning and Development

6   talent management

7   reward

OP&A interface with Executive and Business Line Leaders

The OP&A Leader interfaces with the Executive Leadership Team. They work together across three key areas:

1   strategic alignment and operating model design

2   integrated financial and workforce plans

3   organization optimization

The Give and Get between them is shown in Figure 5.3.5. The steps are numbered to show the order in which they would happen: for example, the Executive Leadership Team gives the OP&A Leader the company strategic plan, which the OP&A Leader then articulates with sufficient clarity to provide the basis for operating model design. They also ensure that the OP&A plan is aligned with the overall business strategy. The fourth step is for the OP&A Leader to instigate operating model design. This is given to the Executive Leadership Team for their input and sign-off.

OP&A interface with FP&A

As shown in Figure 5.3.6, the OP&A Leader and Workforce Planning Leader work with FP&A across two core areas:

• integrated financial and workforce plans

• workforce planning

FIGURE 5.3.5 The Give and Get between the OP&A Leader and the Executive
Leadership Team

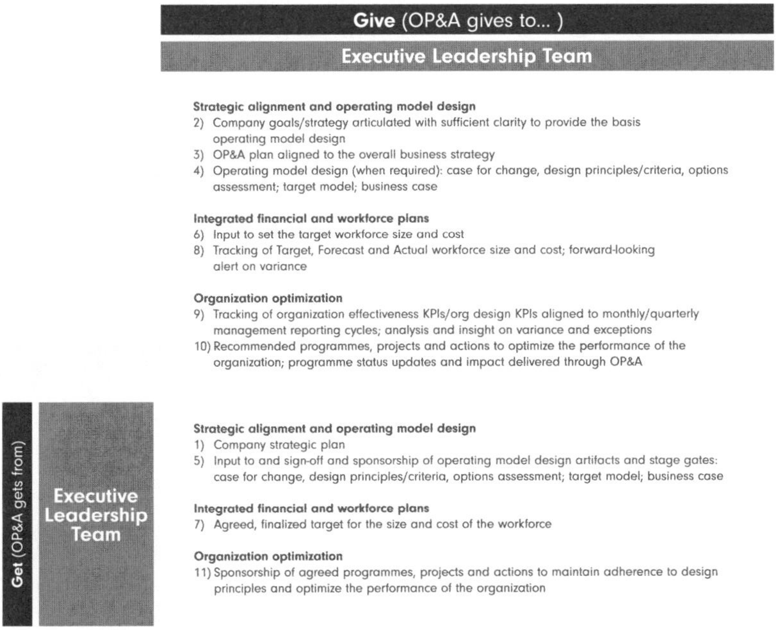

The OP&A Leader and FP&A Leader can work together to define core
concepts and develop one version of the truth for people and financial
data to feed into integrated financial and workforce plans. They 'give' each
other the domain specialism needed for fully integrated financial and
workforce planning: specifically, the OP&A Leader gives FP&A an understanding of the cost, size and composition of the workforce which feeds
into the company and business line financial planning performed by
FP&A. The OP&A Leader is responsible for scenario modelling to optimize the size, cost and composition of the workforce over time. FP&A
provides them with monthly and quarterly business performance data to
enable this.

There is another interface between the Workforce Planning Leader and
the FP&A Leader related to planning the workforce over time. The FP&A
Leader gives the Workforce Planning Leader company and business line

financial targets as an input to top-down demand planning. In return, the Workforce Planning Leader gives FP&A:

- top-down workforce demand projections based on these plans
- workforce size and cost projections based on bottom-up position modelling
- information related to the tracking of Target, Actual and Forecast workforce size and cost over time

FIGURE 5.3.6 The Give and Get between OP&A and FP&A

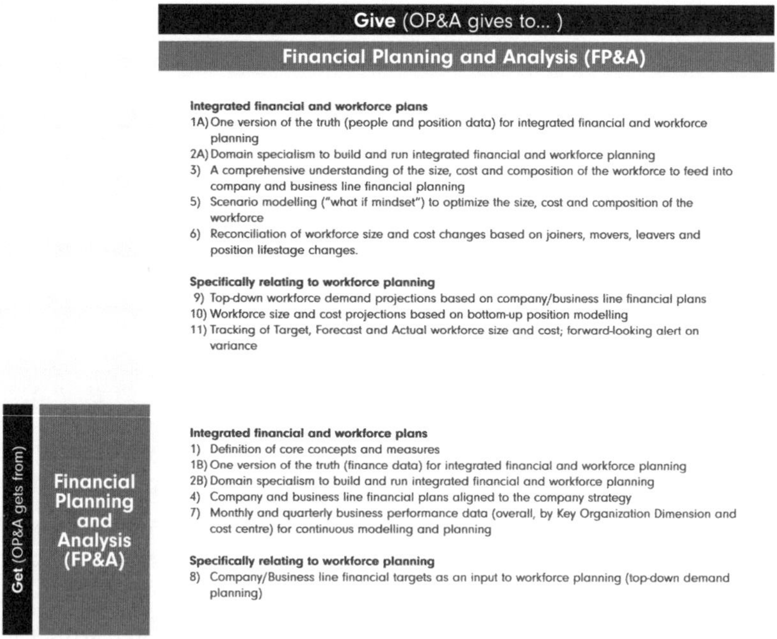

OP&A interface with HR Business Partners

The Give and Get between OP&A and HR Business Partners focuses on three main areas:

1 strategic alignment and operating model design

2 organization optimization

3 workforce planning

I'll start by explaining what I mean by the role of an HR Business Partner. I am referring to someone who sits on a Leadership Team responsible for a function, geography or business unit. For example, they might be part of a Finance Leadership Team or an EMEA Leadership Team. It is a generalist HR role with a holistic view across all people dimensions. The job involves dealing with whatever people-related questions arise, for example dispute resolution or gross misconduct. Often, HR Business Partners need to think with an OP&A mindset. Their role is strategic as well as tactical and reactionary and so much of what they do is relevant to the work of the OP&A Team. They can be thought of as the CHRO for their business area. They are a coach to the leader of that business area, and pull in specialists to support the area as required. They have an overview of such things as reward, and insight into how long people have been in positions, and as such they are perfectly placed to run mini projects to find root causes for problems such as why attrition levels are high or whether reward is fair across an area or function. Part of their role is to report to their Leadership Team on how the operating model is working in their area of the business. In effect, the conversations that the HR Business Partners have with their Leadership Teams are very similar to those that the OP&A Leader has with the CEO, the CHRO and the CFO, but they do it within their scope.

The combined potential of HR Business Partners and the OP&A Team is enormous. In just the same way that OP&A is joined at the hip with FP&A, the same should be true for OP&A and HR Business Partners. The OP&A Team can provide HR Business Partners with the specialist skills required to, for example, perform data analysis or run models to help with the questions that need answering. The HR Business Partners can, in return, help to feed into the workforce plan and role design, based on knowledge of their area of the business. As covered in Chapter 3.3, the Workforce Planning Leader and HR Business Partner are both involved in bottom-up positions modelling. The Workforce Planning Leader sets out the governance structure for this process, but needs the support of the HR Business Partners.

HR Business Partners are typically very busy people. Leveraging the skills and competencies within the OP&A Team can be extremely useful to them and it's up to the OP&A Leader to highlight how mutually beneficial the partnership can be. Due to the intertwined nature of the work, however, the interface can be one of the most difficult to get right. In fact, as I explain later in the chapter, a major driver for rightsizing the OP&A function is the number of HR Business Partners in the organization.

As the HR Business Partner role is different in every organization, no two Give and Gets will look the same. The OP&A Leader and the Workforce Planning Leader are likely to be the two roles most engaged in this interface. These two leaders give the HR Business Partner best practice tools, frameworks and methodologies in organization design and workforce planning. Not all the work is done by OP&A, and one of the responsibilities of the function is to uplift the capability of the doers such as the HR Business Partners. Figure 5.3.7 shows an example of how this Give and Get could work. When it comes to strategic alignment and operating model design, the HR Business Partner provides the OP&A Leader with the business line strategic plan. The OP&A Leader then articulates this with sufficient clarity to provide the basis for operating model design and revises the operating model design if required. When it comes to workforce planning, the Workforce Planning Leader gives the HR Business Partner a gap analysis between the internal supply of talent and the target workforce, as well as the plan for closing these gaps. The HR Business Partner then agrees to sponsor these plans for bridging the gaps.

In terms of organization optimization, the HR Business Partner gives the OP&A Leader the business priorities, challenges and requirements for OP&A support. The OP&A Leader can then track organization effectiveness KPIs according to these requirements and recommend programmes, projects and actions to optimize the performance of the organization. The HR Business Partner can then agree to sponsor these programmes, projects and actions.

OP&A interface with Talent Acquisition

The Give and Get between OP&A and Talent Acquisition focuses on closing the gaps in supply and demand, as shown in Figure 5.3.8. The Workforce Planning Leader analyses the internal supply of talent and identifies talent demand and supply gaps and gives these to Talent Acquisition. The workforce plan highlights the labour need and OP&A analysis can show how much of the gap can be covered by internal moves. Talent Acquisition then gives the Workforce Planning Leader data about the availability and cost of external talent, the cost of recruitment and the time it takes to recruit. All this feeds recruitment plans. Talent Acquisition also supplies the Organization Design Leader with standards and frameworks to feed into role descriptions and role data (including reward benchmarks).

FIGURE 5.3.7 The Give and Get between OP&A and HR Business Partners/Business Line Leadership

Give (OP&A gives to...)

HR Business Partner / Business Line Leadership

Strategic alignment and operating model design
2) Business line goals/strategy articulated with sufficient clarity to provide the basis operating model design
3) Operating model design (when required): case for change; design criteria; model evaluation

Workforce planning
5) Analysis of gaps between internal supply of talent and target workforce size and plan for closing gaps (buy, build, borrow, bind...)

Organization optimization
8) Tracking of organization effectiveness KPIs/org design KPIs aligned to monthly/quarterly management reporting cycles ; analysis and insight on variance and exceptions
9) Recommended programmes, projects and actions to optimize the performance of the organization; programme status updates and impact delivered through OP&A

Additional elements
- Recruitment plans based on the workforce plans to close talent demand/supply gaps (where demand > internal supply)
- Forward-looking analysis and to inform talent management strategies (attrition, tenure, age, ultimately flight risk)
- Inputs to talent reviews: Role match analysis to identify potential succession candidates and development requirements
- Training needs analysis based on identified gaps; prioritized weighting of competencies and prioritization of roles

HR Business Partner / Business Line Leadership

Get (OP&A gets from)

Strategic alignment and operating model design
1) Business line strategic plan
4) Input to and sign-off and sponsorship of operating model design artifacts and stage gates: case for change, design principles/criteria, options assessment; target model; business case

Workforce planning
6) Sponsorship of agreed plans for bridging talent demand and supply gaps

Orginization Optimization
7) Business priorities, challenges and requirements for OP&A support
10) Sponsorship of agreed programmes, projects and actions

Additional elements:
- Outcomes from performance reviews, e.g., overall performance ratings
- Outcomes of talent reviews (e.g., confirmed succession status and development actions)

If candidate source data is provided, the Data Scientist or Data and Tech Leader can provide insight into the effectiveness of each source. For example:

- the one-year churn
- likelihood of promotion
- level of performance
- cost of hire
- Time To Productivity

A small amount of data can provide a great deal of value if used well.

FIGURE 5.3.8 The Give and Get between OP&A and Talent Acquisition

Give (OP&A gives to...)

Talent Acquisition

2) Forward-looking recruitment plans based on the workforce plans to close talent demand/supply gaps (where demand > internal supply)
4) Consistently defined role descriptions leveraging the OP&A data model
    -Role data (including reward benchmarks), position data, activities/accountabilities, competencies
6) Insight into the effectiveness of talent acquisition sources

Talent Acquisition

Get (OP&A gets from)

1) Data to inform strategies for closing supply-demand gaps
    -Availability and cost of external talent
    -The cost of recruitment (e.g., partner, vendor and channel access costs)
    -The time to recruit

3) Input to standards and frameworks (e.g., job descriptions)
5) Adherence to standards and frameworks (e.g., reward benchmarks), and input for continuous development

OP&A interface with L&D

The OP&A interface with L&D focuses on closing competency gaps, as shown in Figure 5.3.9. Once competency gaps are identified, the OP&A Team can share these with the Learning and Development Team and identify who has what gap alongside the roles which need to be prioritized.

The Organization Design Leader can also work on a training needs analysis based on the identified gaps to see who needs what training and development. The L&D Team then executes and operationalizes this by rolling out the L&D plan, ensuring necessary programmes are run and that people are getting the training they need.

As is the case with all the Give and Gets outlined in this section, this interface is not set in stone. If your L&D function is strategically focused, they may perform analysis themselves rather than relying on the OP&A Team to do it. In some instances, the L&D Team may identify gaps in the plan rather than the OP&A Team. It depends on how the functions are organized and the competencies of the people within them. Some people are very good at analysis and drawing out conclusions, and others are extremely good at operationalizing and making things happen. They are very different skillsets, so decide where these tasks should sit within the context of your own organization.

OP&A and L&D also work together to track the impact of the L&D plan. L&D supply individual-level data on participation in programmes and OP&A run the analysis and generates insight regarding the effect of participation on competency development, performance, engagement and retention.

FIGURE 5.3.9 The Give and Get between OP&A and L&D

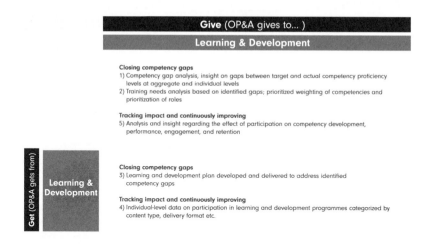

OP&A interface with Talent Management

The Give and Get between OP&A and Talent Management focuses on talent management and succession planning, as shown in Figure 5.3.10. A large part of the Workforce Planning Leader's role is to provide insight to inform these processes. They will provide the Talent Management Team with:

- forward-looking analysis and to inform talent management strategies (attrition, tenure, age, flight risk)
- structured career paths based on defined roles structured by level of work and role family
- role fit analysis to identify the extent to which individuals possess the competency proficiency levels required for their current role
- talent risk analysis: specific individuals or areas of the business where individuals have no identified progression routes

In return, Talent Management devises strategies for retention, motivation and engagement of workforce segments and outcomes from performance reviews.

When it comes to succession planning, the Workforce Planning Leader supplies Talent Management with inputs for talent reviews such as role match analysis to identify potential succession candidates. They can also supply succession risk analysis to identify specific roles or areas of the business which are at risk from low succession readiness.

FIGURE 5.3.10 The Give and Get between OP&A and Talent Management

Give (OP&A gives to...)
Talent Management

Talent Management
1) Forward-looking analysis and to inform talent management strategies (attrition, tenure, age, ultimately flight risk)
2) Structured career paths based on defined roles structured by level of work and role family
3) Role fit analysis to identify the extent to which individuals possess the competency proficiency levels required for their current role
4) Talent risk analysis: specific individuals or areas of the business where individuals have no identified progression routes

Succession Planning
7) Inputs to talent reviews: Role match analysis to identify potential succession candidates and development requirements; individuals categorized by succession status for specific roles (e.g., ready, ready with development, long-term candidate)
8) Succession risk analysis: specific roles or areas of the business where risks are faced due to low succession readiness

Talent Management
5) Strategies for retention, motivation and engagement of workforce segments/people based on analysis of role fit and talent risk classification
6) Outcomes from performance reviews, e.g., overall performance ratings

Succession Planning
9) Outcomes of talent reviews (e.g., confirmed succession status and development actions)
10) Regular status updates on individual completion/performance against development actions

Get (OP&A gets from) — Talent Management

OP&A interface with Rewards (Compensation and Benefits)

Large organizations often have a specialist Compensation and Benefits function with a remuneration committee where decisions about pay and bonuses are made. For these organizations, the OP&A function probably wouldn't need to be involved with compensation and benefits. For smaller organizations without such committees, it does make sense for OP&A to interface with the Reward Team. The OP&A function is analytical in nature and holds the reward data within the role grid. Data Science work can provide insight into the impact of different incentive programmes. The function also has people with the necessary competencies to run models and bring in external benchmarking data. The Reward Team contributes by bringing its expertise on external benchmarks, as shown in Figure 5.3.11. The decision to incorporate this interface needs to be made based on the size of your organization and organizational culture.

FIGURE 5.3.11 The Give and Get between OP&A and Reward

Give (OP&A gives to...)
Total Rewards (Compensation and Benefits)

1) Consistently defined roles (role grid) to provide consistency for managing and applying reward frameworks
4) Reward benchmarks linked to defined roles
5) Model cost impacts of alternative reward models to inform the company's reward model
7) Analysis of consistency/compliance with agreed reward models (e.g. consistent application of grade/bands; role reward parity; benchmark thresholds)

Total Rewards (Compensation and Benefits)

2) Best practice reward frameworks to support desired outcomes (talent acquisition, retention, career development)
3) Authoritative external benchmarking data
6) The reward framework/model to be applied across the organization (with approval by executive/board oversight)

Rightsize the OP&A function to deliver the work

How you size the OP&A function depends largely on such things as the number of your employees, the number of business units and the number of different geographies you operate in. It's worth mentioning up front that depending on the complexity and scale of your organization, you may only need fixed roles in your function, so rightsizing it will be a doddle. The OP&A Leader, Organization Design Leader, Workforce Planning Leader and Data and Tech Leader are all fixed – in other words, for each one, there is only ever a single position, and the number of positions doesn't vary according to the volume of work. These core roles may well be sufficient for organizations employing up to approximately 2,000 employees. For larger organizations operating in a greater number of geographies and with more business units, variable roles such as the Organization Design Consultant and the Workforce Planning Consultant may be needed to support the core roles. For variable roles, the number of FTEs required varies by a volume driver, and the larger your organization, the greater the number of consultants you are likely to need. OP&A functions are unlikely to ever need more than 15 to 20 people, even for large-scale organizations that employ more than 500,000 people.

Determining the number of these variable roles really comes back to that vital interface between OP&A and the HR Business Partners. The larger and more complex the organization, the greater the number of HR Business

Partners. The greater the number of HR Business Partners, the greater the number of OP&A heads required to offer support. Given this, it makes most sense to select driver and ratio analysis from the full suite of FIDRAM right-sizing methods described in Chapter 1.2 to determine the number of FTEs required.

A sensible ratio might be five HR Business Partners to one consultant, but don't take this as read. One of the golden rules of rightsizing is not to blindly follow a single number. Always consider the wider context to determine whether the ratio makes sense in all scenarios. For example, how will the Workforce Planning Leader and the Workforce Planning Consultants work alongside the HR Business Partners when balancing the needs of the top-down plan with the bottom-up modelling? Does it make a difference where the HR Business Partners are located?

How much can I outsource?

This is a big question I am often asked. Do all the roles need to be perma-nent, in-house roles, or can it work to have a core team and hire outside help as necessary? I'll start with the roles included in the initial scope. In my opinion, the OP&A Leader, Organization Design Leader and Workforce Planning Leader must always be in-house. Supporting consultant roles can be either in-house or externally sourced. The key is to size your OP&A func-tion according to the day-to-day, 'business as usual' demand. Fewer people are needed in this context than in one of large-scale transformation or mergers and acquisitions, but in these instances, the team can be augmented with external management consultants.

You may also find that you need to outsource work if you cannot find the right people to fill the roles. As I explain in Chapter 5.4, finding people with the required attributes for these roles is not easy. Sometimes, bringing in external resource while you continue the search is a great idea.

There is also the important question of how much you can afford. You may find you need more than one Workforce Planning Consultant or Organization Design Consultant, but that you can't scale as quickly as you need to because of cost constraints. In cases such as these, augmenting with management consultants when necessary can be an excellent solution until you do have the necessary budget to recruit more people. In Chapter 5.4 I give specific advice on how to work with management consultants.

Develop organization effectiveness KPIs
and reporting format and frequency

Much of the work of the OP&A function involves monitoring the organization. This isn't just about providing insight, but about curating that insight and getting leaders to understand progress, issues and where action is recommended. Too much data can lead to overload and paralysis. The OP&A Leader should act as a curator, deciding who needs to be made aware of what, and for what purpose. This is done by establishing KPIs and deciding who needs to be aware of them. Establishing KPIs at the initial stage has further benefits:

- It allows you to identify any data access, availability and quality issues.

- It provides the opportunity to socialize measures with stakeholders.

- It gives you the chance to test and refine reporting formats and frequency.

The development of these KPIs is informed by two key factors:

- the availability and accessibility of data

- existing organization guidelines, principles and priorities (e.g. managerial spans or DEI)

What follows is a list of sample KPIs I hope you might find helpful to apply to your own organization.

Workforce size, composition and cost:

- total headcount
- total FTE
- proportion of part-time employees
- proportion of contingent employees
- total compensation costs
- average compensation per employee
- Revenue per FTE

Workforce age and tenure:

- average employee age
- proportion of employees in each age group
- proportion of employees in each generational cohort

- average age to retirement
- average tenure
- proportion of employees within five years of retirement

Reporting structure:

- proportion of People Managers
- average span of control
- total number of layers
- proportion of employees in top five layers
- proportion of micro teams
- proportion of one-on-one reporting relationships
- reporting grade compression
- reporting grade dispersion

Gender diversity:

- proportion of female employees
- proportion of female employees in top three layers
- proportion of female People Managers
- proportion of female high potential employees
- percentage compensation difference

Ethnic diversity:

- proportion of employees from ethnic minorities
- proportion of employees in top three organizational layers from ethnic minorities
- proportion of People Managers from ethnic minorities
- proportion of high potential employees from ethnic minorities
- percentage compensation difference

Activities:

- number of activities per employee
- number of employees per activity

- proportion of processes categorized as fragmented
- proportion of activities conducted at the right level
- number of activities with multiple people accountable

Competencies:

- proportion of employees with high/medium/low role fit scores for their current role
- proportion of employees with 80 per cent role fit scores at a higher level
- proportion of competencies without people possessing required proficiency levels
- proportion of positions without a succession candidate
- proportion of people without progression/development routes

Final thoughts

There is a lot of detail in this chapter. My hope is that it provides you with a 'starter for 10'. For most of us, this is preferable and less daunting than a blank piece of paper. I hope it helps to get you over the feeling of not knowing where to begin, or that you don't have the time or energy to get started. So here is a solid start: a list of roles with defined scopes and lists of accountabilities. Equally important is how these roles fit together. How do OP&A roles fit alongside the HR Business Partners or the Learning and Development Leader? None of us in an organization is an island. The Give and Get matrices give you this detail. They may not quite fit your own organization, but I hope they will give you a starting point for debate.

I constantly advocate the discipline of getting the detail right. I advocate designing meaningful, motivating roles – roles that do great work. In this chapter I define four roles which I believe are great roles. Roles lots of people would love to do. Are they challenging? Yes. If they weren't, they wouldn't be desirable.

We are almost there. The 'only' thing left is to get the function live and see the value flow. I'll describe this process in the next and final chapter.

REMEMBER THIS

1   As with any organization design, there is no 'right' way.

2   The four primary roles are OP&A Leader, Organization Design Leader, Workforce Planning Leader and Data and Tech Leader.

3   You can start with just two roles and add more as you scale.

4   The objectives of the OP&A Leader, Organization Design Leader and Workforce Planning Leader are broadly similar, but those of the Data and Tech Leader are somewhat different.

5   There are seven key interfaces to define between OP&A and the rest of the business.

6   The OP&A Leader curates insight based on KPIs to get leaders' attention focused on the right things at the right time.

5.4

Stage 3: Making the OP&A function real

Introduction

There is a time for everything. A time to learn, reflect and develop. A time to turn learning into designs, then plans. A time for stakeholder discussion, refinement of your plans and designs. A time for committing to a set of decisions. And a time for action. A time for doing the do. For getting it done.

You should have everything you need, or, at least, as much as you can reasonably expect. Are there still uncertainties? Sure! Are you a little nervous? I hope so. You wouldn't care if you weren't.

This is the most exciting part, but it can also feel daunting. You have your roadmap and you've done the detailed design for the function, but how do you put the roadmap into practice? How do you implement the plan laid out in your business case? What do you need to think about as you're doing it? What should your priorities be? There will still be many specifics to figure out. How will you roll out an initial programme of work? What HOWWIP questions will need to be addressed? What do you need to think about when interviewing for OP&A roles? How will you get people successfully through the onboarding process?

Getting your OP&A function up and running is like performing a dry run for the types of tasks the function will be responsible for at an organization-wide level – transitioning from the design phases to implementing the design in practice. My intention is for this chapter to transform what might at first feel overwhelming into a process that can be performed in bite-size, achievable chunks. Remember that we tend to overestimate what we can achieve in the short term and underestimate what we can make happen in the long term. At the end of implementing your roadmap you will look back and marvel at what has been accomplished.

Determine the initial programme of work for the OP&A function

In Chapter 5.2 I discussed how to define your roadmap to full OP&A capability. But there is a significant amount of preparation needed before you take the first step. This is where you think through the practicalities of how things will work on a day-to-day level. You'll remember from Chapter 5.2 that there are three on-ramps to pick from. There is not the space to consider each in turn, so below I focus on competency design and demonstrate how to prepare for rolling it out in the organization. The principles and thought processes can be applied to whichever on-ramp you have chosen.

Attempting to roll out competencies across an entire organization all at once would be a mammoth task. It would also be unlikely to result in the best framework for the organization. Instead, apply an iterative approach. This allows you to obtain feedback and figure out what works and what doesn't. The idea is to continually improve the process and iterate the taxonomy as you roll out to increasingly large numbers of people. Remember that in agile methodology, shipping something earlier is preferable to waiting for perfection. If you followed my recommendations in Chapter 5.2, you will have set out a timeline for implementing each step of your roadmap in your business case. In the example I gave, I suggested that each phase of the journey would take four to nine months. Make use of this time to learn and improve. Break the work into sprints so that it feels less daunting. Is it better to roll out function by function? Role family by role family? Or sub-role family by sub-role family? With each roll-out, learn and iterate for the next.

The first step is to get a draft taxonomy in place. This shouldn't be a process performed by senior stakeholders alone. Tempting though it might seem to involve just a handful of people to quickly map out a taxonomy, it won't save time in the long run. It's crucial to engage stakeholders at all levels of the organization. Get input from those who are close to the work to ensure completeness and that the language used will resonate and make sense to everyone. Identify two or three respected people in the role family or sub-family and ask for their input.

Once you have a draft taxonomy in place, the next step is to have it sense-checked. Roll it out to the first 10 people in the family or sub-family to get their feedback. Again, choose a combination of more senior and junior people to ensure that it makes sense across the board. Once everyone is happy, this becomes your prototype that you use to roll out to the next raft of people within the role family and the process is repeated. You will speed up as you go along, and eventually you'll be rolling out competencies for two or three families or sub-families at a time.

As you progress, gather feedback and record any objections so that you can refer to them later. There may be numerous WIFM and WAMI questions (see Chapter 2.3). For example:

What's In it For Me (WIFM)?

- If I attain these skills, will I be able to do my job more effectively?
- How is this framework going to help me progress in the organization?
- How is it going to help me build my skills in the future?
- If I attain these skills, will I get a pay rise?
- If I attain these skills, will my work be more enjoyable?

What is Against My Interest (WAMI)?

- How will I free up my time?
- If I don't have these competencies, does that mean I'll be made redundant?
- Will the competency framework be used for pay and reward?
- What if I am not able to learn new skills?
- If I've got all these competencies already, does that mean I won't be put forward for any Learning and Development initiatives?

Make a note of these questions so that you can pre-empt them and offer reassurance with the next roll-out of competencies. Throughout this process you will not only be developing the competency framework but also communication strategies. Your goal is to get buy-in and bring everyone with you on the journey, so think about what communication strategies work best and aim to improve how you do things with each new roll-out. Employing the WIFM and WAMI frameworks is a great way to build real empathy and demonstrate to people that you are genuinely interested in their views and concerns. Dozens of these sorts of questions will arise when thinking through the practicalities of how OP&A will function on a day-to-day level.

Address HOWWIP questions

In Chapter 2.2 I introduced HOWWIP questioning – an acronym for How it Will Work In Practice. During Stages 1 and 2 the issue of whether something is practical or not will have been addressed only partially. Now is the time to think through a raft of HOWWIP questions to ensure that nothing will be allowed to fall through the cracks.

There are many HOWWIP questions that could be asked when implementing your OP&A function. In Chapter 2.2 I introduced the HOWWIP log – a place to record questions related to the practicality of an issue or process for you to return to later and address. I suggest that you keep this by your side as you make your OP&A function real and remember to give each concern a priority rating so that you can manage the order in which things are dealt with. The following are the sorts of questions that might come up:

- I'm the leader of, for example, the Marketing function. I have a surge in demand and need to add 10 positions. What do I do?

- The bottom-up numbers are out of alignment with the top-down projections. Who is responsible for reconciling and approving this?

- Competency assessment has identified that someone doesn't have the necessary skills and they are nervous they are going to get fired. What should they do?

- Adam and Bridget both think they are responsible for a certain activity and tensions are rising between them. How should the OP&A function address this?

- How do we go about adding a new role to the role grid? Who develops the draft? Who approves it?

- New technology has presented us with an opportunity that requires a strategic shift. How do we work that through?

- We want to enter a new market or geography. How do we plan for this?

What follows is an example of an interface ball game to bring HOWWIP questions to light (introduced in Chapter 2.2). It is an excellent way to bring the Give and Get matrices alive.

The interface ball game

As a reminder, this exercise allows people to discuss and visualize how they will interface with each other and identify any potential problems or conflicts. It ensures that each matrix is watertight. You will have thought through the Give and Get matrices between OP&A and the rest of the business in some detail during Stage 2, so use these as the starting point. This game involves a lot of role play, so once you've got people in the room, start with a few icebreakers to create a relaxed atmosphere. Then get people to role-play how they will work with each other on a day-to-day basis. Below is an example of how a conversation might go between the Head of Learning and Development and the Organization Design Lead.

Head of L&D: I've got to create training programmes – what will you give me to help me to do this?

Organization Design Leader: I'll create the competencies, and I'll give them to you.

Head of L&D: I'll sense-check to see if you've missed anything and give them back to you.

Organization Design Leader: I'll input them into the competency framework and then run surveys to calculate actual proficiency levels. I'll use a combination of employee self-assessment, manager and 360 feedback. Once this is done, I'll assess individual and team scores so we can see which team members have reached the required skill levels and where the gaps are.

Head of L&D: I'll build training programmes based on the results to address the gaps. I'll run the training programmes once we're happy with them.

Organization Design Leader: I'll then rescore them and let you know how well the training is working (in other words, how the proficiency levels are improving with time) so that you can make any necessary tweaks to the training programme.

OP&A Leader: We will also check whether those who attend your training, and truly engage in it, are more likely to stay. In other words, does training reduce churn? We can also test for promotion prospects. We can pull the data together to improve the business case for more L&D.

These sorts of role-play conversations will probably throw up many WIFM and WAMI questions. For example, a WAMI question from the Head of L&D could be whether they are losing scope and power. Up until now, competencies may have been entirely their domain, and sharing responsibility for them may not appeal. On a more positive note, from a WIFM perspective they may see that this process will elevate the importance of competencies in the organization and help them to get a budget.

Don't overlook your external partners when doing this exercise. While not considered in Chapter 5.3, where the focus was on internal interfaces, it is important to think through how the OP&A Team will work with external management consultants. Up until this point, consulting firms may have been hired on a regular basis to do much of the work of the OP&A function. They may be alarmed by the idea of losing work and have many WAMI questions to that effect. In many instances, consulting partners will still be needed to augment the core OP&A Team on an advisory basis, especially in times of large-scale transformation or mergers and acquisition. This leads me to my next HOWWIP question – how the OP&A function should work with management consultants.

How should I work with management consultants?

Far too often, people fail to maximize the potential of the relationship with consulting partners. Speaking as a former management consultant who loved their job, I can say that they are often workaholics – insecure over-achievers who work too many hours a week and spend a lot of time away from home. Mostly, they only ever want to please and solve the issues they are faced with in the best way that they can. In my experience, it can be difficult to speak up if you feel wrong decisions are being made because you don't want to upset your client. Remember that management consultants have the luxury of being able to dedicate all their time to the specific problems and issues you ask them to focus on. In this respect, they differ from people within the business and therefore in the OP&A function, who jump from meeting to meeting and need to think of a million things at once. Management consultants are expensive, so make the most of them. Be clear from the start that you see the relationship as a partnership and that you value their views. A lot of time can be wasted and value destroyed from failing to take this approach.

Another mistake which is often made is bringing management consultants in before you are ready for them. Make sure they have access to the data they need from the moment you bring them in. I can't begin to think how much time and money is wasted by management consultants having to hunt around to source the right data. Having it prepared will save at least a third of their time.

This leads me to another point: be mindful of management consultants' time. I am often struck by how conscious people are of doctors' or lawyers' time. Most people understand that appointments cannot overrun, or that their lawyer can't be expected to be at the end of the phone 24/7. The same is not always true for management consultants. Yes, they work long hours, and yes, they are well paid, but be careful not to abuse them. There is some-times an expectation that the consultant will work 18-hour days – they're away from home, so what else are they going to do? But this won't build strong rapport and trust.

Selecting the right people for the OP&A Team

Finding the right people for your OP&A Team is critical for the success of the function. Ideally, you want the function to be made up of people with a broad range of backgrounds. As this is a relatively new function, it's unlikely that you will be able to recruit from another organization's OP&A function into your own, so think outside the box and aim to spot people with the right aptitude and mindset which will mean they can make a success of the role. A degree of upskilling will be needed with whomever you hire. For example, a candidate from FP&A is likely to need training in workforce planning and/or organization design. Look for people who enthuse about data and analytics. They need to be strategically focused. They also need to be comfortable with building rapport with a range of different personalities and across all levels. Do you think they will be equally comfortable with the Janitor, Financial Controller or a Non-Executive Director?

Start by looking inside your organization for people with an FP&A back-ground. They are likely to have the future-focused mindset necessary for a great OP&A Leader or Workforce Planning Lead. Equally, an HR Business Partner who already thinks about many of the aspects of the OP&A mandate could make a great Organization Design Lead. As well as recruiting from within, you will also want to source at least one external candidate to bring new ideas and fresh perspectives. Someone with a management consulting background who wants a better work/life balance could be a great option for an Organization Design Lead. They will have developed many of the required attributes in their work with clients and are likely to be highly skilled present-ers with excellent persuasion skills. They should be able to listen, digest and build relationships with people at all levels of the organization.

Below I outline the types of attributes to look for when recruiting for each role. Use these lists as cheat sheets when you are selecting and inter-viewing candidates. The competencies outlined in Chapter 5.3 feed into these attributes, but remember that when you're hiring, you're looking for attributes and people who will be able to build the necessary competencies.

As can be seen from the lists below, the attributes needed for an Organization Design Lead and a Workforce Planning Lead are quite different. Someone who would perform well in organization design might not be brilliant at workforce planning, and vice versa. This is worth mentioning as these two roles can be combined into a single role in the initial stages of setting up the function. Be aware that if you have chosen to go down this route you may find it harder to fill this position.

As you scale, consider hiring more junior candidates to support the Organization Design Lead and the Workforce Planning Lead. These are exciting opportunities for graduates or people with one or two years' experience. They can learn a lot, and do a lot of the heavy lifting, documenting workshops and meetings and generally making the function more efficient.

Attributes needed by the OP&A Leader

The OP&A Leader needs strong programme management skills. Look for the following attributes:

- strong presenting and persuading skills, including the confidence to present to the CEO and board at a moment's notice
- ability to tell stories, applying the Pyramid Principle
- sufficient understanding of data and analysis to draw conclusions and tell stories
- ability to deal with political situations and have difficult conversations
- ability to build rapport with people throughout the organization and become trusted
- ability to understand and execute strategy. They don't need to be industry specialists, although this is desirable to be able to understand the work
- ability to deal with ambiguity and think in concepts
- ability to debate and understand and articulate a view even if they don't agree with it (a good screening question can be to ask candidates to give both sides of the debate for legalizing drugs – can they argue both for and against, and persuade you both ways?)
- ability to straddle multiple layers of the organization
- ability to be hyper-structured and detail-focused as well as think through things at a high level

- ability to take ownership (note that some people with management consulting backgrounds can struggle to do this. They need to switch from making recommendations to owning it themselves)
- an expertise in organization design, workforce planning or analysis, or the ability to learn all three

Attributes needed by the Organization Design Leader

The Organization Design Leader needs to be able to talk to the business, running workshops and using data to tell the right stories to influence and persuade. Whereas the OP&A Leader needs strong programme management skills, the Organization Design Leader needs strong project management skills. Look for the following attributes:

- ability to think from a systems perspective (see Chapter 1.1), drawing connections and understanding how a change in one part of the system can have an (often unexpected) impact elsewhere
- ability to understand data and analysis, and draw conclusions
- strong workshop facilitation skills
- ability to feel comfortable sitting down with individuals at all levels of the organization and in all functions to understand the detail of their role. For this you need good communication skills and an ability to build rapport
- ability to tell stories with that data, using the Pyramid Principle
- a good understanding of language, good editing skills and the ability to structure thoughts. These are all important skills when building taxonomies
- expertise in organization design
- a thorough understanding of the macro operating design and micro detailed design processes
- an understanding and appreciation of financial planning

Attributes needed by the Workforce Planning Leader

The Workforce Planning Leader needs to be skilled in running a process on monthly, quarterly and annual cadences. Look for the following attributes:

- strategic thinking and understanding of the talent landscape

- ability to have strategy conversations and challenge the business to put strategy into practice
- ability to challenge initial executive assumptions
- a good command of numbers, data and mathematics for modelling tasks and performing driver analysis
- a process-driven mindset to help with running the top-down and bottom-up planning. As part of this they need to be good at meeting deadlines and chasing other people to perform tasks on time

Attributes needed by the Data and Tech Leader

One of the main objectives of the Data and Tech Leader is to ensure that the right people have access to the right information at the right time. Look for the following attributes:

- ability to understand the HR landscape and HR systems, working in partnership to set up the data flows
- a firm grasp of governance and data security (including Infosec) and how to set up permissions
- demonstrable understanding of the importance of data integrity
- an understanding of the concept of the golden thread of data
- a trustable individual – the nature of the data they are dealing with is highly sensitive
- an understanding of how to answer questions with data and build stories, using the right sort of visualizations to answer certain types of questions
- an understanding of how to build effective dashboards, using the tips discussed in Chapter 4.3
- an ability to build automated data flows
- an agile mindset and ability to build a visualization with incomplete information. This is necessary to facilitate discussion and figure out whether the visualization is the right one for the story which needs to be told
- sufficient confidence to be comfortable in a workshop environment with senior stakeholders
- an ability to write basic scripts. They don't need to know how to build a data warehouse, but scripting skills are helpful. For example, would they be able to create basic calculations in Tableau, run Python scripts or write

basic expressions in orgvue? It is likely that the person applying for this role will have these skills, as most analytics courses and programmes now teach you how to do this

- an understanding of how to combine different datasets and blend different data

- an inquisitive mind with a thirst for learning

- an enthusiasm for data and answering business questions with it

- an ability to explain a statistical concept to someone who is not mathematically minded. Can they explain why standard variation is relevant? How would they explain variability of data to someone with no background in statistics? Can they explain the material difference between median and mean, and why it is important (think back to the example of Elon Musk walking into a bar in Chapter 4.3)?

Final thoughts

This has been a book about time: about short-term and long-term thinking. I've looked at the difference between operational and strategic workforce planning. I've looked at how to optimize over time to continuously improve. I've looked at the importance of productionizing data and operationalizing analytics so that it is repeatable *over time*. I've also looked at agile ways of working and the importance of implementing change at speed. As shown in this chapter, implementing an initiative quickly rather than waiting for things to be perfect enables faster feedback loops and continuous improvement.

I am continually struck by the number of executives who don't think about the impact of time on the organization. They are stuck in the present, with their focus firmly fixed on quarterly reviews and quarterly budgets. They live week to week and month to month and very rarely think beyond the quarter they are in. This 'what now' thinking has its place, but allowing it to dominate your mindset and being blind to whatever might lie around the corner is extremely dangerous.

Remember JCR Licklider's wisdom that people overestimate what can be done in a year and underestimate what can be done in five or 10.[1] Another lens on this is the overuse of the term 'strategic'. People use it to make them sound and feel good. It's a great way to win a point in a verbal sparring session: 'Yes, but strategically we should…' Often, people are simply pointing out something that's important, or they use it to double-down on importance: for example, 'It is strategically important we do ...' It might be crucial, but it doesn't mean it's strategic. Richard Rumelt, the great strategist and author of *Good Strategy, Bad Strategy*, states: 'the core of strategy work is always the same: discovering the critical factors in a situation and designing a way of coordinating and focusing actions to deal with those factors'.[2]

At its core, HR is a People function. A function to get a group of humans working together to transform a range of inputs into more valuable outputs. Other humans benefit from these outputs, often (in business at least) for a price (the price being what your customers pay for the value you give). A price less, given the valued benefit, than they can get elsewhere, and typically beyond what they could ever dream of themselves. The role of the strategist is twofold: first to determine what value to create, where and for whom; second to determine how to do that in a superior way to another 'group of humans' (i.e. your competitors). A strategy is a *design*, it isn't just a plan. As Rumelt states, you are designing a 'coherent approach to overcoming critical obstacles' with a 'tightly crafted and integrated set of actions... strategies are more designs than decisions'.[3]

It is your group, the set of humans we call our colleagues (be those employees, contractors or suppliers) that come together and 'do' those integrated sets of actions. Who does what? Where? What competencies do they need to do it? In what number? In what structure? These are HR questions. More accurately, they are OP&A questions. And they are pretty fundamental. Most organizations have a group of people responsible for planning cash, expenditure, investment and profit over time. They are also responsible for tracking its success, modelling scenarios and presenting options to the board. They help the Leadership Team to plot a pathway forward. I have never seen this questioned. On the contrary, I have seen how people value it, and take it as a given. It is called FP&A. All this, in my view, is why having an OP&A function is so crucial and fundamental to helping your organization achieve and execute on its strategy. Many organizations continue to fail in this mission, as can be seen in the decreasing amount of time companies stay in the Fortune 100 list (see Chapter 1.1). Everything I have written about in this book should enable you to pivot strategy and execute it more quickly, to decrease your chances of being disrupted and losing out to existing and new competitors alike.

In many ways, OP&A is only the beginning. In 2020 Gartner introduced the idea of extended planning and analysis, or xP&A, which it defines as 'an extension of Financial Planning and Analysis beyond the finance department'.[4] For Gartner, this extension could be into any area of the organization that produces business plans in line with organizational strategy, be that Sales, Marketing, Operations or HR. For me, there is nothing more exciting than an organization united through 'What-If' thinking. One which scans the horizon with a heads-up mindset. There is no doubt in my mind that organizations which manage to permeate these mindsets throughout every function and level will be the ones to succeed and thrive. They will be the ones to enjoy the journey to their success.

REMEMBER THIS

1 It is now time to implement – time to 'do the do'.

2 Focus on getting the right people into your roles. They will come from a range of sources.

3 Use management consultants well and effectively. They are too often misused (and abused).

4 OP&A requires What-If and heads-up mindsets – impacting the future, not just the present.

5 OP&A is core to maximizing the value from your most important resource – your human resource.

Notes

1 Quote Investigator (2019) People tend to overestimate what can be done in one year and to underestimate what can be done in five or ten years. https://quoteinvestigator.com/2019/01/03/estimate/ (archived at https://perma.cc/TVD2-USLA)

2 Rumelt, R (2012) *Good Strategy Bad Strategy: The difference and why it matters*, Profile Books Ltd.

3 Ibid.

4 Gartner (2020) Innovation insight for extended planning and analysis (xP&A) www.gartner.com/en/documents/3992338 (archived at https://perma.cc/NQK7-RMSR)

GLOSSARY

actionable insight Information derived from analysis of data which informs decisions and enables action to be taken

activities One component of the 'organization system' framework: the work conducted, and the accountabilities held, specified within value chains and processes

actual data Data which describes observed status which is compared to target or forecast data to identify gaps

agile methodology An iterative approach to project management which allows teams to self-manage how they get work done. The methods involve itemizing tasks into distinct phases

amortization A way of calculating the reduction in an organization's intangible assets over time

Analyse–Design–Plan–Monitor (ADPM) A process for managing continuous improvement, similar to the well-known management discipline Plan–Do–Review

Application Programming Interfaces (APIS) Interfaces between systems which pull data and follow set rules to allow systems to talk to each other

as-is The organization at the current point in time, against which planned changes can be described and projected

assumption A number or event that it is predicted could happen in the future which is used as an input to a plan, model or projection. It is something which is assumed will be true but is not certain

balance sheet A financial statement which shows the total assets a business owns versus its liabilities and the amount of shareholder equity

baseline A dataset specifying the 'as-is' organization at a point in time from which you can project, model and monitor trends and changes

behavioural competencies Attributes which shape behaviour. They show *how* an individual performs their work, conducts themselves and interacts with others

bottom-up Can be thought of as aggregating. Going from the lowest level of aggregation to the highest level of aggregation

capability Systems, processes and people within an organizational unit which, in combination with the competencies of those people, deliver organizational goals

career path mapping A data-driven process used to understand which roles people in the organization could perform in the future, given their current competency proficiency levels

case for change Document which lays out why organizational change is necessary and what the benefits of the change will be

cash flow A financial statement that shows where cash is coming in from and how it is being spent

ceteris paribus A Latin phrase meaning 'all other things being equal' which is applied when assessing the impact and volatility of assumptions in sensitivity analysis

cognitive competencies Competencies which relate to behaviour with a focus on cognitive functioning, for example how someone thinks about and solves problems

competencies One component of the 'organization system' framework: the skills, knowledge and behaviours that need to be possessed by people to perform in the role

current asset Either cash or something which can be converted into cash within a year or less, such as stock or investments which can be sold off quickly

data controls Calculations which can be used to shine a light on quality issues and/or inconsistencies

data foundation All of the components including the definitions of the properties, the datasets and how they connect

data warehouse A system used for data and analysis and reporting, built into fact tables where factual information is recorded and dimension tables for analysis and managing this data. Facts and tables are connected through relationships to form a star, with the fact table in the middle and dimensions radiating from the central point

Decisions, Outputs and Tasks (DOT) dimensions A way to dimensionalize activities

depreciation A way of calculating the reduction in an organization's tangible assets over time

design criteria Critical business goals used in the design process to evaluate different design options and decide which should be chosen

design option A schematic or conceptual model which defines the high-level structuring of an organization

design principles Measurable rules which organization designs should conform to (e.g. maximum number of layers)

dimensionalize The process of applying dimension or category labels to nodes for comparative analysis, e.g. adding 'strategic', 'operational' or 'transactional' to activities within a taxonomy

dimensions A way of categorizing measures to answer business questions. A dimension can take the form of textual categories such as categorizing 'gender' into 'female', 'male' and 'non-binary'. Values can also be categorized into 'bins', e.g. categorizing salaries into: less than £20,000; £20,000–£50,000; greater than £50,000

direct costs Costs that can be directly attributed to producing the service or product that brings in your income

Diversity, Equity and Inclusion (DEI) Initiatives designed to support groups which have historically been marginalized or underrepresented. Diversity refers to the differences between people. Equity refers to the need to remove barriers in some people's way to ensure every individual has a fair chance of success. Inclusion refers to the need to foster a sense of belonging

Earnings Before Interest, Tax, Depreciation and Amortization (EBITDA) This metric gives an understanding of an organization's growth and its potential to generate cash, and should not be misunderstood as the equivalent of free cash flow

epics Used in agile methodology as a way of breaking down a backlog of work

feature (macro operating design) An item which can be incorporated into part of a frame to describe how a specific part of the organization will operate

feedback loop A looping process whereby a system's outputs are fed back into the system as inputs

financial modelling A method used to understand likely future financial performance across a range of different scenarios

Financial Planning and Analysis (FP&A) A role within organizations that performs financial budgeting, planning and analysis to ensure the future financial health of the business

fixed roles A role for which the number of positions is one. The number of positions doesn't vary as a result of planned activity levels or output volumes. These are typically senior-level roles, e.g. Chief Finance Officer, Chief People Officer

Fixed Roles, Incremental Percent, Driver Analysis, Ratio Analysis, Activity Analysis, Mathematical Modelling (FIDRAM) The six data-driven methods to rightsize the organization

flight risk The probability that an employee will leave in a given time period

frame (macro operating design) The highest-level definition of an organization design model

gap The difference between defined target data and observed actual data

generic business skills Technical competencies that cut across different role families

Give and Get matrix A tool which visualizes and supports interface design. It summarizes what each organization unit gives to other units and what is received from those units

goals The aspirational and directional results you want your organization to achieve based on your vision and strategy

golden thread of data A map showing how data flows from its source to each of the areas where it is processed, controlled and consumed

Goldilocks Dilemma The principle of not doing too much, and not doing too little. This is the art of getting things 'just right'

graph database A database with nodes, edges and properties to represent and store data. In D-DOD, we call the edges 'links'. Think of this as a spider's web or a network diagram where the node is a point and the link also holds data

gross profit Sometimes referred to as the operating margin, this refers to the profit made by an organization once all direct costs have been subtracted from the revenue

heads-up mindset A mindset used to scan the space in front of you so you can foresee what's coming and have confidence in your decisions

How it Will Work In Practice (HOWWIP) A method of articulating how the target organization design will work in practice. Addressing HOWWIP questions makes organization designs tangible and is used to remove ambiguity

hybrid design A design option formulated around a primary frame with secondary features embedded into that frame

'Imagine you are moving house' An exercise used to establish your case for change which is helpful for identifying current strengths and weaknesses as well as what you should be doing but aren't

impact assessment A data-driven method used to understand how individuals will be affected by a transformation process. Impact assessment is done at both an individual and an aggregate level

indirect costs The money needed to keep a business operating, but not as a direct result of producing your product or service. They are the same as operating expenses, and are sometimes referred to as Selling, General and Administrative costs (SG&A)

Individual Activity Analysis (IAA) The process of collecting data to understand the actual work activities consuming the time and cost of the workforce

inputs Raw data, metadata and assumptions which are inserted into a financial model and that you expect will affect your future performance

intangible asset An asset which is not of a material nature, such as copyrights, patents or brand recognition

interface design The connections between people in terms of their interactions and responsibilities. Interface design is used to understand how items of work (or the information needed to progress work tasks) are handed from one team or person to another

Internal Rate of Return (IRR) The rate (expressed as a percentage) at which a project breaks even using cash flow over time. The calculation does not factor in external considerations such as inflation

Kanban A generic scheduling system developed by Taiichi Ohno to improve the flow and structuring of work. Cards are used to track the flow of 'things'. In the context of agile working, these 'things' are work items like features or tasks. An example is structuring work into 'Now, Next, Later' and putting items into the relevant bucket. Work is pulled forward depending on the urgency of the feature or task

Key Organizational Dimensions (KODs) The key lenses used to view your organization and measure performance. Common examples include business unit, function, geography, customer segment and managerial level

lagging indicators Measures or outcomes that have already occurred, for example a previous year's profit or revenue

leading indicators Measures which can be used to predict future outcomes, for example a predictor of future client churn and therefore future revenue

links Links, containing data, form the many-to-many connections of a graph database, e.g. people to activities. One person has lots of activities and each activity is linked to lots of people. A link value might be how much time is spent. In data science links are more formally known as 'edges'

macro operating design The first stage of the D-DOD process. It involves articulating strategy; developing the case for change; setting design criteria and design principles; evaluating and selecting design options and signing-off the business case for change; iterating the design and creating a business case

Making it Real The third and final phase of the D-DOD process. This phase puts plans laid out in the macro operating design and micro detailed design phases into action

Management Complexity Index (MCI) An index to quantify the burden faced by individual managers as a result of structural reporting relationships. Components of the index include reporting distance between managers and team members, team tenure and working hours overlap

many-to-many relationships Relationships where many categories have many relationships (links) with many other categories, e.g. the relationship between people to activities: there are many people (in a people dataset) conducting many activities (in a process taxonomy)

master data management A way of structuring data in a robust and logical way to control it and ensure uniformity and quality as well as consistency in how the information is understood. This is both a management and a technical process

matrix design A design option with positions having multiple reporting lines

measures Indicators providing insight on the organization and the workforce. Usually calculated by applying simple statistical techniques to properties, e.g. average span of control, percentage of female employees

micro detailed design The second stage of the D-DOD process which details the macro operating design. Roles are designed with OAC data, processes are optimized and the key organization dimensions are built out according to rightsizing projections

Net Present Value (NPV) A way of calculating the time value of money, and therefore the present-day value of an investment using the WACC. The calculation is important to accurately predict when investment will be returned

neural networks Models which mimic the functioning of biological neurons to generate predictions

node The smallest 'thing' in a dataset you have information about, such as an individual employee in a people dataset. Nodes have properties attached to them, e.g. for people: name, salary and date of birth

non-current asset Assets which cannot be converted into cash within a year or less or sold off quickly, such as property

Now, Next, Later A framework used for prioritizing work, often used in the Kanban approach

objectives One component of the 'organization system' framework: measurable and time-specific results that need to be achieved

Objectives, Activities and Competencies (OAC) Three components of the organization system. In D-DOD, roles are designed with target OAC data and actual OAC data is collected for people. Analysing gaps between targets and actuals informs action planning to optimize the performance of the organization

operational workforce planning Workforce planning performed over a time horizon of 12 to 18 months at the Role, Position and People level

operationalization of analytics The process of making analytics techniques continuous and repeatable

options A set of choices you make in light of different scenarios. A scenario is a range of things that might happen to you. Option analysis looks at decisions that could be made in different scenarios

organization system The framework used in D-DOD, comprising six interrelated components: Roles, Positions, People (RPP) and Objectives, Activities, Competencies (OAC). Each component is defined with data, enabling gaps between role targets and people actuals to be measured and managed

outcomes A result which is predicted through modelling scenarios based on inputs and assumptions. Scenario modelling results in a range of different outcomes

payback period The length of time it is expected to take to recoup investment costs over time. Payback period is calculated by subtracting annual cash flow from the decreasing cost of an investment over time

people Individual employees or other workers, e.g. contractors engaged by an organization

position lifecycle management The six stages that a position progresses through from being envisaged to being demised. Analogous but different to an employee lifecycle

positions The specification of roles with a defined scope of responsibility (e.g. territory coverage) and location in the organization hierarchy

productionization of data The process of regulating data processes to allow the continual updating of data and generation of insight

profit and loss statement (P&L) Sometimes referred to as an income statement, this financial statement shows you whether you have made a profit or loss over a specified period

profit margin A metric used to determine whether revenue has exceeded cost, and by how much

property The information held about nodes, such as the salary or age of a person

random forest model A supervised machine learning algorithm which is based on decision tree algorithms

Real Option Pricing (ROP) An economic technique used to value options. Value is based on the level of risk involved in an option (risk being the number and range of possible outcomes or the variability of possible outcomes). The higher the risk, the greater the option value

Reduce, Reallocate, Improve and Invest (RRII) A framework of eight process enhancement levers which can be pulled to alter the amount of effort required for each activity

release train A way of prioritizing a backlog of work in agile methodology. At the end of each release train, the product or code is 'shipped'

requisite level of work The one to eight levels of work described in Elliot Jacques' requisite organization. The level is defined by the complexity, time horizon and impact of the work

Responsible for, Approving and Doing the work (RAD) An accountability matrix which defines who is responsible, the approver, and who 'does' the work to support the person responsible

Return on Investment (ROI) A way of understanding the return you will get on an investment as a percentage. ROI is calculated by dividing the net income by the initial cost of the investment and multiplying it by 100

revenue The money a company makes from its operations

rightsizing The method of determining how many full-time equivalents (FTEs) are required for each role and in aggregate for the organization

role cluster A grouping of roles within the same role family and at a comparable level, used for workforce planning

role criticality Role families can be segmented to understand critical roles. This is done using four key drivers: scale of impact; time to productivity; growth; and prevalence

role family A grouping of roles with similar competencies

role fit score A measure of how closely an employee's actual competency proficiency data fits the target requirements for their role

role grid A structured grid used to organize roles according to role family and level of work

role match score A measure of how well an employee's actual competency proficiency data fits the target requirements for other roles in the organization

roles Defined jobs needing to be performed for the organization to deliver its strategy. In D-DOD, roles are designed with OAC data. The specification of the exact scope of each role (e.g. territory coverage) is done by breaking roles into positions

Roles, Positions and People (RRP) Three components of the organization system

scale of impact The positive side of impact considers the financial benefit a role-holder could bring to the organization when performing well in their role. The negative side considers the risk the organization would face if the role-holder failed to execute their responsibilities correctly

scenario modelling A scenario is a range of things that could occur in the future. Scenario modelling involves changing a range of inputs and assumptions and seeing the impact on different outcomes

sensitivity analysis The process of changing inputs such as assumptions in a systematic way and seeing the impact of changes on outputs

slice and dice Cutting data in different ways (e.g. by dimensions) to see it from a variety of viewpoints and enhance understanding

span of control The total number of direct reports supervised by a people manager

specialized functional skills Competencies relating to specialized functional knowledge and technical abilities

sprint Used in agile methodology. A backlog of work is prioritized into 'release trains'. Release trains are, in turn, broken down into shorter, time-boxed iterations known as 'sprints'

star schema The model most often used to create a data warehouse. Star schemas consist of fact and dimension tables and are often visualized as a star, with a fact table in the middle and dimensions radiating from the central point

strategic workforce planning Workforce planning performed over a time horizon of two to 20 years at the levels of Key Organizational Dimensions, role families and role clusters

strategy The plan defining how an organization will achieve its stated vision; how the organization will win in its chosen markets

supervised learning Refers to when a machine learning algorithm maps inputs to outputs and uses these datasets to learn over time

swing rating method A weighting method used to prioritize such things as objectives and competencies, where the most important objective or competency is given a score of 100 and other objectives or competencies are rated relative to that

systems thinking A way of cutting through complexity by understanding how things relate to each other as a system, and the impact that a change in one part of the system can have elsewhere in the system

tactical workforce planning Workforce planning performed over a time horizon of four to eight weeks at the people level

talent marketplace The number and identity of employees possessing sufficient proficiency to be considered for defined roles. Understanding who the potential individuals are can therefore be thought of as creating a 'marketplace'

tangible asset An asset which is of a material nature and decreases in value over time due to wear and tear

target data Data which describes the required status that actual or forecast data is compared against to identify gaps

time horizon The distance into the future you want to plan for

Time To Productivity (TTP) The average duration in months from a position opening to a new position-holder performing productively in the role

to-be A snapshot of the projected state or target design of the organization to be implemented in the future

top-down Can be thought of as disaggregating, going from the highest level of aggregation to the lowest level of aggregation

transactional database A database used to record transactions or events, such as when someone joins or leaves an organization

unsupervised learning A machine learning technique where models are left alone to uncover patterns in data. Unlike supervised learning, which learns by mapping inputs to outputs, learning occurs without the use of an output variable

value chain The definition of the top-level, end-to-end steps through which the company creates value

variable roles A role which requires a varying number of positions according to planned activity levels or output volumes

vision Sets an organization's direction, giving clarity on where it wants to get to and why it wants to get there

Volatility and Impact Category (VIC) A way of categorizing assumptions in sensitivity analysis. Assumptions can be categorized according to volatility (or uncertainty) and impact, and those with high levels of both can be isolated as the ones to focus on

Weighted Average Cost of Capital (WACC) A calculation used to understand and weigh the cost of capital according to the amount of debt and equity used

'What-If' mindset A dreaming mindset used to think about what could be possible in the future

'What is Against My Interest?' (WAMI) and 'What's In it For Me?' (WIFM) Analysis considering a situation from someone else's personal point of view. Anticipating responses to these questions enables the potential upsides and potential downsides perceived by others to be identified

working capital The money tied up in the ordinary course of running a business, such as the money tied up in stock.

INDEX